More praise for *The Early Arrival of Dreams*

"Rosemary Mahoney writes of China and the Chinese with sharp-eyed sympathy. She has a good novelist's way with eloquent detail, remarkable characters, and narrative flow. *The Early Arrival of Dreams* is a delight."

John Barth

"An extraordinarily moving and sensitive account of a young American teacher's effort to work in China and learn from those she came to know—a sensitive, thoughtful, beautifully rendered story, and a fine novelist's sensibility brought to the tradition of personal, documentary writing."

Robert Coles

"Rosemary Mahoney has written a dispassionate, honest recollection of her teaching year in modern China. She tells some memorable, and often horrifying stories with understanding and sympathy, and always with the art of a skilled fiction writer."

Doris Grumbach

"*The Early Arrival of Dreams* is a joy—a journey of discovery for the reader, as it was for the author. Mahoney's account is distinguished by intelligence, and a fierce sense of the comic and the absurd, yet tempered always by compassion. The author is no 'China expert' but an alert, sometimes bewildered, traveler with a novelist's ability to bring to life the sights, sounds, and textures of contemporary Chinese life. A wise and spacious first book."

A. G. Mojtabai

THE EARLY ARRIVAL OF DREAMS

OF DREAMS

A YEAR IN CHINA

工作证

ROSEMARY MAHONEY

FAWCETT COLUMBINE · NEW YORK

AUTHOR'S NOTE

For the writing of this book I have relied on journals I kept while in the People's Republic of China, on letters I wrote from Hangzhou, and on memory. Some of the conversations here are re-creations. Many names have been changed and several identities have been altered to protect the privacy of the individuals.

A Fawcett Columbine Book
Published by Ballantine Books

Copyright © 1990 by Rosemary Mahoney

Library of Congress Catalog Card Number: 91-70647

ISBN: 0-449-90655-8

Cover design by James R. Harris

Cover photo: © Superstock

Manufactured in the United States of America

First Trade Paperback Edition: March 1992

10 9 8 7 6 5 4 3 2 1

For Ming Yu

ACKNOWLEDGMENTS

For their assistance I am grateful to Nona Rohan Mahoney, Mary K.S. Parkman, Christine Mullin, Mary and Coburn Ward, Roger Messick, and my brothers and sisters: James, Sheila, Stephen, Elizabeth, Ellen, and John. I am particularly grateful to Betsy Lerner, my editor, for her patience, generosity, and guidance.

CONTENTS

THE EARLY ARRIVAL
OF DREAMS

SHY, QUIET, MODEST

When I met Bai Yiping in the parking lot of a restaurant in Boston, I was struck once again by her youthfulness—at forty-three she had the face of a college senior; I told her this, she smiled politely, nodding her acknowledgment. "But you," she said softly, encircling my wrist with her fingers, "look tired after your year in China." The intimacy of the gesture surprised me; it didn't match what I remembered of her.

An English teacher at Hangzhou University in the People's Republic of China, Bai had spent the past year studying Women's literature at Harvard University as part of the Radcliffe College–Hangzhou University Academic Exchange Program. While Bai studied at Harvard, Christina Mungan and I spent the year teaching English at Bai's university in the city of Hangzhou.

Though in Hangzhou I became friendly with Bai's husband, Huang Zhiye, I knew little about Bai herself, only what I recalled from my first meeting with her in China, nearly a year before, several days prior to her departure for the United States. I remembered her as formal and deliberate, guiding Christina and me through the steaming streets of Hangzhou, her short black side-parted hair like a glossy helmet on her head, the back of her white cotton blouse transparent with sweat. She spoke softly and cautiously and with a shadow of a smile, as though her words held a hidden meaning for us, if only we would be clever enough to grasp it. She had the distant, instructive manner of one accustomed to addressing large groups of students, and when she spoke, her eyes seemed to focus not on us but on whatever lay just behind us. She apologized for things; for the unmitigated stares our foreign faces inspired, and for the inadequate size of her apartment, where we would later have tea with her husband and son. More than once she apologized for the overwhelming heat.

"My thermometer reads thirty-nine degrees Centigrade today, but on the radio they tell me it is only thirty-seven. On the radio perhaps the temperature never goes above thirty-seven, for if it goes higher than this, it is officially too hot to work and the workers must be allowed to go home. I am sorry your first days in China are like this. I think you are not used to such heat."

It wasn't the heat that took getting used to, but the fact that there was no escaping it; few buildings here were air-conditioned, and even in the shade the temperatures were menacing. As foreign teachers, Christina and I had been given an apartment with the luxury of an air conditioner in one room, but the machine was ancient and functioned properly only five minutes at a time before, with a shudder and a startling bang, it began to blast hot air into the room. Some days it shut down completely.

Softened by the scalding sun, the pavement gave slightly beneath our feet; bicycle tires left grooves across it. In the shade of a sycamore tree at the edge of the road, a frail old woman in black trousers and a white blouse sat on a stone wall, her tiny hands resting on the head of her cane, her slippered feet barely reaching the parched red ground. Her breathing was shallow and labored.

"The heat is too terrible for some of the older people. I have heard that several of them have died this week because of it." As Bai spoke, an elderly farmer harnessed to a cartful of cabbages approached us in the narrow street. His blue shorts were soaked, and his bare shoulders, crossed with heavy ropes, were burned and blistered. The sweat of his upper lip had dampened his cigarette. He stopped to rest for a moment, to light a fresh cigarette and rearrange his ropes. When he peered up from under the brim of his hat and found himself face-to-face with Christina and me, he flinched and jumped backward into the handles of his cart. He pointed his cigarette at us and roared to Bai Yiping, "Are these two your cousins?"

Bai gazed vacantly at a point just above the farmer's head. Her reply was stiff and even: "They are not my cousins."

"What are they, then?"

"Foreigners."

The farmer squinted at us, puzzled and suspicious. Then, slowly, a smile of recognition and amazement spread across his wrinkled face.

Bai led us away by the elbows. "Never mind, please. Perhaps some farmers forget their manners. Perhaps some farmers have never seen a foreigner."

Bai's speech was riddled with the word *perhaps*, which she intended as a buffer, a way of muzzling criticisms, but she used it so often and so consistently that it turned against her and betrayed her posture of dispassion. In the end *perhaps* was a sign that Bai felt strongly—or strongly critical—about things; wherever the word appeared, I made a mental note and put *definitely* in its place. When Christina commented on a Chinese-made English typewriter for sale in a shop window, Bai said, "It looks fine indeed, but the people are perhaps reluctant to buy such things as this, for they are expensive and the quality is perhaps poor."

But for a few wide boulevards, Hangzhou's streets were narrow and close, crowded with one-speed bicycles, tiny Japanese cars, and double-length buses that eased along their routes with the imposing grace of hippopotamuses in water. Bicyclists pumped along with their purchases strapped to the backs of their bikes or dangling in baskets from their handlebars. Workers on pedal wagons hauled towering stacks of bricks and cakes and milk bottles over the rough streets. Sweating peasants carried baskets of fruit suspended on shoulder poles, and children played on the sidewalks while their mothers washed clothes and cooked and threw basins of dirty water through doors and windows into the gutter. Everywhere long lines of bicycles stood parked in assigned spaces on the sidewalks. For a few cents an old woman with a red arm band would watch over the bicycles, keep them straight in their rows, and cover them with a plastic sheet in the event of rain. On street corners signs in both English and Chinese exhorted citizens to promote hygiene and preserve nature by refraining from littering and spitting: Honor to Those Who Pay Attention to Hygiene—Disgrace to Those Who Don't! Do Well in Sanitation—Build Up Socialist Civilization! Grated spittoons were built into the sidewalks, and trash cans in the shape of roaring lions appeared every fifty feet. Elderly workers waving red flags stood on corners directing traffic and admonishing offenders.

As we crossed over the elevated footpath above a busy intersection, I glanced down and saw a knot of people in a heated argument on the street corner below. A skinny young man in a mustache and tight pants shouted angrily at an older female traffic official, stamping his foot and wagging his finger repeatedly in the woman's face. The woman shouted back and threatened him with the little red flag clutched in her pudgy fist; she was stocky and strong and had bristling steel-gray hair. At her side a short man in a muscle T-shirt incited and defended her with throaty shouts of his own, and suddenly, in a frenzy of emotion, he sprang forward and gave the young man a shove and a surprisingly girlish little slap on the chest. The young man looked down at his chest in disbelief; a hush fell over the crowd. Immediately a squint of regret appeared on the attacker's face, and before he could scurry back to the traffic official's side, a general brawl broke out, expanding to include two indignant young women, who, with great vigor and imagination, began shrieking and flailing their arms. The entire group seemed at once thrilled and frightened by the chaos, and there was a kind of camaraderie to the fighting, a feeling that, for better or worse, they were all in this together.

As mysteriously as it had begun, the fight broke up and the participants parted ways, straightening their shirts and patting their hair down.

As we walked down the stairs on the other side of the bridge, I wanted to ask Bai Yiping about the probable reason for such a fight, but I sensed she would think my interest indelicate. Several times when I glanced at her during a lull in our conversation, she appeared tense and preoccupied. Her mouth seemed to settle habitually into a line of apprehension, and her eyes were hooded and weary. She held her purse at waist level as she walked, clutching its handles tightly and with both hands, the way an anxious rider might hold the reins of a skittish horse.

As we boarded the bus that would take us back to the university, Bai said softly and for the third time that day, "I am afraid you will find my apartment small."

Bai and her family lived in a faculty residence in a group of cement buildings near the university, and like most apartment buildings in Hangzhou, this one was stolid and dreary. The stone stairway was musty and dark, like stairs to a wine cellar, and the landings were piled with boxes and bicycles and wicker baskets. On the third-floor landing Bai opened a pocked wooden door and said, "Now we are here." We stepped into a short, dark hallway that let onto six small rooms, which seemed reasonable until I learned that the three rooms toward the end of the hallway were occupied by another family entirely and that Bai's family possessed only two of the rooms and a tiny cement kitchen. The kitchen, appointed with a deep soapstone sink and a gas stove, had the barren feel of a potting shed. The cement walls were so damp that green fungus sprouted near the ceiling. The north wall held a bleary window no bigger than a cookie sheet. At the end of the hallway, behind a saloon-style door, was the shared toilet. Bai's other rooms were only slightly more comfortable, but they were considerably brighter, and I could see that she and her family had possessions they valued: a small refrigerator, a color television, a sewing machine, an antique chest, some photographs on the walls.

Bai introduced us to her husband, Huang Zhiye, a professor in the Foreign Languages Department at the university, and invited us to sit at the table, which had been set with dishes of fruit, plum candies, and meat buns. The table was only big enough to accommodate three people, so Huang sat in an armchair, and their son, Huang Ming, sat quietly on a bed in the corner of the room. As she dropped lumps of ice cream into two glasses of China-brand cola, Bai talked about her son: He was hardworking, he was too shy for a boy of sixteen, he needed to practice his English. She hoped he would become friendly with us while we were here. Throughout the afternoon she badgered him to speak English with us, but he responded only by smiling at the floor and shrugging his refusal. He had long legs, even teeth, and a beautiful honey-colored face, which he hid from time to time behind a newspaper.

Huang Zhiye, dressed in white shorts and plastic slippers, was cheerful and loose-jointed and solicitous. He offered us a bowl of black grapes and advised us to eat a lot for the sake of our strength. He asked us were we pleased with the teaching assignments we'd been given. We told him we hadn't been given teaching assignments yet, that we still had no idea who or what we were to teach. Huang frowned and hugged the bowl of grapes to his hip. "No one has told you?"

We confessed that in the three days since we'd arrived, no one had come to see us about academics. It was September 1, and still we didn't know when classes were to begin. Bai Yiping said, "Well, there is still time yet. To tell you the truth, we ourselves sometimes don't know even two days in advance when we will resume teaching again. But someone will announce it at least the day before it arrives, and so you see, there is no need to worry."

Huang was still frowning. He was an emotional man, far easier to read than his circumspect wife. "Who came to meet you at the airport?"

"No one."

"The Foreign Affairs officers did not meet you?"

Christina and I told him about our two-hour wait at the Hangzhou airport and about the three kind men from Wuhan who had given us a lift to the university, and about the visit we'd got from Yang Shiren, the director of the Foreign Affairs Office, later that first night. Huang glanced surreptitiously at Bai. Bai cleared her throat, put her palms down flat on the table, and began to speak with consummate Chinese diplomacy—a dizzying blend of appeasement, contradiction, dismissal, and defense. "In China, you know, communication is sometimes less than excellent. It must have been a misunderstanding. You were very patient. You misunderstood him. Or you may say that he misunderstood you. Also, Mr. Yang is quite experienced in his post and always operates with foreign visitors in mind. Also, he is perhaps a forgetful person. But it is his job to make things comfortable for you. I am sure he had an explanation for not coming to meet you."

"Yes, he said he thought we were coming the next day, and that as soon as he heard we had arrived, he intended to come right over, but then he discovered that his son had borrowed his bicycle and he had no way of getting to our building."

Huang winced in apparent disgust but refrained from telling us what we later learned for ourselves: Yang Shiren lived directly behind the campus, not a mile from our building, and indisputably within walking distance.

Bai offered us some bananas and flipped the subject to America and Harvard/Radcliffe: Where would she live? What would she eat? Would things be expensive? She asked us about academics and the weather. And crime—she had heard unsettling things about shootings and stabbings, and she had heard that everyone in America had a gun. And she had heard, correctly, that Wan Jie, her predecessor on the exchange, had had her pocketbook yanked from her shoulder in broad daylight on the streets of Cambridge. I wanted to point out that Miss Wan's misfortunes could not have been too unbearably bad, for despite them she had chosen to stay in Cambridge another year beyond her initial appointment at Radcliffe, but I said nothing; I realized that Wan's decision to stay in Cambridge was informed not by the level of crime in America but by the lack of opportunities available to her in China. Had Miss Wan been robbed of all her worldly possessions, she would still have chosen to stay.

Bai confessed she was eager to be going, but nervous. She had rarely been out of Zhejiang Province and had never been in an airplane. Nevertheless she was thrilled and thankful for the opportunity to go to America.

From the safety of his straw bed Bai's son observed us with the unexpectant gaze of a man adrift on a flat sea. He sat with his knees together and his feet apart and the newspaper wrapped across his lap, like an apron. Minutes before Christina and I left, he sighed and came awkwardly to the table. Bai Yiping watched him with love and apprehension, waiting to see how he would perform. Haltingly he said to

Christina, "Do you come from America?" His voice was surprisingly soft and soothing, like a young girl's. Christina told him she did come from America. "Oh," he said, and retreated to the bed, satisfied that his task for the afternoon had been successfully completed.

Bai appeared suddenly self-conscious and perplexed, uncertain as to whether she should be made proud or embarrassed by her son's modest effort.

Some months later in her first letter to me from Cambridge, Massachusetts Bai Yiping wrote of her life in America and expressed, among other things, her astonishment at American advertising. "What a lot of methods to attract customers to buy—sale, special, rebate . . . % off, even free!" She told me of the endless amount of reading required in the courses she was auditing and how American students had assured her that it would not be a crime if she neglected some of the books on the reading list. Bai said it pleased her to walk the streets of Cambridge and Boston. She wrote, "I always feel I am walking in a big garden with different architectural houses," and she marvelled at how uncrowded the streets were as compared to China's streets. She discussed briefly some American food she had tried at my mother's house and commented on our dining customs: "Four candles were set in the middle of the table, just the scene I saw in foreign films."

Now, in the Boston restaurant, Bai joked easily with a busboy and ordered baked scrod after a cursory glance at the menu. Her manner was both more direct and less severe than it had been a year ago, though her attire was noticeably unmodified.

Bai had spent the summer working as a maid for a wealthy couple in a small town on the Rhode Island shore; she found the town boring and the couple demanding. She commented on the man in the couple: He was a professor, an important person in his field. His wife was a business woman many years younger than he. He was growing old and intolerant. He liked all things just so.

Bai balanced her fork on the edge of her plate and smiled behind a corner of her napkin. Over dessert she asked me about my life in Hangzhou and seemed amused by my general impression of China. She sipped from her glass of Coke and said what she had said several times already in various ways: "In a few years the Chinese will not be so courteous or innocent as they have been. Things will change very quickly. People will continue to become business-minded and selfish, more like in America."

Bai spoke with ostensible despair, but I had a strong feeling that she took a kind of pride in such a change, as though she believed it might finally demonstrate the competency and modernity of the Chinese people.

Toward the end of the meal, when I mentioned in passing Ming Yu, a young English teacher in the English Department at Hangzhou University, Bai's face fell. "I am acquainted with Miss Ming," she said guardedly. "Some years ago she was my student, and also my husband's student."

I said that if that was the case, then Bai and her husband must be very good teachers, for Ming Yu's English was beautiful.

Bai pounced at the comment. "True! In class Miss Ming is an excellent student, but in life I am afraid there is something the matter with her thinking. She talks what is in her head, and at the wrong times. She wears Western clothes; perhaps she spends too much time with foreigners. She is not like Chinese. She has odd ideas. She is young and distracted. You may say she is too free."

Baffled by the turn in the conversation and by the apparently passionate thought Bai Yiping had devoted to the matter of Ming Yu, I said nothing. I had hoped to suggest Miss Ming as the perfect candidate for study in America; but it was clear that even here, where one was free to speak,

Bai would not agree, and I sensed that whatever I could say about Ming Yu she would pit herself against.

As if reading my mind, Bai Yiping said with grave finality, "No. It is not Miss Ming's time to come to America."

On my way home that night I thought about this and about my friend, Ming Yu, and I felt uneasy. I couldn't help but be reminded of the last letter Bai Yiping had sent to me in China, sometime in April, a letter in which she detailed the reading she had done, mostly about the women's movement in America. She had read de Beauvoir's *Second Sex*, and for her own amusement she read essays on women in Shakespeare. Bai felt she had learned a great deal from American women, whom she described as, "self-assured, ambitious, and forward-looking," and she noted what a contrast these qualities made with those of Chinese women, who were "shy, quiet, modest." She said, "it is by no means good education, especially for women, to be timid and withdrawn." In America Bai had found a confidence and courage she had not previously had in China. She described herself as being more forthright in America. Above all she was impressed by the defiance American women displayed in the face of authority, for in her opinion "Chinese women usually show too much respect for superiors."

But regardless of what she had learned during her year in America, Bai Yiping was still a middle-aged Chinese woman, and her views on Ming Yu's behavior reflected that.

YANG
SHIREN

The Hangzhou airport, a gray cement building with red velvet curtains stretched tightly across its tall windows, had all the charm of an abandoned factory. Scattered in the fields around it, as if for moral support, several single-story cement shelters stood, windowless, square, and solid.

It was 98 degrees on the last day of August and unbearably dry. Dressed in long pants and tops with long sleeves, Christina and I followed a crowd of Chinese travelers out of the small plane, across the cracked pavement of the landing field, through the double doors of a shelter, and into a low-ceilinged room appointed with wooden benches like pews from a Quaker meeting hall. Iron ceiling fans rotated lazily above us, and though the room was filled with people, it was strangely quiet here. A teenage customs officer in a visored cap and baggy green uniform stamped our passports and waved us into a hangar, where our luggage had been flung into a heap. Weary travelers dug through the luggage pile for their belongings, scrambling over suitcases and tossing aside whatever didn't belong to them. A tiny grandmother in black trousers and smock leaned against the cinder-block wall and shouted orders to a man I imagined was her grandson, indicating with the tip of her cane which part of the pile she thought he would be wise to delve into first. In old age the woman's bound feet had assumed the cylindrical shape of dinner rolls; I had to force myself not to stare at them. Her gray hair, raked flat against her scalp and twisted into a knot, was smooth as marble. She had tiny ears and a handsome brown face.

Earlier, on the plane, I had seen this grandmother eating something shiny and black, like snake or eel, from a plastic container and inspecting a watch she had brought home with her from Hong Kong. She chewed contemplatively as she held the watch up for examination by the light of the airplane's window, and her chopsticks manipulated the slippery eel with finesse, as though the sticks were an extension of her bony fingers. She muttered something to the grandson, and dutifully he fastened the watch, like a handcuff, to her fragile wrist. She held her brittle arm up and watched in fascination as the second hand swept along its tiny circle. She checked the back of the leather watchstrap, fastened and unfastened its gold buckle several times, plucked out its stem, and rushed the hands through all the twelve hours, a trick that made the corners of her mouth curl up into a bemused smile. Another bite of eel, an utterance to the grandson, and he removed the watch from her wrist. It was a big-faced man's watch and it lay heavily in the palm of her hand. She stared at it for a long time, considering it, then she lay the chopsticks down on the tray table, and with both hands she pressed the watch to her hearing aid. She shut her eyes and listened, open-mouthed, to the ticking. When the grandson attempted to speak to her, she silenced him with an upheld hand. Eventually she put the watch into its velvet-covered box, tucked it carefully away among her possessions, settled back into her seat, and turned an indifferent gaze on the cottony clouds that wiped the wings of the plane and on the mountains of China passing below.

In the dark hangar the grandson, heavy-faced and fortyish in a suit and tie, clambered awkwardly over a duffel bag and heaved a suitcase higher onto the pile. Christina and I abandoned our shyness and joined him, and when the grandmother crowed impatiently behind us, he grinned sheepishly. He was sweating and harried. At one point in his search he knelt unwittingly on the tip of his own tie, and when he tried to lift his head, the tie stopped him short with a jolt, like a leash.

Christina and I carried our luggage out to the front of the building, where a crowd of people in white shirts stood in the blinding sun waiting for friends and relatives. We stacked the luggage against the building, sat on it, and stared at the rocks and bricks and debris that lay around the ground like the fallout from a bombing. The earth here was hard and dry, and the crabbed branches of the few mongrel bushes were choked with bits of windblown trash. In a field across a narrow road men and women worked in straw hats, ignoring the airport and the taxi drivers, the travelers and the two silver planes parked in the lot behind them. The dry fields were an ocher color, flat as the close blue sky and bounded in the distance by gently swaying poplars. Not far from where we sat, the paved road narrowed further and became a dirt path, and occasionally a farmer rounded the bend on it, seeming to appear out of the bushes, leading a donkey trembling under the weight of a two-wheeled cart piled high with stones. The donkeys picked their way gingerly down the road as though their pointed hooves were bruised and sore. A hot wind blasted dust out of the fields in sheets.

As far as we could see, no one had come to meet us. In the parking lot three men in white shirts sat smoking in a white Japanese van with the motor running and the windows rolled up tight. The driver got out and approached us with the high-stepping gait of a horse. "Excuse me," he said, glancing nervously from Christina to me and back again, "are you Miss Clark?" Earlier I had seen this man self-consciously waving a piece of cardboard with *Judy Clark* printed neatly across it in red crayon at travelers who passed out of the building. We told the man we were not Miss Clark, and he smiled, as though the news pleased him. "I am from Wuhan Medical College," he said. "Excuse me." He returned to his smoky van.

Christina looked at her shoes. She was slight and blond and had a fine-boned prettiness. She had high cheekbones, a long neck, and a long straight nose. Her hair framed her face in delicate curls, and she walked like a ballerina, on the balls of her feet. At some point during our two-day trip she had told me that her mother was from Sweden, her father was from Turkey, and that she—by some odd twist—had been born in Oklahoma and raised in Canada. She had a distinct but unidentifiable accent—a little bit of England, where she'd studied for a year; a little bit of Calgary; and a little bit of Cambridge, Massachusetts, where she'd lived for the past few years. She was intelligent and scholarly. She made notes to herself in the margins of *The Economist*. Her clothes were expensive. At twenty-two she was four years younger than I. Beside her on the luggage I felt like a rough dunce. I didn't like being thrown together with a stranger under such intimate and extreme conditions. I preferred to travel alone. If I made mistakes, I wanted them to be mine, and I sensed Christina felt the same way. We sat on our bags, sweating and doubtful and looking away from each other.

Earlier that morning, from our hotel in Hong Kong, I had placed a telephone call to the head of the Foreign Affairs Office at Hangzhou University to reconfirm that we would be arriving at the Hangzhou airport at two o'clock. When I got through to the university operator and told her I wanted to speak to Mr. Yang, she said, "What Yang?!" Her voice was thin and buzzed like raw electricity in my ear.

No one at Radcliffe had told us Yang's first name. "I don't know what Yang," I said. "Yang is all I know." A crackling silence underscored the distance between Kowloon and Hangzhou; then came the operator's emphatic, "Miss! In China, Yang is the same as Smith! If you do not know the first name, I cannot help you!"

An hour passed. The three men in the van smoked with devotion and gazed at us through the dirty windshield. The crowd of travelers around the door had dissipated in a cloud of dust, laughing and shouting, dragging their bags into taxis and vans, piling them onto pedicabs, or simply hauling them happily down the road on foot. There was something distinctive about the shirts the people wore, and after some thought I realized it was not merely that they were uniformly white but that every last one went untucked, the apparent fashion, and the shirts had no tails but were simply chopped off at the hip and hemmed, like Mexican dancing shirts. Their pants were gray cotton, their shoes were vinyl sandals, their heavy black hair was cut in two or three variations on the basic soup-bowl motif—these features combined to lend them the look of the hard-bitten religious.

Eventually Christina and I got off the luggage and went in search of a bathroom. Behind a wooden door in a neighboring building we found a bereft cement cell with a broken sink on the wall and a mossy trough in the floor for a toilet. We washed our hands at the sink and somberly reminded each other not to drink the water. I put my hand to my face—it was burning hot and so was the top of my head, where the sun had been driving into it like a hot nail. Reluctantly we returned to our luggage, to the heat. I wanted to speak, to say something that might be comforting to both of us, but I was afraid of my voice, afraid it would betray only fear and regret.

Another half hour passed. Again the van driver approached us. "You are waiting for?" he said.

We told him.

"Aha," he said, "I have been waiting for Miss Clark,

but I don't see her now, so of course we can drive you to your university."

We leapt up and threw our bags into the air-conditioned van before the man could change his mind. He proposed waiting a bit longer in case the friends from our university were on their way. Politely we agreed that this was wise, and we stared out the windows at the flat fields, and the farmers in the patched blue rags. Eventually the driver said, "We'll begin," but as soon as he shifted into gear, the van stalled, and he had trouble starting it again. As if on cue, his silent companions jumped out and disappeared under the hood; amid their tapping and banging and testing of wires the driver peered over his shoulder at us and said with a nervous grin, "We are just now having a little rest before we go!"

The apartment Christina and I shared in the Foreign Experts' Building at the university was dark, gloomy, and hot. It had two bedrooms, a living room, a bathroom, and a small kitchen reminiscent of the bottle-washing room in a country creamery; the floor was cement, yellow tiles ran halfway up the walls, a low counter supported a deep sink, and two metal elements hooked up to a keg of gas. We had pea-green wall-to-wall carpeting, bamboo-patterned wallpaper, and brown Naugahyde armchairs and couches. There were two small desks and two single beds, unaccountably spread with terry-cloth beach towels. The heavy red velvet curtains that stretched across the windows in the living room were like stage curtains—they would have made an excellent dress—and when drawn open or closed they spanked up a cloud of dust.

We pointed out to the two young maids who had helped us with our luggage that the door to one of the two bedrooms was locked. They said, "Blankets and bedding are stored there," and to prove it, they pointed to the blankets stacked up as high as the small window in the door and rattled the doorhandle and shrugged. The blankets and bedding would stay where they were. We would simply have to turn the living room into a bedroom.

The maids brought us two thermoses of hot water and left us alone. While Christina began to unpack her things, I sat in an armchair, exhausted, trying to collect my thoughts, to calm myself. Idly I stretched out my arm and pulled open a wooden cupboard built low into the wall beside me. In it I found a box of mysterious orange powder spilled across a shelf, a box with *Obesity Pills* printed across it in shaky English type, and a map of the world in Cyrillic with the Soviet Union situated prominently in its middle. These seemed ominous artifacts to me, and the room felt hopelessly dark—a good place for brooding. I shut the cupboard, leaned my head against the back of the chair, and went over the few facts I knew for certain: where I had come from, where I was, and how long I would be here. As I was thinking, I saw, from the corner of my eye, a white sneaker hurtle down past my window.

I didn't get up. Why upset what little remaining sense of order I had with another new surprise? I ignored the sneaker and stared out the window. From where I sat I had a partially obstructed view of two pine trees within our compound and, just beyond the compound wall, of an enormous gray apartment building with the two-dimensional look of a stage set. The cement staircases in this building were exposed, and on the third-floor landing I could see two young parents arguing, while their muddy-faced child howled between them. The child's gaping mouth was a spot of red in an otherwise colorless picture, and the three wretched voices echoed spookily up the stairwell. Just to their left a middle-aged woman in a white blouse and heavy black-rimmed glasses stood cooking in her kitchen. I could hear the sound of her wok searing the vegetables she threw into it, could see the steam rising up in front of her face in great billowing bursts. A stout husband appeared and disappeared behind her in his undershirt, dutifully passing her utensils and ingredients. Outside the kitchen window a dried fish hung stiff on a piece of twine.

Next to the apartment building stood an empty seven-story red-brick building from which the windows had been removed. Men in blue clothes were working on the building, but their progress was notably slow, and weeks would pass before I had a sense whether the building was going up or coming down or in a state of renovation. On our trip from the airport I had noticed scores of buildings like this, and everywhere there were deep pits in the ground and piles of tools and building supplies. Buildings of bright red brick would go up overnight here, long one-story barracks that housed the construction workers, peasants who came into the city to help build the city's modern office buildings and hotels. The walls of these temporary structures were only one brick thick, and in the evenings I could see barefoot people inside them cooking over open fires in the middle of the room.

A second white sneaker flew down past my window. I got out of the chair, went to the balcony door, and after a great deal of heaving and banging, managed to open it and get out into the crushing heat. The air was dense, and the foliage in the courtyard seemed to be baking. As I walked to the balcony's edge, I stepped, to my horror, on the decomposing body of a sparrow, heard its tiny skull crunch to pieces under my shoe. I jumped in fright and clapped my hands over my mouth.

Across the way the cook paused between stirs of her soup to wipe the steam from her glasses and have a look at me. I waved to her, and she responded by disappearing entirely from the window.

Two white sneakers lay sole-up in the weedy courtyard below—I hadn't imagined them—and in days to come I would be unfazed when sliced bread came down and landed on my balcony, and pillowcases, and towels, and one day an entire bedsheet.

The young maids in the Foreign Experts' Building were vigorous and loud. That afternoon they burst in and out of our rooms with lamps and tables and linen, talking at the top of their voices, laughing, moving things and taking other things away. They watched us carefully and uttered a cautious "Hello" whenever we looked at them. They were called Xiao Zhen and Xiao Zhou, and when I asked them how old they were, they narrowed their eyes in suspense and said, "Guess!"

I guessed seventeen, which I thought was several years older than they looked. They snorted and laughed and hugged each other in sheer amusement. "Ha-ha!" said they. "Twenty-one and twenty-two!" They were long-haired and wore white silk dresses as insubstantial as underslips. When they saw among my possessions a photograph of me and my sister together on a beach, they said, "Twins!" I told them my sister was three years older than I. "But how much you look alike!" Zhou exclaimed. "*Too* much alike!" Zhen added definitively.

That evening a man appeared at our door: Yang Shiren, the head of the Foreign Affairs Office. "Also known as Jack," he said, heartily shaking our hands. He was a small man with a disproportionately large head. His hair was raven black and backswept, his teeth perfectly white, his cheekbones high, and his mouth parenthesized by deep lines. He had spent a year and a half studying and teaching in California, and his English was excellent. He sat down in an armchair and apologized for not having come to meet us at the airport. Radcliffe College had told him we were coming tomorrow, he said, and when the house workers alerted him we were here, he intended to rush right over. "But then I realized my son had taken my bicycle and I had no way to get here!" he said. He had a thin, reedy voice that whispered up like hot steam from the back of his throat, and he spoke with exaggerated woe, tilting his head and knitting his brows at us in what seemed like a parody of sympathy. He chattered like a chipmunk, had a tapping, distracting chipmunk's laugh. We replied politely to his questions, smiled, and made small talk about our trip.

Despite his garrulousness it was obvious that Yang was in a hurry to get this meeting over with. When we asked him about our teaching duties and about getting the teacher of Chinese that had been promised in our informal contract, Yang's expression soured perceptibly, as though the request had led him off his script for the evening. He fiddled with his watch, and with the faintest shadow of a warning in his voice he said, "Someone will come to see you about a teacher. But now you must be very tired."

The impression I had was that this sort of subject was not to be broached so soon and that it was not for us to ask, but for Yang or someone else to inform us at the appropriate time. It was my first experience with the Chinese method of procedure, a slow, subtle, unbending code that seemed devised to keep the foreigner guessing.

On his way out of the room Yang said with a skeptical smile, "You girls are very young to be teachers!"

BUILDING AND
BUFFALO

The day after I arrived in Hangzhou, I walked around the university in the late afternoon and was struck by the stillness of it—the students hadn't arrived yet, and under the deep-blue sky the campus felt eerie, like a prairie town that had long ago been abandoned in favor of a city. The central courtyard was covered with weedy grass and stunted bushes, crisscrossed with hard dirt footpaths, and ringed with short oak trees and a crudely paved oval. The buildings and grounds of the university were in astonishing disarray; the newer buildings were permanently unfinished and prematurely aged, and the older buildings were dilapidated. The grounds were torn up and littered with construction materials. Some of the classroom buildings around the central courtyard were of plain gray cement, and others—painted a peculiar mango red or canary yellow and trimmed with purple or orange—had a distinctly traditional cast and sloping roofs that flipped upward at the edges, like ski jumps. Doors were unhinged, windows were broken, slate shingles slipped dangerously from roofs. Inside, the buildings were dirty and stark, with mops and old furniture piled up in corners, and the bathrooms at the ends of the hallways were dark and damp and festering. The stairs and floors were covered with dust, and the hallway walls were papered with ragged posters and announcements, many of them years old and peeling, like advertisements on the wall of a subway station.

From the outside the main library at the end of the central courtyard had the hollow, layered look of an urban parking garage. Inside there were scores of tin watering cans piled up in the lobby and skeletons of broken shelves and card catalogs lining the walls and blocking the doors that opened onto the library proper. The area behind the library was like a public junkyard scattered with bricks, broken tools, bicycle parts, rubber boots, a cotton dress, and rolls of wire. Oddly, in the middle of this confusion a brand-new bamboo scaffolding had been erected for what I could only guess would be another construction project. In the distance, near the high cement wall that surrounded the university, two aged workmen chatted idly, rakes slung over their shoulders, backs turned on a roaring bonfire.

Next to the library I found the building I'd be teaching in, the Foreign Languages Department, a brand-new structure that Jack Yang proudly told me had been completed that month. Indeed the exterior of the building was brighter and more cheerful than the others, and several floors taller, but as soon as I stepped inside, I was filled with horror and fascination: it was like witnessing the result of a bad engineering mistake, for essentially only the shell of the building had been erected, and the project had been abandoned—or worse, deemed complete—before any of the finish work had been properly done. There were gaping holes in the ceiling where light fixtures should have been, doorknobs hadn't been put in place, steel wires snaked out of holes in the baseboards, the screenless windows in the classrooms didn't close snugly, and watermarks ran down the new walls from leaks and cracks in the structure. The hallways were strewn with papers, cigarette butts, and watermelon rinds. In the classrooms brand-new desks and chairs made of a cheap blond wood were already cracked and wobbling, and in one room the heavy slate blackboard—not yet days old—had fallen forward off the wall and shattered in a hundred pieces on the cement floor. Everything was covered with a fine white dust; when I pressed my palm against the wall, it came down white as a clown's face.

As I passed by the small reception office just inside the front door, I glanced through the surveillance window and was startled to see an old man in his underwear napping on a cot. He had a fan, a coal stove, a wok, a mosquito net, and a festive banner of laundry drying on a line he'd strung across the room. This guard had turned his little room into a cozy home away from home and wasn't the least concerned that his every domestic move was visible to the passing public. On my way to class on future mornings I would catch him brushing his teeth and combing his hair in the reflection of his tin tea kettle.

On my way out of the building I waded through a deep puddle in the lobby, marveling that classes were soon to begin here.

Before I went home, I took a walk in the big fields to the west of the university; through these fields narrow footpaths had been elevated out of the earth by hand, and in some places the paths were so narrow and so high above the planting plane that walking along them was like walking along the top of a picnic bench. The fields looked exhausted, and the water that gathered in the irrigation ditches was foamy and black. But it was peaceful here, and I felt relieved to be away from the dust and the ugliness of the campus. In the west the sky was turning red, and yellow lights flickered on in the long rows of apartment buildings at the far end of the field. Overhead, flitting bats began to appear. Ahead of me I could see the outlines of a young man, a short old woman, and a water buffalo. As I approached them, I realized the man was using a willow whip to coax the buffalo into pulling a wooden plow. The plow was primitive, the yoke was worn and shiny with use, and the buffalo and his master were up to their knees in thick black mud.

The old woman, dressed in a baggy blue jacket and corduroy slippers, stood watching the struggle from the dry path. She folded her thick arms comfortably across her chest and chatted happily at the man.

The buffalo's progress was painfully slow. He kept stopping to nibble clumps of grass, or to lie down like a drunk in the mud, and at the slightest sign of either diversion the man fell into a fit of shouting that raised the veins on his neck and tossed his stringy black hair forward onto his forehead and into his furious eyes. He snapped the whip down hard and fast on the animal's muddy, hairy back. He staggered around in the mud. He had only plowed six feet behind him, and already his clothes were filthy and he was exhausted. I kept a respectful distance between us and watched in amazement. Presently the old woman shouted and waved me over, not at all surprised to see me here in the middle of this field, as though she'd been expecting me. Her skin was brown and dry, and her narrow eyes were like coin slots in her face.

"Hey!" she said cheerfully, fixing her short gray hair with a bobby pin, "is this interesting?"

I told her I thought it was.

She smiled and nodded and gestured proudly to the plow. "Ever seen this before?"

"No."

"No," she repeated triumphantly, "because you don't have this in your country, right?"

I smiled. "Right."

The woman's laugh was braying and confident and rang in my ears. I walked home feeling oddly ashamed that we didn't have that plow in my country.

THE PEOPLE'S ENGLISH

As Bai Yiping had predicted, before the week's end a smiling member of the faculty came to see me about my work. He introduced himself as Chen Peiling, head of the teaching group I would be a member of in the *Gong Gong Yingyu Xi*, or Public English Department, which, he explained, had been established for those students who majored in subjects other than English. "You may think of it as the people's English," he said shyly, crossing his thin arms and legs in a manner that was pleasantly effeminate. Chen was wasp-waisted and imp-faced with small ears and raspberry-red lips. He smiled habitually and emphasized his words by giving the air a smart little stab with his index finger.

As the head of my teaching group, Chen said, it was his job to inform me that my students would be sophomores from the Chinese and Geography departments, that there would be sixty-seven total, and that their English would not be good. He gave me the textbooks we would use and invited me to a meeting of the teaching group the next morning. When our brief conversation came to an end, Chen walked backward out of the room, half-bowing at me.

Chen was delicate and refined; had he lived in the 1920s and '30s, he would have been a languid, opium-smoking landlord, equipped for leisure with long fingernails and billowing silk sleeves. But in 1987 he was simply a nervous teacher in plastic sandals and a white sports shirt, unaware or unconcerned that his leaking fountain pen had stained his breast pocket.

The primary textbook, called *English—Book 2*, was a collection of short essays, stories, and exercises, some of which were written by internationally renowned writers, some of which had no byline at all. The stories, which took place exclusively in England and America, were morally and politically instructive, and they subtly illustrated that the lifestyle of the West was undesirable and the system unjust. The essays focused on class differences, on crime, on greed, on racism, and extolled the virtues of hard work, generosity, and diligent study. One essay dwelt on the virtual slave status of Chinese in nineteenth-century America, on their role as cooks and launderers in gold-mining villages. Another told the story of Jim Thorpe, who was stripped of his Olympic medals not—in the author's tacit opinion—because he had played semiprofessional baseball but ultimately because he was an American Indian and, as such, not a proper citizen of the United States. A third piece consisted of a letter from a woman who had traveled across America in a covered wagon in 1876; the woman and her family suffered unimaginable hardships in order to settle in the American West for the glory and development of their country. There were stories about Hitler, technology, anthropology, civil war, medicine, the spread of knowledge, and many were told in a socialist voice.

The secondary book was a collection of short pieces designed to accompany a taped voice for practice in listening. The books, printed by a language institute in Shanghai, contained egregious factual errors ("The price of a movie ticket in theaters in American suburbs is $20.00, but in the cities it is much higher; in some cities it is even as high as $9.00."), mispellings, misprints, grammatical errors, wrong answers in the keys, and sometimes whole sections of illegible, ghostlike print. I shoved the book under my chair, planning to ignore it.

The next morning when I arrived at the teachers' room in the Foreign Languages Building, a group of teachers was there milling about, joking and talking loudly. In one corner a laughing older woman with pink cheeks and big teeth was slapping a young man on the wrist again and again as if to say, "You rogue!" The woman's eyes blinked violently, an unfortunate tic that made her appear stunned, as though she had caught a frying pan in the head. Beyond the room's six open windows a construction team pounded and clanked with their pickaxes and shovels in the hot sun; the long wooden conference table in the middle of the room was blanketed with the white dust they stirred up. Several younger teachers used wet rags to wipe down the table and chairs before the meeting began.

When I stepped into the room, the teachers fell silent one-by-one and smiled tentatively at me. A slight young man stepped forward and offered me a chair. "I am Zhen Xinqu. I will be your co-teacher. You are Rosemary." Zhen spoke softly and uncertainly, as though he had no faith in his ability to assist me. I shook his sweating hand and told him I was pleased to meet him, which appeared to confuse and frighten him further. Several other teachers murmured, "Welcome you."

With these preliminaries out of the way, the jolly, blinking woman exclaimed, "Peanuts, how about?!" and in one swift motion she yanked a heavy drawer, curiously full of raw peanuts, clean out of the conference table. She opened a wooden cupboard against the wall, fished a wok out from among piles of books and papers, slammed the cupboard shut, and hurried out of the room and down the hall on her short, sneakered feet. A few minutes later she returned and, without the slightest hesitation or ceremony, she turned the wok upside down and spilled the freshly fried peanuts in a heap on the bare table. She laughed and blinked and chatted loudly. She chewed a handful of peanuts and nudged me in the arm, urging me to take some. She introduced herself as Mrs. Ou. Her English was flawed and her blinking was distracting, but she was the first casual person I had met here and I was immediately drawn to her.

"You know," she sputtered hilariously to the room, "my husband says I should not eat peanuts! He says I need to slim down!" She basked in the group's loud laughter. "Comrade Rose," she said politely, "what would you say about a husband like that?!"

In my opinion Mrs. Ou was not fat; it was only her jovial personality that made her seem so. I told her I thought she didn't need to lose weight, that in fact very few Chinese women appeared fat. She stopped chewing to listen to me. Her eyes narrowed with obvious pleasure. When I had finished speaking, she gave me an encouraging thump on the shoulder with the back of her greasy hand and cried, "True! Only Russian women are fat!"

Chen Peiling, the head of the group, arrived with a cigarette held delicately between two fingers. He urged me to sit at the head of the table, next to several large and threatening pieces of broken glass that had been propped against the wall, and formally introduced me to the group of approximately fifteen teachers, ranging in age from twenty-one to fifty-seven. Chen told them I was a distinguished American person and a teacher of writing and that anyhow I would spend that year helping them all to teach English. From the start I sensed he saw me as an unwieldy curiosity, an expensive, unpredictable, potentially dangerous object that he was responsible for but didn't quite know what to do with. I might have to be cosseted and humored. I might make demands. I might criticize his English. He wouldn't look at me, and when the introduction was over, he leapt into an explanation of the course we would teach, a jumbled mix of reading, writing, speaking, listening, and social study. We were all to use the same textbook, were expected to keep apace in it, and were to devote two hours per week per class to work in the listening laboratory.

Chen spoke with the light and mischievous delivery of a man telling a joke at a party; he grinned wetly, his eyes twinkled, he seemed amused by the thought of his own responsibility. His tone suggested that these orders were not his idea, that they were merely filtering through him from some higher source. He said, "We are also to teach in the manner prescribed by the chairman of the Foreign Languages Department," but his expression seemed to question the mandate. He read the chairman's prescription from a notebook: " 'Read text. Explain text. Explain important points and unknown phrases. Ask students to answer questions at end of text. If students don't understand questions, explain. Do exercises.' "

Chen moved on to a detailed presentation of how he planned to teach the first lesson of the semester to his students, and as he talked, several of the older women—including Mrs. Ou—at the far end of the table drifted off to sleep, while others knitted or whispered among themselves or read books unrelated to the class. One of the women had brought her young son to the meeting, and he now wandered around the room, snapping sticks of chalk and banging the windows closed and open, closed and open. No one objected to the interruption, and the construction workers outside clanked on. In the middle of the meeting two workmen opened the door, marched boldly into the room with their pantlegs rolled up over their bony knees, and with a tremendous shouting and knocking about they dragged the pieces of broken glass out into the hallway. Remarkably the teachers seemed not to notice them, and without a pause Chen Peiling forged bravely ahead with his nearly inaudible presentation.

Several more teachers arrived thirty to forty minutes after the meeting had begun. They entered smiling and not the least contrite or apologetic. When Chen was finished, everyone clapped furiously, and Zhen Xinqu stood up and offered his interpretation of the second text we would teach, an essay entitled "A Brush with the Law," which takes place in a suburb of London during the late 1960s and details the slightly illogical and very unlikely story of a long-haired college student who gets arrested for allegedly stealing milk bottles. In truth the arrest occurs because the youth looks to the police like an itinerant, a "thoroughly disreputable character." The arrest is clearly unwarranted. The young man's middle-class father hires a brilliant solicitor to represent him. In court the magistrate dismisses the case immediately, and costs are awarded against the police. A socialist at heart, the boy sees the injustice in the experience: His release clearly hinges on his family background, his class affiliation, his proper accent, and his father's ability to afford a good solicitor. He says, "Given the obscure nature of the charge, I feel sure that if I had come from a different background and had really been unemployed, there is every chance that I would have been found guilty."

Mr. Zhen's English was excellent, and his explanations of new phrases was perceptive and accurate, but like Mr. Chen, he offered no analysis of the story. When he had finished, Zhen asked the group if they had any suggestions. One older man with a scarred eyelid raised his hand and said, "I have no suggestions, but I am interested in a deeper understanding of the text. Perhaps Comrade Rosemary could assist me with this. Why would this boy be happy to call himself part of the counterculture?" He seemed genuinely puzzled by the boy's confession. I explained that at that time many young people in the West were proud to be part of the antiestablishment movement, that they felt obliged to challenge and inspect the goals and motivations of the people in power.

The man looked cautiously around the table at the faces of his comrades before reacting to my statement with a knowing smile.

An older woman stood up and gave her presentation in Chinese.

After the meeting two friendly young teachers who identified themselves as Margaret and Eileen approached me to say that they were graduate students in English and that if I had any problems or questions about anything while I was here, they would be more than happy to assist me. They spoke perfect English with the angular accent of the American Midwest, and when I pointed this out to them, they fell beside themselves with glee: they had been fortunate enough to have a teacher from Wisconsin some years back, they explained, and ever since, they had tried their best to sound like him.

I asked them why that last speaker had given her presentation in Chinese. Margaret said, "She cannot speak English."

"But she's an English teacher," I said.

Eileen answered, "Yes, it's not her fault. She was trained as a teacher of Russian, but in the middle of her career, when certain foreign policies changed, she was advised that she was needed to teach English. She studied English of course, but it wasn't much use. Several in our group have had the same unfortunate experience."

Later I discovered how true this was. There were older teachers in the group who never once spoke a word of English to me, and the majority of the teaching group, including some of the younger ones who were nearly fluent in English, conducted their classes entirely in Chinese.

MING
YU

I met Ming Yu on the introduction of George Greatorex, an Englishman who lived in the apartment above mine in the Foreign Experts' Building at Hangzhou University. The building—a four-storied structure occupied by fifteen teachers from Germany, England, Japan, the United States, Finland, and the Soviet Union—was surrounded by a tall cement wall topped with shards of broken bottles. The iron gate to the building was guarded around the clock by two elderly men who worked twelve-hour shifts and slept in the guardhouse to the side of the gate. The guards ate their meals from tin bowls there, boiled drinking water for the members of the household, housed the bicycle pump, kept an eye on the parked bicycles, and listened to Beijing opera on an old radio propped on the windowsill. Their main purpose, however, was to keep track of who came and went here, to know what visitors were in what rooms and how often, and in some cases to decide who had the right to enter the building and who hadn't. Chinese visitors were required to identify themselves at the gate and sign their names in a register kept in the guardhouse. University students had particular difficulty getting into the building—some because of the whim of the guard, others because there were specific official orders against them. I discussed this with a student of mine and asked her if she knew why we had guards at our gate. She hedged, then said, "They say they protect the foreign teachers, but I really think they are trying to protect us." Each night at 11:00 P.M. the gate was locked from the inside with a long iron bolt, and if a resident still had visitors at that hour, the guards knocked loudly on the apartment door crying, "The gate is closing! The visitor must leave!"

During my first week in Hangzhou I had noticed George Greatorex around the Experts' Building. He struck me as singular, listless, and somewhat depressed. He was tall and very thin and was forever carrying plates of sliced cucumbers from the kitchen up to his room, where he spent most of his time alone. He had a dark beard and a sallow, sharp-featured face. He spoke softly, swallowing his words in what seemed like an effort to foil eavesdroppers. His unwavering gaze missed nothing. The first time he spoke to me, from a distance in the courtyard, I thought he was talking to himself; naturally I ignored him and walked out through the gate.

Mr. Greatorex had heard that I had studied writing in an American university, and early in September he came to my door and asked if I might be willing to look at the poetry of a young Chinese teacher in the university, Ming Yu, a friend of his who wanted very much to go to the United States to study creative writing. His friend, he said, was intelligent and talented and needed to leave China in order to realize her potential. When I agreed to talk with Miss Ming, he asked if I would mind greeting her at the gate to our building rather than waiting for her in my room, in order that the gatekeeper might see her with me. His reasoning was that if Miss Ming entered the building alone, the gatekeeper would naturally assume she was going to see Mr. Greatorex, a practice she had already been reprimanded for several times by the university security officers, who had lately been monitoring her appearances here and had told her, in no uncertain terms, that her visits were inappropriate. According to Mr. Greatorex, one night as Miss Ming passed their office on her way home, the police called out to her and nicely asked her to come in for a "little chat." Once inside, their tone changed. They told her she must stop spending so much time with the foreign teachers, that they were a bad influence on her, and that it was particularly unseemly for a young Chinese woman to be spending time alone in the apartment of a foreign man. She had, they assured her, no idea what a foreign man might attempt under such conditions. In short, foreigners could not be trusted, and Miss Ming, at twenty-seven, could not be trusted to know as much.

Despite my uncertainty about Mr. Greatorex, I was curious and so agreed to meet Ming Yu at the gate.

The armchair in my room dwarfed Miss Ming when she sat in it, and only because of her high heels did her feet touch the floor. She was small and graceful, with heavy, waist-length hair and a slight, appealing overbite. She wore a gray skirt, a red blouse, and a pair of wire-rimmed glasses secured to her person by a chain worn around her neck. On such a delicate face the chain was incongruous; it hung down limply along either cheek like a disguise, making her appear older than her years. To the right of her small mouth three dark freckles formed a kind of triangle in an otherwise unblemished face. She spoke softly and thoughtfully with the accent of a British broadcaster. Her sentence structure and her vocabulary were elegant, making me self-conscious about my own sloppy speech. She was nervous; so was I. When I spoke, she snapped her fingers softly in her lap, again and again, as though this would help her to remember what I said. Her eyes were keen with interest and concentration.

I offered her a glass of water, which she held in both hands and drank carefully and all at once, in what resembled an act of obedience. From the wrist down her hands were swollen and pink, as though they had been immersed in boiling water. The fingernails were broken and the knuckles were scarred and callused; they were the rough hands of a laborer, which Miss Ming clearly was not. On a cold day much later in the year she would hold her hands up to me and say, "In winter I wash my clothing and vegetables in cold water, and then I get this . . . frostbite. In winter my hands are never warm." The hands were the only ungraceful thing about her.

"Your room is very, very comfortable," she said softly, looking around with genuine wonder, and I felt ashamed for having thought the room dim and drab.

We spent some time discussing various writers. She liked Henry James and Hemingway, whom another American teacher had introduced her to a few years back. She read Yeats and Browning and Shelley. I gave her books by Elizabeth Bishop and Mavis Gallant and some poems my sister-in-law had written, and when she glanced at the poems, she said in surprise, "They're typed."

I asked Ming about her wish to study writing in an American university. She hesitated a moment, then explained that in China no one studied creative writing. The opportunity did not exist. If anyone suggested such a thing, she would be laughed at.

She said, "Chinese do not believe such a field of study is useful. 'What good is it to study writing?' they say. 'If you want to be a writer, you simply write.'"

I told her that many Americans shared that sentiment. She said, "But at least some of you understand that it is useful." She explained that she had already applied to the writing program at Iowa State University of Science and Technology and had been accepted there with a teaching assistantship. I asked her why Iowa State, and she replied that her American teacher had told her that Iowa had a good writing program.

"I'm sure that's so," I said, and didn't share my suspicion that Iowa State University of Science and Technology was not the same Iowa the American teacher had in mind. I asked Ming if she would go to Iowa; she paused, softly snapping her fingers, considering her answer. "Well, this is not my decision. My work unit—the English Department—decides. They won't let me go to Iowa because they are afraid I would not come back. They told me that if I got married first, they might let me go. They told me they had a good person in mind for me to marry, a man who is now studying in America and who is soon to return to China."

"Do you know the man?" I asked.

"I have never met him, though I have heard his name."

I must have looked incredulous at this bit of information, for Ming went on to tell me that marriage was a common prerequisite of authorities faced with a single person's request to study abroad. For the most part only married people or people with children were allowed to leave the country, the reason being that if they loved their families, they would certainly want to return to China to be with them; a family was a kind of ransom.

"If you had the opportunity to go to America, would you eventually return to China?" I asked.

"I can't say."

"You can't say because you don't know, or because you don't want to say?"

"Because I don't know."

"But if you knew you wanted to stay, could you marry the man they had in mind for you—say, as a convenience—and then go?"

Ming looked quizzically at me for a moment, and when she finally understood the question, she smiled in embarrassment and closed her eyes and leaned her head against the back of the chair. "I could not do such a thing. If I went and never came back, that man would bear the blame for it. He would be expected to be able to persuade his wife to return. If he failed, he would lose face. Even if I did not care for him, I could not do that. But regardless of my wish to study abroad, my department still wants to know why I am twenty-seven years old and unmarried. They try to match me up with various men. They say to me, 'Miss Ming, you are twenty-seven years old and you are not married. Is something the matter? You are not concerned? We would like you to meet Mr. Zhou. He is a professor of mathematics. You will like him.'

"One day the director of my department approached me in the hallway at school and said, 'Ming Yu, I have noticed that you seem unhappy these days. We never see you smile anymore. Perhaps you take your disappointment over America too hard. You must try to learn to accept the things that come to you. You must stop thinking only of yourself. You must begin to think about other people. There are many other people who also want the chance to go to America, people who are older and more deserving than you.' I asked the professor if he thought I was immature. He said he did think so. He said I still needed to grow up and asked if there was anything he could do for me in the meantime to make me feel better. I told him, 'You could send me to America. That would make me feel better.' He said, 'Miss Ming, you know I cannot go against the policies.' I wanted to say to him, 'But everyone knows you go against the policies at all times when it is convenient for you to do so.' " Ming laughed at the thought. "Of course, it would be foolhardy of me to say such an impertinent thing to my superior. Instead I turned and walked away from him. Even that was impertinent."

Ming Yu spoke without bitterness, and I found her remarkably open and accepting. She removed her glasses and rubbed their lenses on the hem of her skirt. Without the glasses she looked young, like a teenager. Her cheeks were round and her large brown eyes were exceptionally clear. As an afterthought and almost to herself she added, "In summer, because I am not married, I must return to my parents' home in Wuxi."

Eventually I asked to see some of Ming's poems. She put her purse in her lap, and as she sorted through its contents, her hair fell around her face in a veil and the ends of it fell into the purse. In the purse I could see a melee of papers, loose bank notes, a hair ribbon, a blue exam booklet, keys, a small flashlight, some photographs, letters bearing foreign postage stamps. She tucked her hair behind her small ears, held some papers to her chest. "I am afraid you will find my poems incorrect. Please forgive me. Now I will go upstairs to visit George Greatorex. Later I will return." She put the handwritten poems on the small table between us and said good-bye. Halfway through the door she stopped abruptly, came smiling back into the room, pulled a plastic bag from the bottom of her purse, and offered it to me. "You may try it," she said with an encouraging nod of her head. The bag was full of soft brown disks the size of coat buttons and dusted with a yellow, pollenlike powder.

"Is it something to eat?" I asked.

"Yes."

"Is it mushrooms?"

"Yes."

I looked closely at it and thought it wasn't mushrooms at all but smoked meat. "Is it really meat?"

Ming smiled. "Yes."

When she had gone, I nibbled one of the disks and discovered, after all, that it was pickled lemon peel.

An hour or so later Ming Yu returned, followed shortly by George. He had brought a liter bottle of beer down from his room, and as he filled three glasses, I noticed that his wrist was thinner even than Miss Ming's and that his fingers were long and paper-white. Somehow he seemed more Chinese than Ming did. His clothes—baggy pants like a surgeon's pajamas, a dingy yellowed T-shirt, and black Chinese slippers—were the same he'd been wearing for days and, as if he had caught me making note of this, he sat down and offered an unsolicited explanation.

"When I first came to China, I took care to wear a jacket and tie, but then I realized how dirty everything was and how filthy the classrooms were and I stopped. Why spoil my clothes? I suggest you do the same." He spoke in a soft, calculated monotone, snipping his words off, pausing a half beat between them—just long enough to draw my attention but not enough to be peculiar or annoying. I had to strain to hear him, which I supposed was precisely his intention; it had the effect of making what he said the more memorable.

George was thirty-three, a Foreign Expert in literature who had taught at Hangzhou University for one year, a year he said he thoroughly regretted. He would leave tomorrow if only the administration would pay him the money they owed him, but each month they told him they would not have his money until the next month, and the months went by, piling up behind him like a stack of dirty dishes. Chinese smiled. They lied. They spat. They were lazy and dishonest. And now Ming Yu could not visit him here because the authorities felt they had to protect her from him. Victorian as they were, their imaginations ran wild. George had tried to practice *taijiquan* with a teacher from the university, but within a few weeks the teacher was directed to stop giving George lessons. The university claimed the teacher was giving university secrets to a foreigner. George asked them what secrets. They said, "Why do you have to ask *us*? You already know what secrets." He asked them again. They said, "You know very well! Students' identification numbers!"

George's laugh was brittle. Here there was a regulation that any teacher employed by the university—including foreigners—would not be allowed to accept outside employment without the university's permission. And if a teacher did decide to accept other employment, such as a tutoring job or a night class, whomsoever he worked for would be required to pay not the teacher but the university for his services. The university would take its cut and give the teacher the remaining amount. If the university wasn't getting money for George's teacher's work, then they would make sure the teacher wouldn't get it either.

In George's evident opinion the university was little more than a money-making machine, and I found it hard not to believe that when I learned from other teachers that the Chemistry Department devoted its energies not to research but to devising new ways of making disposable balsa-wood chopsticks to sell to Japan. In addition, students were charged for the privilege of using the one mainframe computer on campus, and the Foreign Affairs Office was relentless in billing unwitting foreigners for nonexistent services and fees.

George's expression remained virtually unchanged as he spoke. His infrequent smiles were fleeting and closed-mouthed. Occasionally he raised his glass and sipped from it. He said that among the administration and the faculty no one wanted to work more than six hours per week. Professors did as little teaching as they could get away with, and they taught the same course year after year with no alteration, no changes, no modification. He said Ming Yu was a good, creative teacher who worked nearly twenty hours per week and was responsible for many students, but was nevertheless insignificant, underpaid, and dispensable.

In George's view the senior professors had no ambition beyond resting and staying in a cool place, and still they were paid handsome sums by Chinese standards. Administrators were tyrants who dispatched orders with a chilly smile that could disappear in an instant if one had the temerity to disagree with them. Lower-level teachers were fearful and so made no effort to improve their situation or to rectify the inequity. No one was concerned for the intellectual welfare of the students. The teachers read from a book for two hours, and the students tried to memorize what they heard. No one was invited to share ideas—no one had any ideas. The students knew nothing but how to repeat what they'd been told.

I glanced at Ming Yu, hoping to catch a reaction from her, but there was none; though George hadn't once deferred to her membership in the Chinese race, she was unfazed by his criticisms. She listened with calm concentration, her chin uplifted and her hands folded neatly in her lap. She did not strike me as someone who would try to make a good impression at the cost of the truth, but she did seem proud to be Chinese, and these Chinese George was talking about, if what he said was true, were certainly not people to be proud of.

George carried on in his flat and bitter and oddly compelling way. The information spilled out of him, a catalog of injustices and Chinese contradictions, and gradually his conviction, combined with the measured way he spoke, assumed the ring of a courtroom plea. I asked him why he was telling me these things. He shrugged. I asked him if he had told others. He had told some of the foreign teachers and students but said they didn't believe him. They didn't want to believe him. They saw only what they wanted to see.

I wondered aloud how Hangzhou University compared with other Chinese universities. George answered that fundamentally they were all the same, that their offenses varied only in degree, and that the Foreign Affairs Office at Hangzhou University, under its present regime, was particularly ruthless. "Before you leave, they will have tried to cheat you out of your money."

"I don't have any money to be cheated out of," I said. "And besides I didn't come here to make money."

"No?" George said pointedly, his eyebrows shooting upward in a caricature of surprise. "Why did you come?"

"For the same reason you did."

He raised his glass to his lips. "I doubt it," he said smugly. "But anyway, it doesn't matter. They'll anger and frustrate you. You can ask any of the German students here in the university. They'll tell you. They have good insights. They've been treated particularly badly."

I told George I supposed I'd eventually see these things for myself and that until that time I would reserve judgment.

"Prudent," he said dryly, stroking his beard.

George and Ming Yu made plans to meet several days later at 6:00 A.M. at the botanical gardens; they hoped to find a certain expert in *taijiquan* there, a teacher George admired. Before he left, George took a folded piece of paper from his pocket and put it on the table. "You might like to read this," he said. As he went out the door, he glanced back over his shoulder at me and said in a tone suited more to a dare than to an invitation, "Come along to the gardens if you feel like it."

When George had gone, I said to Ming Yu, "That wasn't mushrooms you gave me earlier, it was lemon peel."

Ming smiled deeply, her forearms stretched out flat along the plump arms of the chair. "I know," she said.

"Were you testing me?"

"No. I was agreeing with you."

I walked Ming Yu down to the gate. The night was warm and quiet. The gatekeeper sat in the courtyard on a low bamboo stool with a coil of incense burning near him on the ground to keep the mosquitoes from biting his bare ankles. He nodded as we walked by, fanned himself with a newspaper, spat loudly on the ground.

Ming and I said goodnight, and as I closed the gate behind her, I saw her lingering at the edge of the road looking back at me, as though there was one more thing she wanted to say.

I went back upstairs, thinking what an odd pair she and George seemed.

CORRECT
GOALS

The folded paper George had left on my table was a photocopy of an article headlined, UNIVERSITY PUNISHES 33 FOR GAMBLING, which appeared in the summer of 1987 in the *China Daily*, China's English-language newspaper. Quoting a story in the *People's Daily*, the article detailed the results of a campus raid that had occurred that spring at Hangzhou University:

> Thirty-three students were "expelled, ordered to quit school, placed on disciplinary probation or given a written or verbal disciplinary warning.
>
> "The students reportedly behaved badly because of the influence of decadent bourgeois ideology ... a small group [of students] prized open some empty dormitory rooms to gather there many times to gamble at mahzhong and cards. They also held drinking parties and all-night dances in the dark.
>
> "Some students said the incident had made them realize they must never relax their ideological vigilance against the influence of the decadent Western lifestyle. They must have correct goals in life and study hard for the country's socialist modernization construction."

Except for one or two, my students didn't fit this description; they were neither gamblers nor born-again socialists, they didn't drink or fight or prize rooms open. The only dancing they did was the occasional impromptu waltz in a public park with their roommates in preparation for a time when they would be old enough or bold enough to dance with members of the opposite sex. In class the boys sat in the back of the room, the girls sat in the front, and when I suggested we mix the seating for a change, they tittered and covered their faces. Though they were nineteen and twenty years old, many of them had the physical appearance of ninth-graders, and an alarming number wore the small, horn-rimmed, government-issue eyeglasses that had the capacity to make the most seasoned hooligan seem bookish and diffident. They had a refined appreciation of humor and were particularly delighted by puns and by jokes that relied on wordplay for their punch. They were polite and earnest. They had hobbies. They honored their parents. As for correct goals in life, they seemed to have few goals at all beyond passing their final examinations and moving into an acceptable job. Many of them confessed they had secret hopes of traveling to America, but among the more realistic of the students these hopes fell into the category of daydreams and were appreciated as such, as unattainable, as little more than fantasy. In general, when it came to their own future, the students were unexpectant and fatalistic, resigned to their dependency on their parents and the state. They had little confidence in their ability to change their circumscribed lives or to take control over what would happen to them next. Indeed, when they were finished at the university, they would be assigned to jobs wherever jobs happened to be available and whether or not they wanted them. Not surprisingly, some of my students seemed to suffer a mild depression. The young women looked particularly unhappy, and in unguarded moments they wore sad, pensive expressions on their faces.

Throughout their four years at Hangzhou the university would watch the students carefully, tell them what to do, when to do it, and how to think about it. At 6:30 in the morning loudspeakers blared militaristic anthems across the campus to wake the students and get them started on their day. After splashing cold water on their faces they tromped to the dining hall with their tin bowls and spoons, hurried down a breakfast of rice and fried breadsticks, and began their classes at 7:30. They studied by rote. Some days as I walked across the campus I could hear the sound of students' voices repeating in unison the information they had just received; it was a dragging, methodical chanting that seeped through the open classroom windows and seemed to settle in the leaves of trees. The sound was disturbing, and it stayed with me long after the classes were over. When I asked my students why they studied certain subjects, including English, they answered simply, "We must."

Some students confessed they found their regular classes dull and unchallenging. In my class when I shared my ideas and opinions about our work and asked students to share theirs, or to disagree, they were overwhelmed by the opportunity. When I touched a student's hair to illustrate a point, they exploded with laughter at my familiarity. If I raised subjects unrelated to the text we were reading, their eyes glowed with fascination. Anything slightly unorthodox in class—a comical gesture, a personal question, an illustration on the blackboard—was momentous to them. They were bright and had, through long years of practice, developed an extraordinary capacity for memorization. Though they had difficulty speaking English in whole sentences, their knowledge of English grammar was dazzling, and their ability to parse a sentence was better than my own. Their grasp of geography was good, much better than the average American student's, though in a discussion of the peopling of America, when they asked me where my ancestors had come from and I answered "Ireland," it took them a moment to remember what country that was, and then, with recognition creeping across their faces, they said, "Oh, yes, a province of England."

The students slept seven to a room not much bigger than a 1948 De Soto sedan. Each room had one window, two rows of bunk beds pressed up against the walls, and two rickety tables that doubled as desks for the seven. They kept their belongings on shelves above their beds or in suitcases and trunks piled up near the door. The rooms were so narrow that two students sitting on parallel beds could reach out effortlessly and shake hands. Some students claimed it was a blessing to have so many roommates, for the body heat they generated kept the cement rooms at a bearable temperature on cold winter nights. Like their teachers, the students had dim light bulbs and cold showers, and they washed their clothes in long sinks in the bathrooms. On clear days the dorms were brilliant with laundry draped on drying-racks outside the windows. At 11:00 P.M. the electricity was cut off, the lights went out, and if the students wished to continue reading or studying, they were forced to resort to candles.

For recreation the students played cards in their rooms, read love stories printed on coarse yellow paper, or listened to radios and cassettes. In a university lecture room a black-and-white television had been set up for students' use, but the reception was poor and the selection of programs was limited. On Friday and Saturday nights there were movies in the barnlike university auditorium. The movies were often repeats, and the physical quality of the films was poor: scratched, sometimes broken, and inaudible. The students were so starved for entertainment that they occasionally held talent shows or put on performances for each other. At 9:00 one November night I saw lights glowing in the first-floor windows of one of the classroom buildings, an odd sight at that hour. As I approached the building, I heard the sound of uproarious collective laughter. I squeezed between two shrubs, peered over a windowsill, and saw, to my dismay, that the classroom was bursting with students. Some sat shoulder-to-shoulder in crowded rows, some shared seats with their arms wrapped around each other's shoulders for balance; others sat on desks or on the floor, or stood against the walls. They nibbled absently at salted pumpkin seeds and stretched their necks to get a better view of what was happening at the front of the room: two uncostumed male students aided only by fluorescent lights and a squealing microphone were performing a comedy routine. The smaller of the two was obviously and outrageously playing the role of a flirtatious young woman. He tucked his hands under his chin and his eyelids fluttered and his voice squeaked hysterically as he pranced around his bewildered partner. His timing was masterly. The audience laughed with their mouths open, laughed until they choked, slapped each other on the shoulders, clapped their hands over their eyes, and hugged their sides. They stomped and roared with delight. The weak lights lent their faces a grayish cast, but their joy—so rare—was radiant, and thrilling to see.

With the emergence of Deng Xiaoping's social and economic reforms, the Chinese students had begun to learn about other cultures and countries, and the more they learned, the more they realized how much they didn't have. They knew China was behind the times and they took this personally—it filled them with shame and anger. Though there was a campus Communist Youth League, and though membership in it was considered a prerequisite to a bright future, many students were reluctant to join. Many students had criticisms of their government, of inflation and corruption and "back door" relationships that ruled every facet of the society, but they felt tiny and insignificant in the face of these problems and feared the consequences of outspokenness and public protest. To them the government was like a distant and unyielding father.

In the winter of 1986-87 the brief student demonstrations that occurred in Beijing and Shanghai spread out to Hangzhou and took form in a few thousand students who tromped to the university gate and down Tian Mu Shan Road several evenings in a row with hand-painted signs and crude banners proclaiming *Minzhu* and *Ziyou*, "Democracy" and "Freedom."

Garth Peterson, an eighteen-year-old American studying Chinese in the university at the time, observed these demonstrations and felt that the students at Hangzhou had acted less out of their own political awareness than out of a desire to emulate their peers demonstrating in larger cities. One winter night Garth and his three roommates heard on a BBC broadcast that students in Beijing had been demonstrating for democracy. Several nights later the Hangzhou students began demonstrations of their own. Garth also observed that Hangzhou's students "lacked a coherent and concise proposal for political and social reform" and felt that these demonstrations were chiefly "an experiment with the new freedom of the times, a test of the Deng government's claim of allowing freedom of expression." Garth believed that for the majority of the Hangzhou students the demonstrations were an "unanticipated, exciting diversion from studying." An air of lightheartedness pervaded them, he said.

When I came to know them better, my students told me that in their hearts they considered demonstration a futile effort that could bring only long-lasting trouble to those who participated in it.

When I first met my students from the Geography Department, I thought some mistake had been made, that I'd been sent to the wrong room. I had been told I would be teaching sophomores, and when I arrived, what I found was a group of students so shy and small and filled with awe at my presence that they resembled schoolchildren on their first outing to the zoo. Lined up neatly on their desks they had rulers and notebooks and plastic pencil cases decorated with cartoon characters. They hooked their ragged cotton bookbags on the backs of their chairs. The girls wore homemade dresses and sandals and had straight bangs or drew their hair back loosely in clips and long ponytails. The boys dressed in tight dark pants, cotton dress shirts, and wore their hair in a shaggy, thick-banged style that resembled that of the Beatles in 1965. One or two of the more stylish boys had permed their hair and wore high-heeled boots and colorful T-shirts with English phrases printed across their fronts. One shirt in the back row announced Happy Our Country Being Famous for Its Rich and Strong, and another—almost as if in ironic response to the first—bore the unfortunate misprint Enjoy a Healthy Lie. A few of the students had come to Hangzhou from the countryside, had never seen a foreigner up close, and when I introduced myself, they winced at the sound of my voice and stared at their desks, sweating and trembling and clutching their pens. Every ounce of their energy was focused on me. When I walked down the aisles between the chairs and desks, their heads turned and their narrow brown eyes followed me. When I stood at the front of the class, they stared at my shoes. If I came close to a student and spoke to him, he became entranced by my earrings and gazed deafly at them while I talked. The students brought their spoons and tin lunch bowls to class and tucked them into the shelf in their desks, and when I asked about the bowls, they looked twice at me, as though I had invited them to undress.

I spoke slowly as I told the students about myself, and when I finished speaking, I asked them if they had understood what I had said. They sat wide-eyed and tense with their ears tipped toward me, like deer listening to the distant howling of a wolf. Then, suddenly, there was a unanimous fluttering as they reached for their dictionaries and ruffled through them. While his classmates searched frantically for their words, a tall boy, the class monitor, stood up with his arms pressed stiffly to his sides and said, "Please forgive me.

We do not understand the fast talking." His eye muscles twitched and his voice quivered, and from that time on I spoke unbearably slowly, leaving long spaces between words so that the students would have time to catch them. Eventually, speaking slowly and softly became a habit that stayed with me outside of class and made me sound exceedingly dim-witted, even to myself.

I asked the students how long they had been studying English. The monitor stood up. "Some studied six years, another studied three."

I asked them to tell me their names, and again the monitor stood. "Do you mean Chinese names or English names?"

"Both would be helpful."

The monitor glanced nervously at the boy next to him and back at me. "I apologize. We do not had English names. Do not had a foreign teacher before this."

I thanked the monitor and suggested that some of the other students should try to answer my questions. When I had established that the class wanted English names, I gave them whatever names popped into my head, names of people I had written letters to that day, or singers I had listened to, or brothers and sisters I had. I named the monitor Louis after the American horn player, which pleased him tremendously. There was Maggie and Emmy and Max, Dolly, Jean, Charlie, Elvis and Archie. The class giggled at each pronouncement while the conferee stood silently blushing. As the class progressed, some of the students seemed to forget their shyness; they laughed openly and tried to speak, to tell me in fragmented sentences their experiences in the study of English. I asked them questions about the university and about their families, and though I spoke extremely simply, I found myself stopping to explain even the words I used to explain other words—the class was a minefield of digressions. When I asked the students if they knew the meaning of certain words, they usually didn't, and when they did, it was the dictionary speaking through them. I asked if they knew what the word *quotation* meant, and a tiny girl with a plastic butterfly pinned to her cardigan stood up and said, "Quotation means act of quoting or citing; that which is quoted or cited; the naming or publishing of the current price of stocks, bonds, or any commodity."

"And that means what?" I asked.

The girl stared at me, and gradually her hands began to clutch at each other, and she bowed her head and put one slippered foot on top of the other and raised her shoulders up around her ears as if to protect them from an imminent boxing.

To get an idea what the students knew about writing, I asked them to write something about themselves. These were the results:

My English name is Hank and my Chinese's is Miao Hongwen. I was born on Feb. 23, 1967. Till now I am nearly twenty-one years old. I came from a small town which named Puling, there are all kinds of green trees, clean water, high mountains, especially warm-kinded person. I love my hometown very much. There are six people in my family. Father, mother, three older sisters and I. My father was a senior middle school teacher. He taught geography, and now he has retired. My mother stayed at home, when we were young, she looked after us. Now she sometimes do some housework. Most of her time for a rest. My oldest sister was teacher too, but she teachs picture. She married this year, and lives a happy life. My elder sister is a graduate. She is studying in Hangzhou and learns the same profession as I do. Next summer she will end a students' life and enter the socie. In summer, I used to swim, go fishing, on holiday I go for trips with my father, my father likes travelling, so do I. I often dream of being a journalist. My favourable hobby is psychology. To handle with all different man and grasp their thought. Mention, and their way to deal with the world, is my greatest interest. I like ancient music, particularly some famous music such as ... I like fashion sings too.

Hank

My Chinese name is Zhang Zhihua. I was born on April 23, 1969. My hometown is Wan Jing. east of the ZheJiang. In my family there are five people, grandmother, father, mother younger brother, and me. I have a lot of hobbies such as stamp collecting, sports, playing cards, travel, writing, etc. But my favorite hobby is watching film. I think it can make one in a relation's position. Of course, I mean I only like film, not stay in films. Because I have few music cells, I am shallow in music. Swimming is my likest sport in summer. And I also like football. In summer I always stay at home in day-light. At night, the weather is cool and I go out to play with others. On holiday I always give up studying or doing and walk out to play with myself.

John

My name is Li Hua. I am twenty years old. I was born on 1968 June eighth in Suzhou. There are five people in my family. I have two brothers but no sister. My old brother is a physics teacher and my young brother studies in high middle school. My family love me very much. Especially my two brothers and I are very friendly. we chose november 1rd. as our holiday. In that day we must writer to each other. I proud of my brothers. In holiday I often go to meet my old friends. We feel very happy for gathering together. We talk about everything interesting. And i also go to climb mountain with my brothers. My hobby is travelling so I often go out in Saterday or Sunday.

June

My Chinese name is Sun Mei and born on September 8, 1967, so the day before yesterday I was my twentieth birthday. I came from Wan Chang belongs to Zhejiang province where will take me eight hours to get here by bus. Around my city there are very beautiful mountains and rivers, If you want to see hill, you can't go out the city. My family is very large and there are nine people totally, my grandma, my parents, my three sisters and two brothers. My grandma is 77 years old and my parents are business people. They are all at work except my youngster sister. so the air in my house is always filled with happiness, and we always have good way to make funny. even my grandma make joke with us. I like go outing, so I often go countryside and some other places in holiday. But in summer, even like go swimming with my classmates and friends. To make full use of holiday, I often climb the mountains far away the city. By this way I get endless happiness. In my spare time I like to hear slight music and some others. Also I like ball-sports, but I don't good at it. I like collect stamp too, because I can get a lot of knowlege from stamps.

Pamela

I read some of these compositions aloud, making corrections as I went, and the students listened intently to my voice, delighted by the sound of their own words.

At the end of the class when I told the students they could leave, they sat quietly at their desks and stared at me.

I told them again that class was over and that it was time to go home, and still they stared, and I stared back at them, wondering if I had got the time wrong. I asked the monitor, "Isn't it time to leave?"

"Yes," he said, "it is time to leave."

"Well, then, good-bye," I said cheerfully.

"Good-bye!" the class said equally cheerfully and without making a move to get up.

I thought maybe the custom was for the teacher to leave the room first, so I gathered up my books and papers and went self-consciously out the door with the whole room staring.

As I unlocked my bicycle in front of the building, I glanced up and saw my students' eager faces crowding the classroom windows watching me; and above them on the second floor, students in other classes had also gathered to watch. They seemed to have no reservations about staring, as though they themselves were invisible. I waved to the faces and said good-bye again.

"Good-bye!" they shouted, waving like people departing on a ship.

As I climbed onto my bike, one small girl leaned out the classroom window and cried, "We hope you will like us!" I looked at her; she was grinning and buck-toothed and narrow-shouldered, and her white cotton hairband had slipped down low onto her forehead, like a bandage. At eighteen she looked like a child, and I had a great sense of relief as I thought how different she and her classmates were from American college sophomores, who, on the first day of class, were likely to announce with impassive stares and sullen shrugs that the teacher had definitely better hope *they* liked *her*.

A PROMISING
PARTY

When Yang Shiren, the director of the Foreign Affairs Office, first welcomed the foreign teachers to Hangzhou, he had employed the services of a young, pink-faced interpreter named Xu Ban. Xu had a flat, sleepy face, huge ears, and long arms that extended inches beyond the frayed cuffs of his shirt. He sat blushing on a chair and hugged his knees and trained his olive-black eyes on Yang, waiting to snap up the next sentence. Xu was awkward and self-conscious. When he opened his mouth and spoke aristocratic English in the stuffy, choking style of Winston Churchill, all eyes turned to him in wonder. He had a deep voice and theatrical inflections. The vowels dragged across his tongue, languished and died in his mouth, the *r*'s disappeared completely, and the consonants were hard and penetrating. It was difficult to believe such overmannered speech could emanate from so unprepossessing a figure, and the effect was captivating in the way the voice of a ventriloquist's saucer-eyed dummy is captivating.

Yang's welcome included details of daily life in the university and the importance of the friendship between China and other nations. He described the university as "a key university of higher learning" and fed Xu Ban a broth of pertinent numbers: The university had sixteen departments and thirty-seven specialties, three research institutes, two research centers, fifteen research sections, conferred the master's degree in forty-five subjects and the doctor's degree in ten, a staff of 2,700, student enrollment of 7,700; there were 2,300 students in adult programs; the library held 1.4 million books and 10,000 periodicals . . .

At the close of his speech Yang invited questions. Mitsuko Tokutomi, a Japanese woman who had taught at Hangzhou University a few years previous, raised her hand and sent a pair of silver bracelets jangling down her forearm. She had a wide mouth and dazzling white teeth, and her fiery energy made her seem, at times, more Hispanic than Asian. With blinking innocence Mitsuko said, "I have one question, Jack! This year are you going to keep your promises?"

The interpreter stared at the floor; he dared not translate the question. Yang cleared his throat and answered for himself in English: "Of course, Mitsuko. I always keep my promises."

Mitsuko giggled a rich, long time at this and rocked back and forth in her chair. "That is not . . . ha-ha . . . how I remember it!"

Xu Ban, the interpreter, was one of several young people working in the Foreign Affairs Office, ostensibly helping to smooth the relationship between the foreign teachers and the university—though during his testimony in my room a few days previous, George Greatorex claimed that the Foreign Affairs Office and its workers acted behind a smokescreen of goodwill and that ultimately they only made things more difficult for their foreign visitors, that their role was in truth an adversarial one. They were spies, a finger of the government, a defense. They set up obstacles and pretended to try to remove them. They were expert at giving foreigners the runaround, were evasive and elusive. They opened foreign mail both coming and going, they made false promises, they prevented foreigners from ever seeing the president of the university, who was rumored to be sympathetic to the concerns of foreigners. They were cheats.

Nothing in Xu Ban's persona suggested espionage or calculation. He was said to be extremely popular among the foreign teachers, and the reason for this became quickly evident; he was artless. He lacked the craft of secrecy. He proffered private information about his employers without realizing he was doing so. He was starved for friendship, which he seemed to find most easily among foreigners. He called me Rosie and hooked his arm in mine, like an old friend. He was wide open, and I found it difficult not to speak to him in motherly tones. From time to time I caught myself doting and instructing, chiding and protecting Xu Ban.

Xu rode his bicycle forty-five minutes every day from his home to the university and ate his meals with the maids and the other young Foreign Affairs Office workers in a small room next to the kitchen. At mealtimes shrieks of laughter and shouts of alarm drifted over the transom of that room, along with the sounds of spoons and bowls clinking, glasses breaking, and disco tunes crackling out of the communal radio. Whenever I ran into Xu emerging from a meal, he was red-faced and wiping a mustache of orange soda on the cuff of his sleeve.

In private, Xu was only slightly more relaxed than he was in the act of interpreting; he continued to speak formally and automatically, in the manner of a tour guide. He spouted the edicts and theories he was taught to spout, but often misinterpreted them. He was halfway between cadre and child.

One evening in October Xu Ban came to my room and said, "Rose, I understand that many people who come to a new land suffer culture shock, and sometimes it even makes them want to commit suicide. Rose, if you ever feel that you would like to commit suicide, I hope you will please come and tell me."

I invited Xu to sit down, and we chatted and drank beer from tin mugs. He seemed exhausted and sleepy and kept sticking his fingers behind the lenses of his glasses to rub at his eyes. "Oh," he said, "My eyes hurt today and I feel very tired." I asked Xu if he was sleeping enough at night.

"I sleep eight hours a night now. I used to sleep much less because of my reading, but now I have quit reading so that I can sleep and so that my eyes will not hurt."

I suggested that quitting reading might not be the best solution, that maybe he wasn't reading with enough light.

"Enough light. I should quit reading and then take up sports, and then take back reading again. How is that for a plan?"

"Fair," I said. "What kind of sports do you like?"

"A lot of sports. My favorite sport is table tennis. I play with my brother and my friend on the table at the university."

"I like table tennis. Maybe I could play with you sometime."

Xu's face lit up. "I will beat you definitely in table tennis! Ha-ha. No doubt about it. You can beat me in international chess, naturally, but I will beat you definitely in table tennis. When you are free, eh? I would be glad to beat you anytime."

We set a date to play, and I asked him how he had learned to speak English so well.

He tipped the last bit of beer into his mouth and wiped his lips on the cuff of his homemade jacket. He shifted in his seat and thought. Xu had a habit of winding up for an answer with a deep inhalation, and every answer began with a string of stray words that escaped from his mouth half-baked. He rattled the words off like a poem recited in English class—it was a kind of temporization until the real answer had time to form itself, if ever it did. When he was particularly uncomfortable, Xu's reasoning grew muddled and specious.

Xu swung the mug around his finger by the handle. "Rose, I wouldn't say that my English is that good. Though I consider that my English is pretty good. The first reason

I think is that I studied very hard in college and I had very good teachers who helped me a lot, and the second reason is, as you see, that I work in the Foreign Affairs Office, which gave me a very good opportunity to practice and speak. So I think. And still, the third reason is that I like to study English because I like to talk. I like to talk, so that, I think, is another advantage why."

He sat back in his seat and stared at my face. That was his habit; he stared not to learn something about me but to learn about himself. He scanned my face for reactions to him, for signs of his own character; he was ever watchful lest anyone react badly to him.

"Where did you study English, Xu?"

"Hangzhou. My major was the English language."

"And what kind of books did you use?"

"My textbook was at that time *New Concept English* by Alexander."

"Did you read many novels?"

"Not many at all. I also studied the TV courses. You know, in China we are running short of English teachers. Chinese English teachers, not to mention foreign English teachers, who go without saying. Because the English language instruction only began recently in China, when the door was opened to the outside world in 1979, when Deng Xiaoping became the leader of our country. Russian language is also one of the most popular languages in China. I did not study Russian, though I still consider studying it in future." Xu laughed nervously and stared at my mouth. His long dark bangs lay in a sideswept wave along the ridge of his brow; they were smooth and slick and took the gently curved shape of a starling's wing.

"Why Russian?"

"Oh, first of all I think that Russia is a very good country. Just like the United States of America is a very good country. And China and Russia have a lot of things in common. I need to learn about Russia, as I am learning about the United States. So I think the language of Russia will facilitate my task of doing so."

I asked Xu how he got the job he had now.

"In China when university students graduate they are assigned to posts. So I graduated in 1985 and was assigned to the post."

"Was it the post you were expecting?"

"I thought I might become a teacher of English. So I was a little bit surprised to get this post."

"And were you pleased?"

"Oh, very pleased!"

"What are your responsibilities in this job?"

"My responsibility . . . my title . . . is cadre."

I asked Xu to explain that term.

"*Cadre* is a pretty vague term in Chinese. *Cadre* means 'anybody who is employed by the government.' "

"So you're employed by the government?"

"Yes. The Department of Foreign Languages recommended me. For when I graduated, I was the best student of all. I hope I am not being too proud."

"Not at all," I said. I poured more beer into his mug, and he sipped from it and studied the beer with all his attention. "It is frothy," he murmured.

Xu's mind frequently wandered to tiny details that filled him with wonder, and it was at these times that he seemed most comfortable with himself, most unveiled.

Xu told me he earned a monthly salary of sixty yuan (eighteen dollars), the going rate for recent university graduates. "Ha-ha," he said, "very cheap according to the measure in your country. But of course, in China everything is not expensive and the living standard is very low at the moment. With sixty yuan I can get around very well."

I asked him how many hours he worked.

"Every day we work eight hours. We work six days a week, so that's forty-eight hours. We have Sunday off, and some holidays we have off as well."

I asked him what exactly he did. He answered, "I don't know exactly. I think my name is Jack. Jack of all trades, master of none." Xu laughed, delighted by the colloquial.

"I notice you do a lot of interpreting for the Foreign Affairs Office."

"Yes. And sometimes I translate. One of my major assignments is for the help of foreign faculty at our university. I think I help them in life, in helping them to accommodate themselves in China."

"How long do you think you'll be at this job?"

"Your question is my question. In China if you are assigned to a job, you could possibly work there all your life. Of course you could also get your job changed because of various reasons. So I really don't know."

"How would you change your job if you wanted to?"

"Well, I could ask . . ." He pressed the pad of his thumb against his front teeth, thinking. "Or the government could ask me."

"Might your job get changed without your request or consent?"

"The possibility is there."

"Do you like the job?"

"I like this job at the moment. I like to help foreigners and to understand foreigners and their countries."

"What foreign countries do you think you understand?"

"Well, I can't say that way, but I do think I understand the U.S. better than Russia or Japan, but in fact I don't think I understand that American country very well, because I haven't been to that country. All I get to know is from what people talk to me, from what I read, and from my impressions."

"What are your impressions?"

"My impressions? Oh, let me see. My impressions are first of all that I think that the people of the United States are mostly very outspoken, very active, and to me very friendly. And, too, I am now sensing that the Americans are enjoying themselves very much, I mean those who stay here and who can enjoy themselves. And they help each other a lot sometimes, and they have a sense more of individuality than of collectivism. On the American society I couldn't say very much about it, because I really don't have a good study of it. From my daily association in my daily literature, I think that, as you know, the two systems are quite different—both countries can learn from each other. China is opening its door to the outside world, and you have high technology which China can learn, and we can help each other a lot."

I asked Xu what books he read.

"At the present I am reading English mainly and the essay books. I have books on selected readings in English literature. Let me see, ah . . ." He looked at his knees, recalling what he'd read. He stroked his shirtfront. "Virginia Woolf? Is she someone? You know, I'm not very good at retaining the names of the authors. I just read to find out different expressions and new words. I read a variety of things. And I read a little French. And magazines. Like *Newsweek*. I got *Newsweek* from the foreign teachers at the moment. And newspapers. I read *Hangzhou Daily, Zhejiang Daily* and *People's Daily*."

"Are you interested in world news?"

"Let me tell you, Rose, one of my favorite things is the world news. I'm interested in learning about the world. I hope that our world could be at peace, as every one of us wishes."

"Where do you get world news?"

"Papers, the special page for world news."

I asked Xu what was happening lately in the world. He smiled comfortably at me—he had the answer. "The recent world news is that the American planes attacked Iran."

"Attacked Iran?"

"The plane. Iranian plane." Xu grinned nervously. "Excuse myself!"

"Do you think America was justified in doing that?" I asked.

"Well, I think anything that is good for keeping the Persian Gulf in peace is justified."

I remembered then that on the first day I met Xu Ban, he had told me proudly that he was an officer in the Communist Youth League. I asked him to tell me more about the League. He rubbed his hands together, pleased by the request.

"As you know, I am the vice chairman of the Communist Youth League branch for officers at Hangzhou University. The Communist Youth League is assistant to the Communist party, and if you are a member of the League, you should help the Party as much as you can. Everyone, in fact, should help the Party. I'd like to become a Party member in the future."

"Why?"

"It is a promising Party!" he exclaimed. "At present China is opening the door to the outside world, which bolsters the development of our country. That decision was made by the Party, and the Party is also good at realizing its past mistakes. Take Cultural Revolution, for example. So, the Party can learn from its mistakes and also can change itself and bring China to a more prosperous place."

"What do you mean by 'Cultural Revolution, for example'?"

"Cultural Revolution—a mistake of the Party."

"I'd like to know more about the Cultural Revolution."

"Cultural Revolution." Xu laced his fingers together and stared distractedly at the photographs beneath a slab of glass on my table. With his two long index fingers pressed side-by-side he pointed delicately to one photograph in particular. "Is this your mother?" he asked.

It was my grandmother in a broad-brimmed hat, leaning

on a parasol during the first World War. She wore high, button-up boots and an ankle-length dress with lace cuffs and thirty-eight pearl buttons down its front. Xu leaned over to have a better look at her, his chin nearly resting on the table. The table lamp illuminated the down on his cheek; his skin was pink and smooth. "Grandmother," he said reverently, "in ancient dress." His warm breath steamed up on the glass. He stared, motionless, heavy-lidded, enchanted by the dress.

"Do you like her, Xu?" I said.

At the sound of my voice Xu yanked himself suddenly upright in his chair, all business again. "Yes. And I'm very interested in telling about China's Cultural Revolution. Cultural Revolution took place from 1966 to 1976. I experienced half of the Cultural Revolution. I was born during the Cultural Revolution, in 1966, and of course I was very small at that time. When I was at primary school, we had to lay a lot of emphasis on political studies. At that time the party made a lot of mistakes by putting too much emphasis on class struggle. You know, a class struggle is a struggle between two classes: the capitalist class and the socialist class. But at that time the capitalist class was no longer in existence. So I now think the proposal of class struggle was completely wrong.

"The Cultural Revolution to me was horrible. Because, you know, during the Cultural Revolution I didn't study a lot. Most of my knowledge I picked up after 1979. Because at that time schools didn't run very well. Everyone had to participate in the class struggle. Of course I was a mere kid. I just followed suit."

"What kinds of things were going on during the Cultural Revolution?"

"Criticism. As far as I know from older people, like university professors, many people got criticized. A professor I know had a wooden board hung on him in the street with these words on it: *Fan geming*, 'Antirevolutionary,' and he had to stand before the public every day for criticism. Right here at this university. *Fan geming.*"

"Was he really antirevolutionary?"

Xu shrugged. His laugh was anxious and high.

"What about your parents? What were they doing then?"

"Parents, yes. My father was an engineer at that time and my mother was a worker. They survived the Revolution, like many others. But during Cultural Revolution people could not lead a normal life or go to work. The factories stopped producing. The people had to spend all their time talking about class struggle. People lived a terrible life. You couldn't work or eat well."

"What happened to the antirevolutionaries? How were they treated by the government?"

"Treated very badly. They were hurt. Many went to prison for saying or writing a word against Mao Zedong. So-called antirevolutionaries. But my impression of Cultural Revolution is very vague because I was young."

I asked Xu what he thought was the aim of the Communist party.

"The aim of the Communist party is to realize communism," he said. "Communist society."

"What is communist society?"

"Communist society?" Xu tilted his head toward me but kept his eyes fixed on the carpet. He stretched his arms over his head, arched his back, and yawned sumptuously. He patted his knees, rubbed his eyes, straightened the glasses on his nose—he was keeping himself busy, like a bird tidying its feathers. A strong wind leaned into the building and rattled the tattered screens in my windows. Xu pointed a finger at them and looked at me with wide-eyed astonishment, as if to ask, Can you *believe* that wind?

Presently he said, "Communist society is a society that is best of all. People can get as they like, countries and classes would disappear, people could live happily and there would be no war in the world. A society where people can enjoy thorough democracy and complete freedom. People can enjoy abundant wealth to appreciate and enjoy, people can travel to whatever places they want to. People can live in such a marvelous society where they enjoy friendship every day. I think we will accept this society."

"Abundant wealth?" I said. "What do you mean by that?"

"Society! Abundant wealth!" Xu's hands flew up and landed spontaneously on the top of his head. "Let's not talk about abundant!"

"All right," I said, "but maybe we can talk about wealth. As you know there's a lot of wealth in capitalist countries, and some people are enjoying it immensely, and those people can travel to whatever places they want to. Maybe that's not the kind of wealth you mean?"

"I don't think Americans can enjoy abundant wealth. Can you deny the fact that you have a lot of beggars?"

I could not.

Xu clasped his hands in his lap. "Are they enjoying abundant wealth?"

"As far as I can see, they're not enjoying much of anything, but there are some people who can enjoy abundant wealth."

"In a communist society," Xu said, "the society has the wealth."

"So you mean the collective, not the individual."

"Not just the collective but also the individual."

"Everyone, then?"

"Everyone and no one."

This was beginning to sound deep, like something I had recently read in a lesson on Zen meditation: *There is no bird or air. When the fish swims, water and fish are the fish. There is nothing but fish. Do you understand?*

I asked Xu what prevented Chinese people from traveling freely outside of China.

"Outside of China the question is like this: First of all

China is beginning to open the doors and people could make more money than before, but we still have a large difference between China and the United States, you see. We are still poor. I can't afford to travel outside of China."

"It's a matter of money, then?"

"A matter of money, yes, and in China more people have to work, right? You have to fix out a holiday. I have holidays, but some people at the present time cannot have a long period for holidays where they can travel to a far place like America."

"And that's all there is to it?"

"All there is."

"Who are the members of the Communist Youth League?"

"University students and middle-school students. Young people mostly. The people who are from fourteen to twenty-eight years old. Peasants, soldiers, workers, administrators. All walks of life and who are qualified to become a member of the League."

"What qualifies them?"

"Qualifies them? Hard work. Good marks. Political commitment."

I told Xu I thought the students in my Chinese classes seemed a lot younger than American students and that I didn't notice girls and boys talking together or holding hands, and certainly not kissing, and I asked him why that was.

"At present that is the way it is."

"What about close personal relationships between men and women who aren't married?"

"Not exactly," he said in a delightfully nonsensical way. "You see, it varies from people to people. I don't have a very close personal relationship with any girls at the moment, but some of my friends do."

"Do you have some close male friends?"

Xu brightened considerably at the thought of his close

male friends. "Of course. Friends are a necessity to a person's life. I like to make friends."

"What do you have in mind for yourself for the future?"

"For the future I will try to cultivate myself in a way which is good for the society. To put it more specifically, I think I will try to help the people as much as I can. Still larger, to make China become more and more prosperous. That's my ambition."

"A very generous ambition."

Xu smiled, ducked his head, shuffled his feet. He held his beer mug absurdly high over his head and peered up into it—the kind of test a child does to determine once and for all that the mug is truly empty.

I tried but could not discern what Xu's civic-mindedness meant to him, how deeply and sincerely he felt it, how effective he thought he could be. Like his voice and his parlance, his ambitions seemed oversized and newly adopted. It was as if he had placed a large, stiff-walled hatbox on his head instead of the hat itself.

Because the beer was gone, I offered some orange soda. He said gaily, "I like orange drink. I think Coca-Cola is not good for your teeth, not good for your stomach, eh?"

I asked Xu if he liked wine.

"Oh, no! I cannot sustain it. If I drink even one little wine, I will get intoxicated. Wine has alcohol, and someone has recently told me that alcohol is a drug."

When I told him that beer had alcohol too, Xu put his mug down on the table between us and said resolutely, "Then I cannot have it."

"Xu Ban," I said, "Can you come back tomorrow and talk with me?"

He smiled widely and crossed his legs and smoothed the wing of hair back from his forehead. "Rose," he said, "I can come back any time you want me to. That is my job."

The next evening Xu returned to my room and we took a walk in the rice fields. Hundreds of bats toured over the fields in clouds, like black snow. The weather had grown unseasonably chilly and Xu's nose pinkened in the wind. He was underdressed in a thin white dress shirt and the same gray cotton jacket he'd worn the day before, a shapeless homemade thing that resembled a tinsmith's smock. His skimpy white sneakers squeaked in the wet grass, and possibly the squeaking inspired him, for he began to sing. "The song is called 'A Secret in My Heart,'" he said, "A love song." His voice was clear and high and sweet and carried across the fields toward the ugly buildings that bordered the fields on the west. The bats' flight was erratic and low. Now and again I felt the fan of a wingflap stir the hair on my head, and angular, hurtling objects appeared and disappeared like boomerangs in front of my nose. I struggled to ignore them, to concentrate on Xu.

"Rose," Xu said soberly when the song was over, "Do you miss your family?"

I looked at his pink face and the heavy finger-smudged eyeglasses slipping down his long nose. My family was what I missed most. I told Xu something about them, that my brothers and sisters and I very much enjoyed each other's company. "What about your family?" I asked.

"They are only my father and brother and me. I have one sister, who is five years younger, but she lives in Shanghai. We used to live in Shanghai too. Then my father and brother and I moved to Hangzhou. Sister lives with my mother." He paused, then added, "My father and mother have been divorced some time ago." He studied my face for a reaction.

I tried to conceal my surprise at the news. "How do you feel about the divorce?"

"I feel quite all right."

"Is divorce common in China?"

"It is not common, but it happens more and more now."

"Do you ever see your mother?"

"Maybe I see my mother every few months or so."

"What's she like?"

"Nice, no doubt. She has married again."

"Do you miss her?"

"I should say it is quite difficult to miss someone you do not know extremely well."

We walked quickly now and because the ground was uneven the going was difficult; we were both breathless, and our breathlessness made us sound sad and tearful.

After a long pause Xu said darkly, "I used to have a fear that someone would try to murder me sometime. I could not sleep, for I was afraid if I shut my eyes a person would come into my room and stab me."

I stopped in my tracks. "Why on earth would you think such a thing?"

Xu turned halfway to look at me; his eyes sparkled, the cold made his clothes seem more shiny and threadbare than usual, and he looked much younger tonight than twenty-one. He appeared to be rejoicing in the thought of his own terror. He stuffed his hands into his pockets, and with a sigh and shrug he said, "I am sure I do not know."

IN THE BOTANICAL GARDEN

On the morning I was to meet George Greatorex and Ming Yu and George's *taiji* teacher in the botanical gardens, I woke to the rumbling of pedal wagons passing along the small lane that ran outside our building. It was five o'clock. By 5:30 farmers would begin to gather at the tiny outdoor market on the corner to sell vegetables, eggs, and meat. Some set up picnic tables and served rice gruel, fried bread, and meat buns to people on their way to work. By 6:00 women would be hurrying home with baskets of greens and tiny bottles of milk and yogurt. People greeted each other cheerfully but quickly. No one stopped to converse on these mornings.

I dressed, drank some instant coffee made with musty thermos water, hurried downstairs and out into the courtyard. The sky was a pale lilac color. I took my bicycle from among the others in the rack and went quietly through the gate, hoping the guard wouldn't come out and detain me. The sun was just rising behind the trees and the air was cool and clear. I rode along a back road—already crowded with people bicycling to work—in the direction of Zhejiang University and the botanical gardens just beyond it.

The narrowest, meanest streets of Hangzhou were made beautiful by the sycamores that lined them and the branches and leaves that formed a canopy over them. With their thick trunks of mottled yellow and green bark the trees had a peaceful, noble look. Beyond the trees were the rice fields, and in the distance the gray buildings of Zhejiang University and the short, steep hill that separated the university from the lake. I rode slowly along this road among hundreds of workers. A young woman, who had covered her bicycle seat in the same red-checked material she'd made her blouse from, gasped at the sight of me and went off the road into a ditch. One side of the road was lined with small houses and cluttered yards. In one yard a middle-aged woman brushing her teeth at an outdoor faucet turned to stare at me as I approached. A hen hopped across the yard and pecked curiously at the woman's sneaker. Annoyed by the distraction, she cursed and gave the hen a vicious kick. She wiped her foamy mouth on her forearm, and, toothbrush in hand, she turned back to watch me ride by.

A visitor could spend a day in Hangzhou's botanical garden and still not have seen half of it. There were sections of the garden devoted to each species of plant; a bamboo section, a pink rhododendron section, a rose garden, a peony section, and within each section there were pagodas and benches on which the visitor could rest and observe all this beauty. Hundreds of paths laced the park, and man-made ponds graced it. There were natural springs here, a brand-new swimming pool, and a teahouse. Teams of elderly workers cared for the gardens, hunched men and women who cut the grass by hand with curved knives, like mini-scythes. They crouched under their wide-brimmed straw hats, grabbed a handful of grass, and chopped it off near the roots. Eight of them worked shoulder-to-shoulder in a row this way, sweeping across a field, like a machine. Their bodies were molded into the S shapes of people who have spent their lives raking and weeding, planting and sweeping.

I was to meet George and Ming Yu near the teahouse. I rode my bicycle down a narrow path, left it against a tree, and walked the rest of the way through the bamboo forest. From within the forest the leaves of the bamboo were a diaphanous yellow-green in the sunlight. The slim green trunks of the trees grew so close together, it would have been impossible even for a small child to run among them with his arms raised parallel to the ground. It was dark here, and the bamboo poles creaked and the leaves whispered, and because sunlight rarely broke through the green ceiling, the ground was bare and sprinkled with soft, dead leaves. An eerie mist crept low across my feet. For the first time since I arrived in Hangzhou, I felt utterly alone. I realized there were very few places in the university where I could be by myself for any period of time, and that included—because of the endless string of visitors who came to see Christina and me—my own bedroom. I was enjoying my solitude, and then, just over a rise in the forest, I was startled to stillness by the most improbable sight: Four older women in gray pants and crisp white blouses were silently waltzing together in a clearing. They swayed and shifted in slow three-quarter time, arm-in-arm, smiling, tight-skinned, their feet shuffling through the mist and leaves. They had a spectral beauty, and they danced on and took no notice of me as I passed by.

In the peony garden I spotted Ming and George sitting still and quiet on opposite benches beneath a vine-covered trellis. They looked as though they had been sitting that way for hours. Their bicycles leaned together against a nearby tree. As I approached them, George said softly, "I didn't expect you to make it," which sounded to me like a criticism, as though he was sorry I showed up. I shrugged and thanked him for inviting me.

Ming spread the sweatshirt she was sitting on out farther across the damp bench and motioned for me to sit down on it. Her hair was pulled back in a bun and her eyeglasses dangled like a pendant from the chain around her neck. Her eyes were puffy and tired, and still she managed to look pretty. She wore black trousers, a white T-shirt and high-heeled shoes with buckle straps. "The *taiji* teacher is not here," she said. "I am afraid we have missed him. Or perhaps he has gone to another part of the garden."

George stood and walked to the edge of the trellis, staring out into the mist with his hands clasped behind his back. My presence clearly made him self-conscious. The soft material of his blue cotton trousers bagged hopelessly around his thin legs, and from behind he looked like an old man. We sat this way for several minutes, not speaking. Finally I asked Ming, "Is this where the teacher usually practices?"

Without turning around, George answered for her: "No."

I waited for some elaboration, and when none came, I said to Ming, "Where does the teacher practice?"

"Here and there," said George.

"Is there a reason you've picked here, Miss Ming?"

George answered, "It's as good a place as any."

A mourning dove hooted high up in the limbs above our heads, and sunlight flashed like a thousand yellow stars between the leaves. The garden had the hushed, holy feel of an art museum, and between that and these two mysterious, soft-spoken people I felt like a clumsy intruder. In my increasing discomfort I had to remind myself that they had invited me here.

George sat again on his bench, and Ming looked expectantly at him, waiting for him to speak. He smiled at her. As odd and distant as George seemed, there was also something transparent about him, something soft and sensitive. With his long black eyelashes and blunt nose, he looked like a doe.

I looked out into the mist, hoping to catch a glimpse of someone, maybe of the dancing women again, but the garden was perfectly still. George wandered a short way down a dirt path and back again. He sat down on the other side of Ming, placing her between us, and said, "Look at this. Bench number four."

Indeed, painted in white on the bench was the number four. George covered it with his back and stared strangely at Ming. "*Sì*," he said.

Ming said, "Stop that," and waved her hand at him. To me she said, "He thinks he is frightening me. The number four in Chinese, you know, *si*, sounds the same as the word for 'death.' He is making a ridiculous pun of it."

George leaned forward, suddenly animated, and spoke around Ming to me. "The Chinese are superstitious, despite what anyone tells you about the communists having eradicated superstition. They hate the number four. In Taiwan you'll never see a number-four bus, or if you do it'll be empty, because no one wants to ride it. They think it's unlucky, that it will crash and kill them all."

I looked at Ming, hoping she would confirm that, but she said nothing. Later, when we were alone, she told me that in China, city people were not as superstitious as country people, and that in different places people had different taboos and symbols. In her hometown the teapot was never to be placed with its spout pointing at anyone, and if a family member was ill, a round mirror was hung up on the door to scare away "bad elements." Chopsticks were not to be stuck into a bowl with the two ends pointing toward the sky, for that meant death. Ming said that as a child she liked wearing colorful ribbons in her hair, but because of superstition only red and green were allowed; yellow and blue ribbons meant death; white shoes also meant death. "In my hometown," she said, "the 'don'ts' were more than I could bear."

I asked George if he'd been to Taiwan. He said he had lived there, studying *taiji* and teaching English to rich Taiwanese men and their children. He liked Taiwan, said it was more Chinese than China, more traditional, more artistic, had more of a sense of culture and history. The Mandarin was pure, the people weren't so backward or ignorant. George said he once taught the lazy son of a millionaire, a dull twenty-one-year-old who was married, had a baby, but still lived at home and had to be in by 11:00 P.M. This boy spent all his time bowling tenpins while his young, equally dim wife stayed at home minding the baby.

"He was a skinny little fellow, a weakling, but his right arm was roped in muscle and solid as iron because of the bowling. The boy couldn't tie his own shoe, though. I'd go there, and he'd beg me to talk about England, never wanted to study. When I reminded him his father was paying me to teach him English, he whined, 'I'll pay you more *not* to teach me English.' "

I asked George why he had left Taiwan. He shrugged and glanced around the garden, giving the impression that he was bored with the subject; but I could see that in fact it pleased him to be discussing his own life.

"I thought I'd come to China and see what it was like, see what kind of instruction I could get in *taiji*. That's the only thing that's better here. I'm sorry I came, though."

"I know," I said, hoping he wouldn't go into it.

"The people are like children," he said. "They're rude and dirty. They understand nothing but think they are the only people in the world who understand anything. Their favorite thing is lying down. They lie down whenever they have a free minute. Go to the students' dormitories sometime and you'll see it for yourself."

I had seen it already; the students stretched out on their bunk beds and read magazines. In a way that was practical, for in most rooms there were only two or three chairs for the seven of them. And I had noticed that whenever the house workers had a free moment, they lay down on the couches in the banquet room and spread newspapers on their faces to block out the light. There were tailors at the end of our street who worked outside under a corrugated plastic roof; at rest time they lay down on their cutting tables. Construction workers napped in truck beds; tea pickers rested their heads on a pillow of tea leaves.

I said to George, "You hate it here, but you have to stay to collect your money, right?"

He nodded.

He'd been waiting around in misery for seven months and all for three hundred yuan, about seventy-five dollars. I asked him if he'd done any traveling while he was here. "What would I travel for?" said he.

"Interest," I suggested.

"It's not interesting. It's torture, a pain in the ass. An ugly place. Everything's dug up and plowed over. The public parks are a manipulation, a distortion of what was once naturally beautiful, like putting makeup on a pretty face. The temples and the history have been destroyed. And its impossible to get tickets and impossible to get a hotel room."

"Is that true, Ming Yu?" I said. Ming gave me an enigmatic smile, didn't answer.

George talked on and on about China, without a trace of forgiveness. I wasn't in the mood to listen to him all over again, and since there didn't seem to be any *taiji* teacher here, and since my class would be meeting in an hour, I decided to return to the university.

"I'll come with you," Ming said, tying the sleeves of her sweatshirt around her waist. She turned to George. "Will you stay here, or will you return with us?"

"I'll go to the lake and look for the teacher there."

"Well, good-bye," Ming said hesitantly.

In a faintly mocking voice George said, "Well, good-bye."

As we rode our bicycles home along the narrow road, a small lunch tin bounced and rattled in the wire basket hooked up to Ming's handlebars. She said, "The poems you gave me of your sister-in-law, does she write poetry often?"

"Yes."

"There was a poem about Leningrad. Did your sister-in-law go to Leningrad?"

"Yes, she did."

"She travels a lot?"

"My sister-in-law is adventuresome and travels whenever she has the opportunity."

"I don't have much chance to travel. I go to Wuxi or Nanjing now and then, and to Shanghai. But I don't travel."

"Do you want to?"

Ming looked up from the road and stared at me, perplexed by the question. "Of course I do. I want to see everything, but it is difficult to find the money and time for travel."

We rode on silently until Ming said, "The Japanese beat us. We gave up and did not fight."

This seemed a roundabout explanation for why she had no opportunity to travel. "The Chinese may be too passive," she said. "Do you think similarity between people, similar interests, makes for contempt and competition?"

"I think it does."

"I do too. Though it would seem not, there are many similarities between Chinese and Japanese. But even today there are too many hostilities."

The Japanese subject was one all Chinese seemed to agree on: They were a cruel and cold and calculating people, robbers, rapists, stinking imperialists. Much of this animosity was derived from the memory of Japanese cruelties during the War of Resistance, a memory whose bitterness had been passed on to young people who could not possibly remember.

A topless army jeep with a child riding in its passenger seat veered around us and squeaked its high-pitched horn. The leaves of the trees along the edge of the road brushed our heads. Ming watched the pavement without really seeing it. She told me she had seen films about the persecution of the Jews in Nazi Germany, had seen their misery and suffering, but the effect those films had on her paled in comparison to the effect the Memorial of the Nanjing Massacre had on her. She said that halfway through her visit to the memorial hall she had to stop. "I was seized by an indescribable feeling," she said. "I felt a hollowness in my heart. The Japanese invaders did everything that is forbidden. The more brutal they were, the more honor they got. They animalized themselves and others. Don't ask me what they did. Just consider this: They held competitions among themselves to see who could kill the most Chinese. Two Japanese officers killed more than a hundred Chinese civilians each. The rivers were flowing with dead bodies. Families were forced to kill and humiliate each other."

Ming Yu told me her mother's family had escaped the Japanese on foot and that during their flight her grandfather decided to abandon her mother—then a tiny baby—along the roadside, for in all their hurry he and his wife were finding it nearly impossible to carry her.

"My grandmother put my mother by the road, walked a few steps away, then returned to her and took her up to follow the fleeing people. She couldn't bear to leave the baby. She was in tears and was tired, but she held my mother tight until they finally got to their destination. In that massacre three hundred thousand Chinese people died."

Ming said, "I think people are blinded and influenced by their feelings when they think of the old days. Even the intellectuals cannot guarantee completely reasoned feelings for the Japanese. Theoretically and ideally speaking, people—especially the open-minded and enlightened—should let their hearts come together. Nationality is just a form, a symbol. What is important is not what people have done in the past but what they are doing at present and what they will do in future. When Chinese people remain hostile to Japanese, they have reasons, of course, but history is history. The best thing we can do now is think of each other as brothers."

I had one eye on the road and one on Ming's face. She spoke carefully, respectful of her own words, as though she herself were learning a great deal from them, and she managed to project this without a trace of self-importance. From time to time she lifted a hand from her handlebars to gesture with it. Her hair had twisted out of its bun and was flying freely behind her now, a black pennant flapping in the wind. She could have been speaking to a large crowd.

I asked Ming if some of the hostility the Chinese felt toward the Japanese was not inspired by jealousy of Japan's economic success, by Japan's disproportionate buying power in the world.

"Of course it is," she said. "They are rich, we are poor. Everyone in China wants to have a Japanese car. It is a status symbol."

Hoping to hear Ming's opinion of George Greatorex, I asked her what she thought of the English.

"The English are nothing like the Americans. Shakespeare was English."

I considered that oblique comment. "So Americans are nothing like Shakespeare?"

Ming covered her mouth with her hand to conceal a smile and pedaled harder. "Don't feel bad. A lot of Americans were English once too."

"You have a refreshing sense of irony, Ming Yu," I said.

Ming's voice wavered in her throat as we bumped over a cattle grate, "Have you been to England?"

"Yes."

She nodded thoughtfully. "Your sister-in-law's poems were beautiful," she said.

On the main road near the university and dangerously close to the entrance of an elementary school, we had to skirt a hole in the street big enough to swallow a Cadillac. Someone had placed a few planks around the edges of the hole in an effort to cover it up, but the planks were useless and the hole was menacing and deep. Hazards like this were numerous here. Water pipes were fitted across sidewalks at ankle-height—an inconvenience by day and an utter menace by night—lids were missing from manholes in the middle of the street, and people drove in the dark with their headlights off, switching them on again if they sensed another car approaching. Men smoked in movie theaters, and pregnant women were hired to spray insecticides on crops, a job deemed suitable for them because it required no bending or lifting.

The morning traffic had thickened, and at a large intersection Ming, mid-sentence, collided mightily with a woman on a pedal wagon. Ming and the woman stared at each other, their faces betraying no emotion, not even surprise. I sensed, however, quickened heartbeats, a covert alarm. Ming's knuckles had been hurt in the collision. She climbed onto her bike and started off again, smiling thinly.

"Are you all right?" I asked.

"I'm fine."

"What about your hand?"

"What about it?" she said.

HUANG
THE FAT

Though his colleagues called him Huang the Fat because his face was pudgy, like a tomcat's, Huang Zhiye was actually a very small man. He was soft. His skin was smooth and pink and appeared, at all times, freshly scrubbed. His thick hair was coal-black and short as a schoolboy's. He wore white cotton shirts and stiff brown shoes and a tiny pair of horn-rimmed glasses too small for his fat face; from a distance the glasses looked like swimming goggles. His feet were remarkably small. His voice was high and it broke when he was excited, and he spoke in a kind of staccato stutter that conspired with his various other features to make Huang—at forty-three—seem childlike and vulnerable.

One day at the end of October I was working in my room when I heard a timid knock on my door. I was busy and didn't want to be interrupted, so I didn't answer. The knocking persisted; I ignored it. Eventually, and to my surprise, the door opened and Huang Zhiye stepped quietly into the room.

Christina and I had no choice but to leave our door unlocked because the keys the Foreign Affairs Office promised had never materialized. I had been forewarned that closed doors meant little to the Chinese, that they did not consider it rude simply to walk uninvited into a person's apartment. But this was the first time it had happened to me, and I was stunned.

Huang was stunned. He gasped and leaned against the

door. "Oh! You are only sitting right here! I knocked, but no one answered, so I came in!"

"I see," I said. I couldn't pretend I hadn't heard the knock, for though it was soft, it was insistent and mincing and would eventually have driven me out of the room. Embarrassed and mildly annoyed, I invited Huang to sit down. He sat nervously for several minutes without talking. The top button of his shirt was buttoned too tightly. He hugged himself. He cleared his throat. Slumped in my armchair he looked like a child's toy cast aside.

"My purpose is to ask Christina and you if you will give a talk on any subject for the Foreign Languages Department this semester. It is my job to ask. What is your opinion?"

Huang was a professor of English and in his considerable spare time did translations of popular American novels. His English was quite good, though not as good as his wife's. Since my first meeting with him in his apartment I had talked several times with him; his class met across the hall from mine, and at the end of the period he often waited outside my door to ask if we could walk home together. Because of our connection with his wife, Bai Yiping, Huang seemed to feel a certain responsibility for Christina and me. Several times he had come to our room to see how we were, to offer us the use of extension cords, pots and pans, his wife's boots. More than once before, Huang had mentioned the possibility of our giving a talk, but Christina and I were both reluctant to give one until the spring semester. I'd learned that one Chinese way of saying no was simply to say nothing, to offer no response, and following that formula I had put off answering Huang, hoping he'd relent. But here he was again with his importunate plea: "Please agree to give a talk. You can talk about any subject. No one cares. It is only an opportunity for the students to practice their English. What is your opinion?"

I told Huang that I didn't have time this semester, that

I had also been asked to speak at the Engineering College and at the Medical College, and that I thought he should wait until after the winter break. Three times I said no to him; still he continued to press. Finally I said, "Mr. Huang, it seems you're not going to let me decline," hoping to imply that he was being rude. He laughed softly, implying that I, in turn, was being difficult.

"Are you becoming impatient with me?" I asked.

Huang responded to the question by rubbing his knees and looking vacantly around the room, as though he hadn't heard me. I knew he would be held responsible if the foreign teachers didn't agree to speak in public, and I knew his superiors would not take no for an answer, and I hated to think of Huang being dressed down for a petty failure such as this. Out of frustration I agreed to do the talk.

Huang clapped his powdery hands and smiled. "Fine, and what will you talk about?"

"Con-artistry," I said—the first thing that entered my head.

Huang took a note card and pen from his breast pocket and carefully wrote this down. "And what will Christina talk about?"

"I'm not sure what Christina will talk about. I don't know if she'll talk at all. It might be best if you asked her yourself."

"Surely you could suggest something. I need to tell the department what her subject will be."

"Christina hasn't agreed yet, and I can't decide for her."

"But you are together."

"But she might be unhappy if I put words in her mouth."

Huang stared at the notecard with fierce conviction and poised his pen to write. "What will she talk about?"

"I don't know."

"Surely you can guess."

"I can only guess that she might not want to speak."

"But you are together. You must know."

"In some things we're together, but we also value our independence, especially in matters like this. Christina will want to make the decision herself. I can't decide anything for her. It is the American way."

Huang looked defeated and puzzled, as though what I was telling him was absurd. He understood that we were sent here by the same college, that we had traveled together, that we lived together, that we were approximately the same age, and so, to his way of thinking, one of us should be able to speak for the other. He gave me a fearful smile. "Maybe you could leave her my message? You could ask her to send me a note telling me what she will talk about."

"I'll try," I said.

In the long silence that followed, Huang tapped his fists together self-consciously in his lap. Prolonged silences were frequent with Huang. Suddenly he was struck with an idea, and with a wild wave of his hand he said, "Perhaps you would like to take a trip to Shanghai?!"

"Yes, I would."

"I could take you there on a weekend. In a few weeks I must deliver some translations to the Shanghai Foreign Language School. We could stay overnight there."

"Fine."

"Fine, yes, but please do not mention this trip to the others."

"What others?"

"Any others." Huang raised his short fingers to the side of his mouth and said furtively, "You know, in China it would not seem nice for a married man and a young foreign woman to be traveling together. Things of that nature are very different, very strict, here. People would suspect things."

"What things would they suspect?"

"You are American," Huang said coyly, "So I think you can know."

"I can't imagine," I said.

By way of elucidation Huang told me this story: "My brother lives in Ningbo. His neighbor is married to a good woman but has been having an affair with another woman, a cleaning woman in his work unit, for eight years. Most days at noon the cleaning woman comes to visit my brother's lazy neighbor while his good wife is at work. The wife doesn't know a thing about the affair. My brother would never say a word to his neighbor about it, or to any other person, because the consequences of such a scandal could be devastating to the neighbor's family. Anyhow, for eight years my brother can hear his neighbor and the cleaning woman together at lunch time. The neighbor and his wife have a little daughter. It is terrible." Huang shook his head in disgust.

I thought of Huang's own neighbors. Huang's apartment and their apartment shared an entranceway and a toilet. Their two tiny kitchens were on one side of the short hallway and their bedrooms and sitting rooms were on the other. Huang often left his sitting-room doors open so that he could go freely back and forth to the kitchen while he was cooking. Occasionally when I sat with Huang in his rooms I had seen the dark figures of his neighbors hurrying through the hallway on their way out. They never looked into Huang's rooms or said hello. Huang and they rarely spoke. I had the impression Huang disliked them. There wasn't an ounce of privacy in this living arrangement, but according to Huang, complaints were futile.

"You are American," Huang said, "so you would be used to the kind of carrying on my brother has witnessed." Obviously inspired by the subject, Huang began to discuss the sexuality of America.

"I don't understand," he said, "why so many American writers write about women's legs. They make up whole paragraphs to describe the shape of the legs, the knee, the ankle. They call the legs beautiful. I cannot see the reason for writing such a thing. What do they find attractive about the legs?"

I tried to explain the phenomenon.

"The legs?" he said in disbelief. "What could possibly be appealing about the legs? Chinese men only find the mouth and the face interesting. We would never write about a woman's legs. That would be the same as writing about her elbow." The image sent Huang into a fit of nervous giggling. He pressed his knuckles to his lips in an attempt to silence himself.

I shrugged; to me Huang's point made sense. "What about women's feet?" I said. Throughout history the Chinese had revered women's feet as an object of sexual interest, and this had been one of the reasons for binding them; binding made the foot small and attractive; the smaller the better. "Isn't it true that Chinese would write about the beauty of a woman's foot?"

Huang dismissed the idea with a wave of his hand. "Of course once, but it is not this way anymore. Foot binding was forbidden long ago with the beginning of the Republic. And we don't think about the feet now. That practice has disappeared. It is unfashionable, and women would not submit to it now. Now we would only write about the cheeks, the eyes, the hair, the mouth. Those are the things of interest to Chinese men."

I considered Huang's statement. In the short time I had been here, I had already observed in Chinese men an apparent lack of interest in women they were not acquainted with. I watched for this. I watched the men in the parks failing to notice women as they walked by. I never saw a man glance twice at a woman he didn't know, or stare in an appraising way at her body, or turn his head to look at a face. Chinese men didn't whistle or make catcalls. They seemed uninterested, indifferent. Too, there was an odd absence of sexual publicity here. Advertisements on television and billboards directed the people's attention to ideals of family and comfort, to patriotism, progress, and modernization, rarely to sex appeal. Husbands and wives I knew never touched in public. I would often see young couples kissing in bamboo forests and in boats on the lake, but these couples had known each other for months, if not years, and most of them were destined for marriage. Once, in the city, a stylish young man in high-heeled boots winked unmistakably at me. It was an awkward, amateur's wink that screwed up his face and expressed none of the sophistication he'd obviously been hoping for, nevertheless it shocked me. Here a wink was unaccustomed, unexpected, and prurient as a flasher's self-exposure.

I had noticed, too, that Chinese men were extremely affectionate with each other. They held hands as they walked along the lake, they hugged each other, they hooked arms, they studied on the grass with their legs intertwined, they touched each other's hair, tenderly, the way a mother touches the hair of her child. I had rarely seen such open physical affection among men before, and the sight of two young policemen walking along Hubin Road with their arms around each other's waists never failed to turn my head. In class my male students, eighteen and nineteen years old, often sat with their arms around each other's shoulders, or holding hands, or resting a hand on the knee of the friend sitting next to them. One day when I was telling my class a story about flying—none of my students had ever been in an airplane—I noticed Charlie gently and absently tracing the curve of Archie's ear with his finger. Over and over Charlie traced as he listened, wide-eyed, to my story. To Charlie and Archie the gesture was as natural as the shooing of a fly; to me it was surreal, like an image in a dream, and it so touched me that I lost my train of thought and had to start the story over.

My conversation with Huang Zhiye turned to the nature of relationships between men and women.

"It is impossible for a man and a woman to remain close

friends without becoming lovers," Huang announced with authority. "I have heard reports about Mrs. Petrova, the Lithuanian woman upstairs in this building, and her Bulgarian man friend—I don't know his name . . ."

"Vladimir."

"Vladimir—who lives in the Huaqiao Hotel. It is reported that Mrs. Petrova is married to a man in her country, and Vladimir is married to a woman in his country, but he visits Mrs. Petrova often, and one night he stayed so late in her apartment that he had to climb over the wall to get out, and the guards caught him at this. Another night he stayed until morning. The guards cannot succeed in making Mr. Vladimir leave at the appointed hour, for he curses at them and causes a fuss. Chinese assume that if you stay too long into the night in the apartment of a person of the opposite sex, you are engaging in sexual activities. With these two it was inevitable. They spend too much time together."

I knew Tatiana Petrova well, and though I knew that an intimate relationship between Tatiana and Vladimir was of course not impossible, I thought it was highly unlikely. I asked Huang where he'd heard this story.

"It is reported," he said.

I wasn't certain what he meant by this. I'd heard that if, for example, in the rare event that two students were caught sleeping together, their names would be added in black ink to a shame list posted outside the campus security office. I asked Huang if "reported" meant similar treatment for Tatiana and Vladimir.

He looked horrified. "Goodness, no! No matter what our visitors do, they are still our guests. Besides, no one would bother about what foreigners do among themselves. I only meant the story has been passed along by word of mouth."

"I wonder what Tatiana would tell you if you asked her about it yourself," I said. Huang snickered and looked askance at me; the idea of asking the famously large-chested Lithuanian woman about her reported affair struck him as exceedingly mischievous.

When he had regained his composure, Huang told me he had the impression that illicit sex was rampant in the United States and felt that, in light of this, the controversy over abortion was ridiculous. "All that talk about abortion is silly. All that talk, all that arguing. It is nothing. What is the issue? So many Americans talk about the immorality of it, but look at their sexual habits! What do they expect?"

When I asked Huang about China's attitude toward abortion, he said, "There is no attitude. No one thinks about it. It is very easy to get an abortion here. The government encourages it. They have to. We have too many people to worry about the morality of it. It is not an issue."

"How do you know so much about sex in America?" I asked.

"I translate American books when I am not teaching. That is how I make extra money."

Huang's answer was not unexpected. I knew that his translations included books by Harold Robbins, Robin Moore, and Sidney Sheldon. At that time I happened to be helping my co-teacher, Zhen Xinqu, with his translation of Jackie Collins's *Hollywood Wives*. Because his publisher had told him the book was too long for their purposes, Zhen asked me to help him cut one-third of it without doing damage to the plot. Zhen also informed me that there could be no sex in the translation. As an example of what he meant by sex he said, "Here, on this page it says, *'In the lobby he stood beside her. His fingers slowly intertwined with hers.'* We cannot print such a thing. It is too suggestive." The book was littered with graphic sexual encounters, in comparison with which Zhen's example was delightfully tame. Zhen was obviously too embarrassed by anything more explicit to bring it to my attention. In one afternoon

I flipped through the book and with a red pen I parenthesized all the sex scenes, easily eliminating Zhen's third without altering the plot in the least.

Another acquaintance of mine, Miss Hu, a demure young teacher in my department, was translating an American detective story and was constantly coming to my room, book in hand, to say, "Comrade Rose, what is 'pussy-whipped'?" and "tits," and "blow job," and "sixty-nine," and "cop a feel," and "jerking off," and "good in the sack." As delicately as possible I tried to explain these phrases to Miss Hu, and when it was clear she understood, she never seemed ruffled. If I asked her, "Do these things embarrass you, Miss Hu?" she would push her spectacles up higher on her nose and say soberly, "They are new concepts, but it is my duty as translator." I asked her if such things would appear in the Chinese version of the book; she shut her eyes and shook her head so vigorously that her ponytail swung around and swatted my bookshelf. "Oh, no! No way! That can never happen!"

One day Miss Hu showed up at my door, and before I had a chance to invite her in, she asked, "Rose, why did Americans invent homosexuality?"

I looked hard at her to see if she was kidding—she wasn't. "Miss Hu," I said, "Do you really believe Americans invented homosexuality?"

"Of course! Everyone knows."

I tried then to tell her about the ancient Greeks, the Romans, the homosexuality extant in ancient Chinese literature itself. Hu rejected the news. "Excuse me, Rose, but I think you must certainly be mistaken." When I asked her if there was homosexuality in China, she laughed incredulously and threw up her hands. "Of course not!" she said. "What would be the purpose of it?!"

Now I asked Huang, "Is there homosexuality in China?"

He answered, "If there is, we don't know about it. I never met anyone who was homosexual. I think Chinese just are not this way. We never hear about it, never see it. But we know that it exists in America. Homosexuals and lesbians." He shook his head in confusion. "I can understand how men can be homosexuals because of, well . . . ejaculation. But I cannot guess how women can be lesbians."

The logic of this distinction puzzled me. "Do you mean you can't understand how women enjoy sex?"

"Well, I can understand that women also enjoy sex, but how can they enjoy it without a man?" Huang looked at me, hands folded in his lap, waiting for an answer. For all his apparent puritanism he was willing to discuss the most intimate details of America's sexual practices, and he was remarkably matter-of-fact about it, precisely as he might be in a discussion of auto mechanics. I was reluctant to answer his question. Feebly I said, "If you stretch your imagination far enough, I guess you might be able to think of ways," and quickly, to steer him off of that subject, though not too far, I asked him about pornography in China.

"There is no real pornography in China that I know about. I don't think I have ever seen any. It would be forbidden here." He thought a moment. "This reminds me. When I was studying in New Zealand, a Malaysian friend I had there tried to persuade me to pay a visit to a prostitute. A foreign girl with blond hair! Of course I refused." He laughed uncomfortably and crossed his arms and ankles. "There were also those pornographic magazines in New Zealand that you could buy in any old shop just here and there. Pictures of naked women. Ha! They are very bold."

There was a knock on the door then, and before I could answer it, Ming Yu came into the room in a straw hat and a white silk dress. She and Huang seemed surprised to see each other and greeted each other warmly in Chinese. Huang had once been Ming's translation teacher. They chatted a few minutes, and when Huang had left, Ming said, "When

I was a student here, Huang was one of our favorite teachers. He was refreshing. He didn't recite old information. He did new things. He was entertaining. But he is unhappy in this university."

"How do you know that?" I asked.

"I know," she said enigmatically. "Chinese are secretive people, but in fact among neighbors there is little that can be secret. There are too many neighbors."

I asked Ming, "Is there homosexuality in China?"

"Yes there is."

"Mr. Huang and Miss Hu believe there isn't."

Ming closed her eyes and waved her hand slowly before her face, as if erasing Huang and Hu. "Try to understand, Chinese are prudish. And many people don't know. We never talk about it."

"Do you know any homosexuals?"

"I knew two old women who lived together all their lives and were. And I have a friend who knows a homosexual man in Beijing. But homosexuals in China hide, even intellectuals. You would not often see them or hear them. It is forbidden."

THE EARLY ARRIVAL
OF DREAMS

The more I knew of Ming Yu, the more self-possessed she seemed. Though she appeared physically smaller each time I saw her, her personality seemed larger, and I was increasingly interested in her openness and her uncanny command of English. She had a bright sense of humor and an easy laugh and seemed to have little difficulty understanding my views—in fact she often shared them, and this was comforting in a place where so much was strange and unaccustomed and where curious Chinese behavior was explained away with the dismissive and unsatisfying truism "It is the Chinese way."

Ming was excruciatingly idealistic and honest. Wherever she went, she looked for the truth, and George Greatorex had told me that in the past her inability to lie or to dissemble had brought her more trouble than good fortune. Because her present situation was bleak and limited, Ming spent much of her time dreaming of a life in the future.

In addition to being a poet, Ming Yu was a singer. She had a beautiful voice and was particularly fond of traditional music. Each year the university held a singing competition among the teachers, and invariably Ming Yu won. Too, she had a superb talent for imitating accents, both Chinese and English, and her repertoire included the foreign teachers at Hangzhou and several Chinese leaders. Her imitation of me was so accurate that it filled me with dislike for my own imperious self. She would lower her voice an octave, knit her brows, put her hand flat against her chest, and declare in a disgusted, businesslike way, "How can that *possibly* be true?!"

I came to rely on Ming Yu for answers to Chinese customs that puzzled me, or elements of Chinese life that were unclear. I began to see her as a window on the Chinese life. She answered my questions without fear or embarrassment. When I asked her why my students stared at my earrings, she said, "Because in China only peasants wear earrings. You would never see a teacher or a professor with jewelry on."

I did not ask Ming Yu about her relationship with George Greatorex and rarely discussed him unless she brought him up. I knew only that they were friends, that they spent a lot of time together, and that Chinese tongues clucked over this.

Ming Yu lived in a university dorm for unmarried teachers, a vast three-story cement structure with the cold, damp, unfinished feel of a basement; it was merely a series of floors and corridors and innumerable cement cells. Each floor had a communal toilet and washroom lit by one dim bulb dangling from the ceiling by a frayed wire; these were dank, cavernous rooms unfit to shoe a horse in. The sinks were long soapstone tubs like feeding troughs in a barn, and the toilets, like almost all public toilets in China, were merely trenches in the floor flushed, in theory, every half hour by an anonymously controlled flushing system centered elsewhere in the building. In fact the flushing occurred once a day, and the smell of these bathrooms was sickening and relentless.

Here the unmarried teachers lived two or three to a small unheated room. Electric heaters were forbidden because of the drain on the electricity. There was no hot water in the building, and year-round teachers washed themselves and their clothes in cold water or else boiled their water, a tedious, maddening exercise; the only alternative was the public showers halfway into the city.

The dorm's permanently unlit hallways were reminiscent of city alleys and served as kitchens, closets, and storage rooms. They were cluttered with washbasins, pots and pans, bicycles, open umbrellas, unwanted furniture, baskets, cooking oil, trash bins, clotheslines, and laundry. When I came here in the evenings I walked slowly down the hallway, afraid I'd bump into things, knock them over, step in a puddle of dirty water, or get scalded by the steam of someone's boiling soup. The strongest light in the hallways was the occasional coal fire glowing in a stove or the rays cast out of a doorless room. Now and then faces peered out the door at me, then stiffened and retreated when they saw I wasn't Chinese; foreign visitors were rare to this building.

One day on my way to visit Ming Yu in her room, I had a minor bicycle collision on the wide avenue in front of the university. A middle-aged woman with a cargo of onions strapped to her fender ran the red light and careened headlong into a crowd of bicyclists, of which I was one. The woman's front wheel tangled with mine, we both fell over, and the onions spilled across the pavement. Before she was on her feet again, the woman began shouting and cursing viciously at me. Her face was thick with rage. Preparing for an argument, she collected her battered bike and turned to face me, but as soon as her eyes met mine, her mouth fell open and her hand flew up to cover it. She went crimson with horror. "Forgive me!" she wailed, "I thought you were Chinese!" She dropped her bike with a clatter and stooped to pick mine up. When I tried to help her with the onions, she protested with a flapping of the hands and said, "It is not your job! It is my job! It is my fault!" Her English was perfect.

I carried on through the university gates, puzzled by the woman's reaction.

When I arrived at Ming's room, her door was open and she was sitting at her desk, writing by the dim light. She stood to greet me, invited me to sit at a small table by the window, and offered me tea in a water glass. The casual custom here was to throw a few tea leaves into a glass and pour hot water over them, which made drinking nearly impossible until the leaves swelled and settled at the bottom of the glass. "You may spit the leaves on the table if you don't care to chew them," Ming said. Dropping unwanted food on the table was also a casual custom and was in no way considered rude or unmannerly.

Ming shared her small room with a forbiddingly stylish physical education teacher named Wen Hairuo, who spoke no English but wanted desperately to go to Chicago to get a master's degree in physical education. When I asked her why Chicago, she said, "My boyfriend studies there." When I arrived, Miss Wen had been flipping through a Japanese fashion magazine that Ming told me had cost her a month's salary. Wen was slim and strong, and her hair was so long she was able to sit on the end of her ponytail. She wore an expression of cautious curiosity.

The women's room contained two desks, two wooden stools, and two beds that were merely crude wooden frames with straw mats stretched across them. At the foot of each bed were a few shelves curtained by small blankets; these were their closets, piled high with their clothing and belongings. The room was lit by the same unceremonious sort of bulb that hung in the bathrooms, but this one dangled conspicuously low, grazing my ear as I crossed the floor. The floor and walls were bare but for a poster above one of the desks that displayed various color photographs of Boston and announced in huge letters, THE FENWAY.

The only thing these women had, really, were books, hundreds of them lining the walls in rickety makeshift shelves. There were as many English books as there were Chinese, volumes of Shakespeare, Henry James, Dickens, the Brontës, Austen, Balzac, Sartre, de Beauvoir, Mann, Tolstoy, Chekhov, Wharton, and Steinbeck. The list of books was endless and included *Mao Zedong's Quotations*. When I commented on the Mao book, Ming Yu took it down from the shelf and held it between her rough hands.

"This is my original book, given to me when I was a little Red Guard in Wuxi," she said.

"You were a Red Guard?" I said; I found it hard to believe.

"All children were."

"Why?"

She shrugged. "We were told we must work for the people. We wore red arm bands with slogans written on them; we chanted down the intellectuals and those who were considered capitalists or instruments of imperialism; we denounced our teachers. I remember one week we were told that when we went into our classroom, we should sit with our backs to the teacher, ignoring her if she spoke to us."

"Did you do it?"

"Of course. We were told it was our duty to Mao Zedong and the country."

"How old were you?"

"At that time I was seven. It was 1967."

"Do you remember it?"

"I remember some things. I remember one summer day the conference hall of the county government was filled with people who had come to criticize 'capitalist roaders.' Like many other children I sat on the stairway that led up to the stage at the front of the hall. Every time the name of a roader was called two guards twisted his arms and walked him onto the stage. The audience shouted slogans at him. On his neck the revolutionaries hung a big wooden board with his name and crimes written on it. After the supposed roaders introduced themselves, representatives from different units made accusations, interrupting themselves to ask, 'Haven't you committed this or that crime?! Dare you deny the crime?!' The accused would nod his head obediently, for if he did not, he would get a kick or a blow on the head, or his arms would be held behind his back and pulled upward, so that they looked like the wings of an airplane. I remember children often laughed at other children whose fathers were said to have, 'taken the plane.' "

Through the window we heard people arguing and horns honking angrily on the street that ran beside the university wall. I told Ming then about the accident I had had on my way over and how the woman with the onions had reacted to me. She nodded and said, "Chinese are deferential to foreigners now, but they treat each other badly. You have seen our markets and our shops. Really, there's nothing in them but leftovers. All the best clothing and goods, all the best rice, is exported to foreign countries, while we make do with second best. If you had been a Chinese, that woman would have chased you through the gates of the university."

Ming blew tea leaves across the top of her glass and sipped from it. "Chinese cannot appreciate each other," she said. Self-consciously she shuffled the papers she had been working on and changed the subject. "When you arrived, I was practicing my handwriting. My father insisted I do this. He said my writing was too sloppy and childish from the hand of a twenty-seven-year-old woman. He is correct. If he weren't, I wouldn't heed his demand."

I asked Ming if she had a good relationship with her father. "So-so," she said. "You know, I respect him, but I would not do something just because my father wanted me to do it. I made a mistake about that once and it turned me into a sad, mournful person in dark clothing. I was in love with a boy, an artist with short hair, whom my parents did not approve of. One day I went into town, and because I was in love, I felt very happy and so I bought myself a red jacket, which was unlike me. On that trip to town I lost a bunch of keys, and this made me very worried. I thought it was a sign that something bad would happen to me. When I came home, my father saw the jacket and was extremely angry and said, 'It is not for a young woman to wear red.' Red is the color of wedding clothes. A few days later my boyfriend made me a gift of two pretty teacups. I put them on a table in my room. The next day as I was sitting at my desk something fell off the top of my bookshelf and hit the cups. Strangely it didn't knock them off the table; it only broke the handle off one of them so that I could not hold it to drink. I was forced to throw it away; then I had only the single cup. I was sure now that something bad would happen and I was afraid. I sensed my parents did not like this boy, and I thought that could only bring misfortune to me. Not long after, my parents insisted that I stop seeing the boy. They forbade him to come and see me, and they wouldn't let me go to him, and I was afraid of their anger, so I obeyed them. The boy did not need an explanation for my behavior; he knew what my parents thought of him. Occasionally I still see that boy around Wuxi, but there is no hope for the relationship. It is too late of course."

"Now if you fell in love with someone your parents didn't approve of, would you ignore their disapproval?"

"I could never ignore my parents. That would make me unhappy, but I would try to stand up for myself. These days I try to act as I see fit. Some people don't like this."

"What people?"

"People in the university. In my department a lot of the teachers see me as one of the men, because I don't flirt with men and because I talk to them just as I would talk to women, and in spring when the faculty clean the classrooms, I climb up and clean the windows with the men. Women are not expected to clean the windows; women are expected to dust the rungs of the chairs and such." Ming smiled in self-amusement. She had picked up a bicycle lock and was toying restlessly with it.

"You know, when I came to teach in the department, I went to the first meeting where new teachers were expected to introduce themselves. As soon as the leader had finished his speech, I stood up immediately and introduced myself first. The other teachers were surprised, because it is expected that women will introduce themselves last, after the men have had their chance. A woman should defer and be shy. I was bold. Even as I spoke, I knew I was not acting properly, but I could not contain myself. It seemed correct. Later, when I went home, I began to worry that perhaps I should not have done so. Maybe I have given myself a bad reputation."

I asked her whom she had a bad reputation with. She thought for a while and said, "Anyway I have a bad relationship with Yang Shiren, the head of the Foreign Affairs Office, because I do not agree with him. He has some power over who in the university will be allowed to travel abroad. He is a bureaucrat."

I agreed that it might not be wise of Ming to protest too much, that she could perhaps be more effective if she exercised discretion in her feats of independence. Because the question had been nagging at me, I asked Ming if she agreed with George's general assessment of university life. She touched her ragged fingertips to her lips, considering the question. "The Communist party has a lot of control. The people George speaks of are mostly Party members. No one beneath them can criticize them and so their voices are the only voices that will be heard. It goes on and on this way. It is the kind of cycle . . ." Ming paused and snapped her fingers, searching for the word. "Vicious," she said at last.

I asked how her parents felt about her efforts to study abroad.

She said, "To do my present job properly and wait with

patience for my turn to come is their advice for me. My father would like to see his children go abroad to study, but he also knows the system well enough to understand that it is foolish to hope for the early arrival of dreams."

I asked Ming if she and her father agreed on political issues. She said, "We don't agree, and my father is disappointed that my brothers and I never say anything positive about our government. He is still a very faithful member of the Communist party. He had even written a history of the Party in Wuxi. My brother, who is studying at the East China Normal School recently heard a famous reporter say that the censorship in China is too heavy and that writers here are not honest because they are afraid to speak the truth. This reporter has been in most of the prisons in Beijing for dissenting. He said that much of China's news is either a lie or it is simply not told at all. The reporter knew of a great deal of expensive electronic equipment that had been imported from a foreign country. The goods arrived on the dock of a northeastern port town but went unclaimed. They stayed on the dock for weeks and weeks and were spoiled by the rain. Eventually they were returned to their country of origin. The reporter asked publicly why the people's property had been handled in such a careless way, but his complaint was censored and he was punished. Authorities denied his claims. When my brother told my father the story, he was furious and said, 'You have no way of knowing if this is true!' My father is right, we never know what the truth is. Here the most reliable news is the news that travels on the tongues of the people."

I was fascinated by the ease with which Ming spoke and by her high and heartfelt ideals. I glanced over at her roommate, who had been watching me with equal fascination. She clutched her magazine and inspected me, my face and my clothing, my bracelets and shoes, and when I spoke, she cocked her head abruptly, slightly startled and slightly amused by the strange sounds I made. I wondered if Ming

Yu would have spoken so freely if Wen Hairuo had understood English, and I wondered what they talked about when they were alone.

As Ming spoke, a mouse appeared on the table between us and wandered boldly among the cups and spoons. I looked at Ming, but she went on talking and spinning her bike lock in the palm of her hand, as if the mouse wasn't there. When she saw my amazement, she said, "Never mind; the mouse is not actually a common occurrence." She rolled a peanut across the table for him, then clapped her hands and he disappeared. Ming paused for a moment, looked shyly at me, and said, "I have talked too much." She poured more hot water into my glass.

Before I left that day, Ming gave me this advice: "You must be careful on Hangzhou's streets. When you ride your bicycle in a crowd, mix with it, do not try to resist it. Let it protect you. Don't ride fast. Though, I think you will be tempted to ride fast. Foreigners always ride fast."

DR. FU

Early one morning I was awakened by a shrieking voice that came from behind the gray apartment building across from ours; a woman's voice venting some kind of distress or plea at regular intervals. "Dah-ah-day!" she wailed, "Dah-ah-day!" and the more she expressed her misery, the more rhythmical and unnatural was her cry. It was seven o'clock, the sun was just rising over the roof of the red-brick building under construction beyond our wall, and already I could feel its warmth against my dusty window screens.

I got out of bed, dressed, and went out onto the balcony. The wailing seemed to turn a corner and grow louder, traveling just along the other side of our wall, at the foot of the gray building. It had the round, ringing timbre of a silver flute, and it carried far along the network of alleys and lanes.

The kitchen window across the way banged open, and the bespectacled cook poked her head out and called something down to the wailing woman, who called back softly and rather reasonably now. The cook slammed her window shut and in a minute she was running down the stairs in an apron. At the bottom of the stairway a petite, dark-faced woman with a bowllike haircut came into view and started her way up—it was the wailing woman, carrying on her arm a big wicker basket filled with coffee-colored eggs. The two women met on a landing, eggs went from basket to apron, money changed hands, and each one hurried away the way she had come. The egg seller began wailing out her song before she had even hit the street again.

I turned to go back into my room, and as I stepped toward the door, I felt a sickening thud against my forehead, like the blow of a club, and felt flesh coming off bone. My hands went up to my face, and suddenly my fingers were cold and wet with blood. I had a moment of stunned panic, a familiar, tumbling moment of chaos before the senses could catch up and assess the damage. There was a conspicuous absence of pain, which I took as a sign of deep destruction. I sat down on the warm cement floor of the balcony with my back against the wall of the building and one hand held up to my face in a vain effort to catch the blood, to stop it somehow. I tasted blood on my tongue and felt it trickle down my neck and into the opening of my blouse. If this is really bad, I thought, I'll faint out here and no one will ever find me. An image of the moldering bird I had stepped on weeks before flashed into my mind and quickly out again. I tilted my head back against the building, opened my eyes, and there above me I saw the sharp metal corner of the crank-out window sticking boldly into the balcony. There were three windows like this, bristling with arrowhead corners at eye level; I had walked square into one of them and got stabbed in the forehead for it.

I stood up slowly, pushed the door open, and stepped into my bedroom, and in that same moment two maids, the tall older one named Mrs. Lin and a new one I was not acquainted with, entered through the other door to begin their cleaning. At the sight of me the new maid shrieked and dropped her bucket and scrub brush. Tall Mrs. Lin flung a pile of bedsheets onto the chair, flew across the room on her long legs, and caught me in a bear hug. She shouted for the new girl to call a car and guided me into the bathroom. At the sink she tipped my head back and washed my face with a rag, holding me steady with one hand on the back of my neck. I could feel her hands trembling. I stared at her face in the mirror—it radiated terror, and when she caught me staring, she took a break from the washing to let out a hysterical cackle and went immediately back to work. When the washing was finished, I inspected my forehead; I had a deep vertical slit in my hairline.

A moment later the two maids led me down the stairs, one of them pressing the rag to my head. They tugged and lifted me with such ferocious energy that the soles of my feet hardly touched the steps. In the courtyard a car and driver were waiting to take me to the university hospital. The driver raced through the campus, scattering sleepy-eyed students in her wake.

The two maids had sent Hong Yi, a mature, friendly, English-speaking woman who worked in the dining room of the guest house, to accompany me, and I heard her next to me on the car seat repeating, "Please don't worry," over and over again like an incantation.

The hospital was a small compound of dingy rooms, peeling paint, and cold cement floors, and the hallways were narrow, unlit alleys. A white-capped white-coated nurse led me by the arm into a windowless room, sat me on a stool, took away the rag I had pressed to my forehead, and hurried out. Hong Yi stood against the wall and stared at me. I looked around the room; it was surprisingly bare, with little more to occupy it than an enameled table, a chair, a steel surgical lamp, and one shelf lined with tiny amber vials like the things sold in a traveling medicine show. As in many Chinese rooms, the wall plaster was cracked and lumpy and painted lettuce-green.

A middle-aged doctor came into the room with a lit cigarette dangling from his lip, greeted Hong Yi, and approached me without meeting my gaze. Calmly he inspected my wound.

Hong Yi said, "He is Dr. Fu."

"What kind of doctor is he?"

"I don't know. Maybe the usual kind."

Fu was heavy-lidded and sighed indifferently as he worked. He seemed bored and depressed. He said, "Ha-ha," and took my head in his hands and turned it this way and that, talking at me around the cigarette, poking and peering and saying "Tsk" to my scalp. I had the feeling he was scolding me for my carelessness. Without warning he came at me with a huge pair of shears, preparing to cut off the hair at the front of my head, and to my own surprise I knocked the scissors out of his hand and sent them clattering across the table beside us.

Fu roared with laughter at this, raised his hands in mock surrender, and indicated by pretending to primp in a hand mirror that I was, like all women everywhere, vain. I smiled and nodded and indicated that he was right.

Between laughs Fu muttered something to Hong Yi, which she translated as "Women prefer death than losing their hair."

I looked at the laughing Dr. Fu and thought, Don't you forget it.

With a rough jab Fu applied some yellow ointment to the cut, which burned at the invasion. He handed me an envelope of pills and grinned. His whole approach had changed; he was cheerful as a child now, giggling and eager. His instructions were to take one pill three times a day for six days. I asked Hong Yi what the pills were. "To make the cut better," she said.

"But what are they called?" I said.

"Medicine," said she.

Fu smiled and nodded at the sound of English. Because it seemed the polite thing, I nodded back at him, resolving in my skepticism and mistrust to flush the pills down the toilet as soon as I got home. Fu's parting advice was that I should refrain from showering for a week. When I asked why, Hong Yi said, "Because our water is very dirty and would be bad for the wound."

That afternoon Chen Peiling, the head of my teaching group, canceled my listening class, which met twice a week in the audio lab. The next day when I showed up to teach my regular class, the students stared intently at me, hushed and contrite, with more than the usual amount of reverence, as though they were somehow responsible for my mishap with the window. I told them the story, including how Dr. Fu had tried to cut my hair and what he had said about the vanity of women. The students giggled and tittered at that and whispered among themselves, and, as always, they seemed particularly amused by my confusion and surprise at the Chinese ways. When I told them about my wound, they sucked their breath through their teeth, as though it pained them as much as it did me.

"We are sorry!" they said.

On my way out of the room that day the class monitor came up beside me and said, "Master Rose, you must take care. Be careful to yourself. It would be sad if you had to return to America because you have been hurt in our country."

MARIA

In my group of students from the Chinese Department one girl, Maria, was particularly friendly with me. Every day in class she sat at a desk in the middle of the front row and watched my face for the entire two hours of the lesson. She worked furiously to improve her English. She had a soft, retiring way of speaking, and her words came slowly but with appealing urgency. At times Maria almost sounded frightened, and though I knew she was actually a strong and very curious person, she was easily embarrassed and, like many of my students, easily entertained. She had a breathless, choking kind of laugh.

Except for Huang Zhiye and Ming Yu, Maria was one of the most frequent Chinese visitors to my room and she was certainly the most frequent of all my students, for though I often encouraged the students to visit me, most were hesitant to do so. Some days after class a few girls would go out of their way to walk the block home with me to my building, and though for weeks they refused to come in—saying good-bye at the gate, peering past it to catch a glimpse of the foreign world—eventually a few girls overcame their shyness and came in. Boys rarely visited me.

I realized that many of my students were afraid of intruding and felt uncomfortable in the foreigners' building, possibly because of how the university would perceive their visits. In the spring of 1987, following the students' scattered demonstrations for democracy, China had undergone a period of intense conservativism, of antiforeign, antibourgeois sentiment, and though the mood had now shifted back somewhat in favor of reform, many students—and workers—proceeded with caution in their relationships with foreigners. My Chinese colleagues usually declined my invitations to eat with me in our dining room in the Experts' Building, and the few who did come sat stiffly at the dinner table, staring nervously at the other foreigners and eating very little, so that inviting them there was sometimes more uncomfortable than not inviting them at all. They were as fearful of making mistakes with foreigners as they were of the censorious opinions of the authorities.

One afternoon in October I heard a knock on my door. I had been working in my armchair; there were books perched precariously on both arms of the chair and my lap was covered with papers, and because I didn't want to disturb the order of things by getting up, I shouted, "Come in!"

Slowly the outer door opened, and a whole minute later Maria's thin face appeared around the frame of my bedroom door. I was surprised and pleased to see her and invited her in.

Maria was tall, very thin and straight, and wore squarish horn-rimmed glasses. Her long, side-parted hair hung around her face like the folds of a wimple and always looked recently combed. She had the slow, gliding walk of a heron. This was Maria's first visit here, and she looked terrified. She came into the room and stood before me, staring around her in astonishment. When she found her voice, she said shakily, "Your room is very, very comfortable," echoing Ming Yu's sentiments exactly.

I had learned by now that the room truly was comfortable by Chinese standards. "Thank you, Maria," I said.

"Not at all," said Maria, employing the same phrase and the same methodical monotone she always used when responding to thanks in English. It was a phrase she had picked up somewhere and couldn't let go of, and its mechanical occurrence always amused me.

Maria's gaze lit on the large map of the world that hung on the wall behind my head. She peered at it a long time, stepped closer to it, and peered some more, her slim white hands raised slightly before her. She seemed on the verge of reaching up and touching the colorful continents. She looked thoroughly puzzled. After long, silent deliberation she said indignantly, "Rose, this map is *wrong*!"

I knew what she meant; it was an American-made map, and in its laughably self-important way it had North America situated smack in its middle. China and the Soviet Union appeared sliced in two at either end of the map, and the map's Mercator projection made everything else look flat and disproportionate; Greenland loomed like a great purple cloud at the top of the world. But of course this ethnocentric arrangement of the world was not unique to America, for Chinese maps placed China as near to the center of the world as it could possibly be, and the Russian map similarly favored the Soviet Union.

After we had established that map was not exactly wrong, Maria slid down into the chair opposite me, and we began to chat. I put my books and papers on the floor and poured tea for both of us from a clay pot. The pot seemed to baffle Maria. She lifted it by its handle. "Where did you get it?" she said.

"In the market."

She removed the lid of the pot and peered into it, as though she had never in her life seen such an odd contraption. "But why do you not just put the leaves in the teacups and fill them with water?"

"I don't like tea that has leaves floating in it."

Maria returned the pot to the table. "Only old men use the teapot," she muttered.

"Old men are smart."

Maria said, "God!" as though my old-fashioned ideas were insufferable. As she sipped her tea, she picked up a *Newsweek* magazine that lay on the table between us. On its cover was modern-day Cher, looking cool and smug. Maria held the magazine up close to her face and stared through her glasses at Cher. Like many Chinese, Maria had the ability to appear thoroughly alone in a room when captivated by something visual. Gradually she came nose-to-nose with Cher's glossy image. She began to frown, and asked in her fainting voice, "Rose, is this woman American?"

"Yes, she is."

"But she is frightening to look at!" Maria returned the magazine to the table and told me she was really only interested in seeing foreign women who had blond hair and blue eyes.

"You like that?" I said.

"Yes. It is very beautiful."

"Why is it beautiful?"

"It is different. More pretty. Sometimes we think it is best."

I thought of what the Japanese teacher, Mitsuko Tokutomi, had told me about the great numbers of Japanese women who, with surgery, were having their eyes rounded and their noses narrowed and lengthened in pursuit of more Caucasian facial characteristics; it was a look the Japanese also considered more attractive than their own. I mentioned the practice to Maria and she cringed and put her hand to her pale throat. "I have heard about it," she said.

"Do Chinese women do that?" I asked.

Maria said she had never met a Chinese woman who had had her face changed and that to her the procedure seemed "terrible."

Miss Hu, the translator I was acquainted with in my department, had told me a story of a Chinese girl who had "suffered ugliness" all her life and had finally decided to have her eyes surgically altered to improve her appearance.

But sadly her operation went badly, and when the bandages were removed, the woman discovered "that her ugliness had only been increased." In her despair and shame she flung herself from the top of a building, but survived the fall with a broken neck, and now she was not only ugly but crippled as well. Miss Hu had eagerly pointed out for me the moral in this story.

I asked Maria if she would ever consider having her face changed. She shot me a disdainful look. "Never!"

I peeled apples for both of us. Maria held hers like a weighty rock and approached it with nibbling, occasional bites. I asked Maria about herself, about her family and her life. When I asked her who her friends were in our class, she answered, "I have no friends at this university. If you would get too friendly with somebody in the university, soon they will find a way to make you look bad. If you would tell someone a secret, later she will tell other people."

My impression had been that there were strong friendships between pairs of girls in my class, that only one or two of my students could be called loners, and that these pairs of friends did everything together; they arrived at class together, sat next to each other, and went to lunch and dinner and movies together. Even Maria appeared to have what I had assumed was a close friend in another girl in the class named Helen.

"What about Helen," I said. "Isn't she your friend?"

"Helen in my roommate," Maria corrected. "I have to be her friend."

"But you like Helen, don't you?"

After careful thought Maria said cautiously, "Helen is humorous."

I asked Maria why anyone would want to make her look bad by revealing her secrets. She answered that the students were in competition with each other, that everyone wanted a good job when they finished at the university, and that good jobs were scarce. "If I told one of my classmates that I did not like a certain teacher, the classmate might go and tell the teacher that. If you tell secrets, you will probably be sorry. You will get into trouble and wish that you did not tell. If they could make another person look bad, they could make themselves look better."

It reminded me of stories I'd heard about cutthroat medical students in America who sabotaged each other's experiments and tore pages out of library books to hinder their classmates' academic success. In China, college graduates were assigned to jobs, and naturally the more favored students got the better jobs. But I was confused by what Maria was saying, for I had thought Chinese friends were fiercely loyal to each other, that friendship in China was not something to be taken lightly. I thought Maria was overcautious. I asked her if she had friends at home in Nanjing.

"Yes. My friends there are old friends." She added, "Here I do not become friendly with anyone unless they are in the higher level of grade than I am."

"Why is that?"

"The fourth-year students can help me. And also they like me."

"How can they help you?"

"They can give me advice about what to do. They can tell me how to study well."

"Do you think other students feel the same way you do about telling their secrets?"

"I don't ask them," Maria said.

She told me she thought a few of them felt the same way she did, but pointed out that her case might be different because of her connection to the army. Her father had been an army officer, and though he had died of cancer some years before, her family was still connected to an army work unit in Nanjing, and her mother now worked in the army's boot factory. She said, "We could have privileges like other people in the army, and I think other students are jealous, so they would try to attack me."

I asked her what the privileges were.

"A better job," she said. "Everyone could get a better job."

Maria seemed obsessed with the idea of a good job. "What kind of job do you hope to have when you finish at the university, Maria?"

"I want to go to the television and say the news."

"You want to be a television newscaster?"

"Yes."

Maria told me it cost her seventy yuan per month to live and pay for her schooling in Hangzhou, and that her mother provided fifty yuan of that every month while the government provided the standard 20 yuan. Maria said she had very little money to spend, that she couldn't afford luxuries. Books were expensive. Even a movie was expensive. She said she thought that because of this, many students in the university were spending their time "trying to get money" instead of studying hard. They thought good grades were useless and would do nothing toward getting them a better job. Other students had expressed similar feelings. One unusually politically minded boy told me that in his opinion students were unwilling to study hard because although prices were rising, there was little increase in the people's pay and that this was especially true for intellectuals. He said the students felt frustrated when they thought about the poor wages they had to look forward to and that many students simply wanted to give up studying and go into private business. "But in fact," the boy said, "they have no capacity for doing business. They are naive."

As far I could see, Maria and her classmates were not taking part in the business-for-profit trend. They were not the young people I saw in coffeehouses in the city at night, people who spent their money on modern clothes, cigarettes, and beer. My students didn't wear sunglasses and Western fashions. They were, in many respects, conservative and old-fashioned.

Maria said, "I study ancient Chinese, so after I graduate, I will probably work in a library. I will sift ancient books and it will be terrible!" She told me that most students had no idea what awaited them when they graduated in 1990, that China had a five-thousand-year history, that it carried "a heavy traditional culture," and that "reformation" was difficult.

When I asked Maria if she liked the university, she responded with a horrible look of disgust. "No! It is poor. It is unclean and the food is bad. Also, the condition of teaching in our school is poor, almost all teachers, including our Chinese teachers, stay in a rut and makes less effective teaching."

Many students, she said, had lost interest in studying, because although the government was implementing educational reforms, the results were virtually invisible. Furthermore educational funding had been cut in recent years.

"The treatment of the teacher is low, the quality of teacher is poor. These make the university poor. Many people are worried about it. But we all have confidence if the government could keep doing the education reform to the students, we would have improvement."

Maria looked at the apple turning brown in her hand, and her mind downshifted to simpler things. "At home my mother cooks. I miss my mother. My mother loves me very much. And my brothers and I are very close. I am proud of them and they are proud of me."

During this visit it occurred to me that the students who visited me preferred to come here alone, and I got the impression that they didn't want their classmates, not even the friends they stuck close to, to know they had come to see me. I realized they were worried about getting the reputation as worshippers of foreign things, but once they were here they relaxed. At the beginning of the year I had felt frustrated by my students' seeming lack of individuality and by their apparent inability to speak for themselves, but I had since learned that that was a situational phenomenon, that the "rules" of the group imposed constraints on them, and that when they were alone with me, they were actually quite individualistic.

Maria stared now at the books I had stacked on the floor next to my chair. Among them was a book of historical Chinese photographs, pictures of Liberation, World War II China, and the Chinese military. I had bought several such books at the New China bookstore in the city, and each new book fascinated me more than the last. Though I couldn't understand the texts, I was enthralled by the grainy black-and-white photographs, and I developed a particular fascination with Mao Zedong's countenance, with his photographic presence. I could spend hours looking at Mao's face; in some photos he looked like a plastic doll, in others like a postmenopausal woman. Sometimes his hair looked like a black beret sloping off the side of his head. He had a growth the size of an M & M on his chin and his teeth were like little thorns in his mouth. In most of the photos he looked soft and hapless and uncoordinated.

"Are you reading the book?" Maria said, pointing at the photography book.

"I'm looking at the pictures," I said. "Would you like to look at it?"

She nodded and took the book in her hands, and I leaned over to look at it with her. In one hazy photograph at Yanan six men stood before the wing of an airplane in thick winter clothing. One of them was so bundled up in jackets and snow pants that he looked like an effigy. His arms stuck straight out from his sides, like a swollen tick's. I laughed and put my finger on the man's face and murmured, "Look at *this* fat fool."

Maria looked at me; she was mute with shock. "You cannot say 'fat fool!' " she cried. "He is our greatest leader, Mao Zedong!"

I looked again at the photograph. I could barely make out

Mao's puffy features beneath the brim of his cap. I couldn't have known it was Mao from just glancing at him. I apologized to Maria and said I hadn't meant to offend or defame him, but that she had to agree he certainly looked stout.

Maria's face was red with shame. She pointed to Zhou Enlai, also present in the picture, and said, "Yes, but even Zhou Enlai, our most handsome leader, also looked fat in this picture. Mao Zedong was not fat. He was a great leader."

Maria's loyalty fascinated me. Not long before that afternoon a student in the Geography Department had worn a lapel pin to class with Mao Zedong's pudgy face printed on it in warm colors. The character *zhong*, "loyal," appeared three times on the pin beneath Mao's image. The student who wore the pin was the most rebellious in the class. He wore tight jeans and sharp boots and had his hair done in a permanent wave. He was not a diligent student, was always the last to class, and was the one who said most often, "I am sorry, teacher, I do not have the answer." When I saw the Mao pin on his lapel that day in class, I was curious. I pointed to the pin and said, "Bill, where did you get that?"

Bill laughed loudly, surprised at my interest and pleased at the opportunity to bring attention to himself. "It is our great leader, Chairman Mao Zedong! Ha-ha!" There was bitter derision in his laugh, and the students sitting next to him tittered nervously, reluctant to side with him, but also finding it difficult not to see humor in this.

"Do you admire Mao Zedong?" I said.

Scowling, Bill unhooked the pin from his jacket. "I wear it for a joke," he said, handing me the pin. "You may have it."

I took the pin from Bill and turned it over in my hand; it was very old, made of ceramic, and possibly even valuable. I handed it back to Bill and told him I thought he should keep it, that some day he might want to have it. But he insisted that I take it and shoved his hands into his jacket pockets, turning his head away from me when I held the pin out to him. We were already four minutes into our class time, and not wanting to drag this little scene out any longer, I accepted the pin and slipped it into my pocket.

"You can wear it in America," Bill said. "Also as a joke."

At the end of class I asked Bill where he got the pin. "My grandmother gave it to me when I was a small child," he said.

"Did your grandmother think it was a joke?"

Bill's face grew very serious. "Of course not," he said.

Now, in my room, I asked Maria, "Do you really think Mao was a great man?"

She said, "Of course."

"What do other students think about him?"

"Also that he was a great man."

"What about the Cultural Revolution?" I said.

Maria snapped the photo book shut. "What about *Liberation*?!" She was daring me to insinuate further that Mao might not have been what he was said to be. She would defend him to the last.

Ming Yu, too, was one of the few people I met who defended Mao. "People forget," Ming would say, "the good things Mao did. This often happens in history. As soon as the person dies, they find out the bad things about him. No one talks about the great poetry Mao wrote."

Maria put the book back on the floor and fell silent. "Rose," she said softly, "I love a boy."

"I'm happy to hear it, Maria."

"Thank you," she said sadly, "but I think the boy does not love me, for he sometimes will not speak to me when other people are near."

"He's just shy," I said. A few days previous Maria had asked me to go to a movie with her in the city. Now I suggested that she invite the boy to come along with us.

"Oh no!" she gasped. "He would never come. He would be very embarrassed of you."

We talked a bit more about the boy, and then the typewriter on my desk caught Maria's eye. "Did you bring it from America?" she asked.

"Yes."

"Would you allow me to try to do it?"

"Of course." I got her a fresh piece of paper, and she sat stiffly in my desk chair and studied the keys. Eventually she lifted her hand, poked at a key, and yanked her hand back fast, as though the machine had singed her finger. After three or four minutes of trying, she had typed out the message "Hello, Rose," and each time she made a mistake, she gasped in horror and wrung her hands. She asked me to type something. I typed, "Dear Maria, someday you'll be able to type 55 words per minute."

When she saw how fast my fingers flew across the keyboard, she could hardly contain her astonishment.

On her way out the door that afternoon I gave Maria a shirt that someone had sent me from America, something I wouldn't have worn myself. She seemed not to be able to believe her good fortune at being presented with such a thing and she thanked me again and again and said loyally, "I will not tell any of the others you have given me this gift."

IN THE
CITY

A few days after Maria's visit Ming Yu asked me to go into the city with her. We met at the gate to the building; she wore a black skirt and a cotton army shirt the color of peas, with flaps over the pockets and stiff cuffs and collar. "That shirt looks nice," I said. Ming blushed. "It's American."

As we rode down a narrow lane, I saw a woman emerge from her house carrying a live rat caught in a steel trap. She placed the trap on the sidewalk and matter-of-factly began stabbing the rat through the belly with a long, stiff wire. She glanced idly up and down the street as she stabbed, looking to see what friends of hers were out and shouting hello to those who passed by. Spotless white T-shirts flapped on a line behind her head. The rat squealed and twitched, then lay limp. I was horrified by the sight and looked at Ming Yu.

"I should say the rat situation is worse than the city makes believe," she said apologetically.

Despite the many traffic wardens and police scattered throughout the city there seemed to be little order to the traffic on Hangzhou's streets. Streetlights were planted only at the busiest intersections, and even where they did exist, bicyclists and truckers were constantly running the lights and coming nose-to-nose with each other. Many drivers seemed ignorant of the ways of the road, operating their vehicles as though for the first time. They blasted their horns and flashed their lights and proceeded fitfully down the road. Even the bicyclists seemed unsure of themselves. Near the lake a middle-aged woman pedaled calmly ahead of me, when suddenly, and for no apparent reason, she bounced up onto the curb, grazed two trees, and landed in a heap on the sidewalk with twigs and leaves tangled in her long hair.

At a large intersection Ming and I handed our bikes over to the care of a parking official and walked up Liberation Road. Hoping to buy a knife, Ming brought me into a musty little shop squeezed between two restaurants. Every imaginable cutting implement hung in somber display on the shop's dark walls: knives, swords, saws, scalpels, sabers, and scissors, and there were stacks of them in wooden shelves and pigeonholes behind the sales counter. The shop was filled with customers straining to be waited on, and it was nearly impossible to reach the counter, behind which a single sullen salesgirl in a silk dress fanned herself idly and sipped from a bottle of orange soda. When a customer asked to see a knife, the girl turned slowly, plucked one off the shelf between her thumb and forefinger, and sent it clattering onto the counter. She yawned and sipped and fanned. She glared balefully out the dusty window. Her large black eyes were sharp and set wide apart. A woman studying the shop's various wares put her Chinese movie magazine down on the counter, and in an instant the salesgirl snatched the magazine up and flipped defiantly through it, deaf to the customer's pleas.

Ming struggled skillfully up to the counter and poked the girl in the forearm. "Comrade," she said, "please show me a cleaver."

The petulant comrade hitched up her bra strap, took a lazy step backward out of Ming's reach, and turned another page. "We don't have any cleavers," she murmured.

"But I see them behind you," Ming protested.

The girl raised the magazine in front of her face. "It's rest time, then."

Ming knocked on the counter. "Where's the manager?"

"Out!"

"Get someone else, then."

"They're all out."

Ming whisked me into the street. "The girls in the state-run shops are at their most disagreeable at lunchtime."

I had noticed that myself. I knew by now to stick to the private shops when I could.

In many of the city's smaller shops the cashiers sat in wooden booths perched high up in the corner where the walls met the ceiling. I asked Ming if this practice was a safeguard against holdups, and without a trace of pride or self-righteousness she answered, "In China we do not have holdups." I looked skeptically at her; she was serious. "The punishment for that crime is very severe here."

The salesgirl would attach the customers' payment to a string driven by a motorized pulley above her head, the string shot the money up to the cashier, the cashier calculated the change on her abacus, and sent the money and receipt speeding back down the way it came. In some shops the string moved very fast, and if the customer didn't pay attention to where he stood, the money flew down and slapped him hard on the back of the head. Occasionally—doped by isolation and the rising heat—the cashier fell asleep in her box, and the salesgirl had to reach up with a yardstick or a cane or another handy prod and give the box a bang to wake her up.

Merchandise in these shops was rarely displayed within the customer's reach. There were no aisles to go up and down, there was no browsing, no perusing nor reading of labels here. Self-service was out. Everything was parked securely in glass cases or on shelves behind the sales counter, which made official assistance a necessary fact of Chinese shopping and Chinese shopping the adventure that it was. The Chinese salesgirls were like an imitation in miniature of their country's own government; if you wanted to get their attention, you had to shout or poke them in the arm. And there was always a reason you couldn't have the thing you wanted, including that a salesgirl decided that the color of the thing simply didn't suit you; the shirts you wanted to buy were intended for men, not for women; or that another kind of sweater was selling much better this month. The salesgirls were quarrelsome and brusque. They had hostile stares. They saved the last cotton skirts for their sisters, their mothers, their number-one aunts. They resented the customer's existence and snoozed and daydreamed their way through the day. If politeness and helpfulness went unappreciated, why bother with them? And if the chance for promotion was slim, why be industrious?

Ming Yu and I went to the live market set up under a long A-shaped tin roof near the center of the city. There were doves' eggs here, pied and tiny, and hens' eggs, five different sizes of dried shrimp, fresh shrimp waving long feelers, live crabs, several kinds of dried mushrooms, ginger, garlic, onions, potatoes, lettuce, mustard greens, live hens, live doves, long gray fish flapping their tails in shallow tins of water, live turtles, eels, legs of pork, gizzards, and the large purplish heart of an unidentified animal, chicken livers, roasted chickens and ducks warming under heat lamps, apples and pears and grapes, tangerines, pomegranates, pineapples, and persimmons: all evidence, I thought, of Zhejiang Province's renowned prosperity.

At the exit to the market Ming spotted one of her students, a lanky boy sitting on a curb, gnawing a baked ear of corn he'd bought from a vendor. He seemed shocked to see Ming there and stared at her with his mouth half-open and corn kernels stuck to his lips and face. He wiped his free hand on the thigh of his trousers and raised it uncertainly at Ming Yu. She nodded at him and hurried on without speaking.

When we were out of earshot, Ming said, "I don't like my students to see me outside of the classroom."

"Why?"

"Well, in one way we consider the teacher to be master. The teacher should always be held in a dignified light. Teachers don't like to be seen doing human things. They don't like students to see them eating or drinking, and they don't want the students to see them with their girlfriend or boyfriend. I should think it would be a bit embarrassing to be seen with a husband or wife. When I see students outside of class, I try to ignore them. Sometimes I will talk"—she took my arm and steered me gently up another narrow street—"but that boy was eating. I hate it most of all for my students to see me eating."

I hurried to think of the ways I behaved with my students, the distance between us grew narrower as the days passed. It was so easy to entertain them, to make them laugh, that the temptation was sometimes too overwhelming, and I allowed myself to get carried away with stories and antics. At times I didn't feel much older or wiser than the students. After class I walked home with them, showed them the tricks I could do on my bicycle (which they considered a marvelous but unladylike talent), taught them jokes and slang phrases, and on a rare occasion I spoke Chinese with them, which they found indescribably comical. I knew enough never to eat in the classroom. George Greatorex had warned me about this: at the beginning of his first semester he had made the mistake of bringing apples to class and eating them during the five-minute breaks. Eventually he received a note from one student to the effect that his apple eating was unbecoming behavior from a teacher. But George had also confessed to me that his students—graduate students—were often unfriendly and critical of his teaching methods. One day during a writing exercise he noticed a young woman in the second row staring intently at him; her notebook lay unopened on her desk and her pen remained zipped in its case. He asked the woman why she was not writing. She said, "I have nothing to write." George assured her that if she tried, she would be able to think of something. She said, "I can think of nothing." George said, "You are obliged to write something. It's your job as a student." Reluctantly the woman opened her notebook and began to scribble. At the end of the class the students laid their papers on George's desk and filed out of the room. George flipped through the papers and found that the hesitant young woman had written the single sentence: "You are a mean and nasty old man."

Despite all of this, whenever students came to see me in my room, we ate apples and pears, sometimes made *jiaozi*, and drank orange soda together, and nobody seemed shocked or embarrassed. I told Ming this. She turned her inscrutable dark-eyed gaze on me. "You're lucky," she said. "You're foreign."

We turned down a busy, walled street on our way to the bird market, our final stop. Two men passed us pulling a cartful of hot tar. The cart was unforgivingly heavy. One man pulled it while the other steered from behind. They moved like speed walkers, almost at a run, their knees locking beneath their weight, and when they reached a slight downgrade, they had no choice but to run lest the cart crush the man in front. The men were wiry and strong, like most of the laborers in the city, like most Chinese, and that was no wonder—every single task here was a physical one.

Along the walls of this street various exhibitions of sports photography, artistic portraits, calligraphy, historical photographs, and documents were hung in glass cases. The most puzzling and arresting exhibit of all was a panel of gruesome black-and-white photographs shot at the scenes of automobile accidents and bicycle mishaps, documentation of what would befall the traveler if he did not take care on the road, if he did not, as the sign instructed, Pay Attention to Safety! There were pictures of trucks overturned in gullies, jeeps with bicycles crushed under their back wheels, twisted bodies of children lying like rag bundles in the road, and bloody, featureless faces that had shattered windshields. The pictures were brutal and obscene and that, it seemed, was the point. But despite this scare campaign the citizenry continued to hurl themselves along the roads with the same heedless abandon they practiced in littering and smoking.

When I drew Ming's attention to the gruesome pictures, she shrugged and said, "It's usual. No one pays attention."

"Don't you?"

"I am afraid I do not. Not always."

That was true. Ming was easily distracted. While her mind wandered to important subjects, she lost keys and crashed into people on the road. She was the kind of preoccupied soul who gave poets their reputation for mooniness.

On a quiet, narrow street we found the bird market, where independent vendors competed side-by-side for the business of sportsmen, bird lovers, and gardeners. Some vendors spread their wares on the sidewalk; others were ensconced in wooden stalls. There were bamboo fishing rods for sale and clay flowerpots, hand-carved stone seals, bonsai trees, tulip bulbs, gingerroot, orange trees, flowering plants, straw crickets' cages, and tin basins full of exotic fish. The far end of the street was devoted entirely to birds. One man sold sparrows, another sold the popular *huamei*, and a third sold scores of purring pigeons he kept five to a cage the size of a hatbox. A variety of delicate wooden birdcages hung above the heads of the vendors, cages with ornate hand-carved trimmings, green sandpaper perches, hand-painted feeding pots, and ingenious doors that slid up and down.

In the alley behind the booths a crowd of blue-capped men stood smoking and picking their teeth, gazing proudly at their own birds who sang in cages hung along a fence. These *huameis*, more like robins than sparrows, were too large for the small cages—some had hardly enough room to turn around in. Their tails got caught up on the perches, and their big yellowish beaks clicked awkwardly against the bars, but the adoring men didn't seem concerned.

I asked Ming why there weren't any women at the bird market. She said that in China, birds were a man's sport and that women weren't to be interested in birds.

A little farther along the alley a fat man with thick lips and a sagging face sold puppies out of a cakebox. He poked and teased the puppies and held them up for his customers to see. He lifted a black one with white-mitten paws. "It's fat," he said. A bald-headed man leaning on a cane took the puppy roughly in his hands, turned it over in his palm, and pinched one of its paws hard between his yellowed fingers. The puppy yelped and the two men laughed a false, humorless laugh intended for each other. The customer threw a few dirty bills on the table and carried the puppy off by the scruff of the neck. This was the first dog I remembered seeing in China. When I asked why, Ming said, "Dogs are not allowed in the city. There's no room for them. They bite people and transmit disease. They used to be a hazard, so they are forbidden now. Besides, no one thinks of them as pets. People eat them."

I told her I thought that was a loathsome practice. She laughed and said, "It has a strong flavor and it is considered a good thing to eat in winter, for it has the ability to make a person warm. It makes the skin and the lips warm."

I told her it would be impossible for me to eat a dog, since I thought of them as pets, a man's best friend, and so forth.

"I have heard this of course. 'Man's best friend.' I have even seen photographs of Americans with dogs in their houses and walking with a dog attached to a rope, and they allow the dogs to sit in their laps and on their beds. Chinese would not consider this. The pets we consider are crickets, goldfish, and small birds."

Nothing that didn't fit safely under an overturned teapot, I thought. Nothing that barked or bit.

As we returned to our bicycles, Ming and I saw, in an open square near the bus terminus, a crowd of people gathered around two young boys—one approximately twelve years old, shirtless and small, the other a bit older and bigger. The crowd, four people thick, had tightened to a tiny circle around the boys, leaving them little space to work in. They appeared to be doing a kind of gymnastic and magic act, a medley of tricks and feats designed to shock and entertain. The younger boy, dressed in tight red sweatpants and lace-less sneakers, sat on the street with his skinny legs stretched out before him in a stiff V. On the ground between his legs he performed sleight of hand with three plastic rice bowls and three sponge balls. He was sharp-elbowed and skinny. He dazzled the crowd with an unintelligible sort of auction-eer's chatter. His thick hair—so black it was blue—grew flat along a grain and lay like a beaver's pelt on his head. His short bangs stuck straight out over his forehead, forming a visor for his piercing black eyes.

There was something strange about this boy. I moved closer to get a better look at him; across his chest and nip-ples was a rash of welts and calluses. His neck was rubbed red, and beginning just under his right ear a vicious scar ran a jagged course down to his collarbone.

The boy's speed and finesse with the sponge balls was mystifying. The flourish of his hands was graceful, almost balletic: Three balls appeared to be under one bowl, one ball under each; two balls under one bowl, two in his hand and one in his mouth; three in the waistband of his sweatpants. The audience wagged their heads sheepishly, duped by a child.

He rapped on an overturned bowl with a knuckle. "Are you in there?!" he said. His voice was high and chalky, a sea gull's screech. "Or are you here?!" With a fan of his hands all three bowls flipped upright, yielding nothing. He crossed his arms and stared at the bowls in a theatrically baffled way. He scratched his head and appealed to the crowd. "Who knows where they are?" He had a fierce cry but an utterly vacant expression, as though he were sitting alone in a windowless room trying out the possibilities of his own voice. He stared dully at the spectators' knees. The loose tongues of his sneakers stuck up into the air, like bleached goat's ears.

At the edge of the circle the boy's partner sat bored on a duffel bag, watching the show from the corner of his eye. He scratched at his neck and scowled at the people behind him when, in their effort to get closer, they kneed him in the back. This boy was tough and dark and brooding. He had a schemer's curling lip and longish black hair that fell over the collar of his shirt. When the younger boy swept up his effects and leapt to his feet, the partner got up and with great confidence they pushed the spectators back to widen the circle.

By making themselves conspicuous these two little boys had gained tremendous power. In a place where the invisibility of the individual was the ordering idea, they commanded attention. Their mad courage was a threat.

From a burlap bag the young boy took five long, thin wires; held them up over his head; and introduced them to the crowd. "Observe!" he shrieked. "Wires!" He cinched the wires around his chest, twisting their ends tight around each other at his sternum, like a tie wrap on a bread bag. The wires bound him tightly and cut into his skin. He manipulated them gingerly until two wires were positioned directly above his nipples and three directly below and he tugged his nipples out between the wires until he had created what resembled tiny breasts pinched between the closing blades of scissors. He grimaced in pain. His partner watched in the same bored way he'd watched the sleight of hand.

I looked at the faces in the crowd; they were at once disgusted and delighted by the spectacle.

I caught the eye of a grinning man directly across the circle from me. His face fell and he looked self-consciously at me, and at the people standing on either side of him, then shuffled out of the line of my gaze and hid himself behind two women.

The boy stood in the middle of the open space, raised his hands over his head, and with one inhalation and a powerful heave of his chest he popped the wires free. He sat on the ground, pouting, annoyed, and looking—at last—like the very small boy he was.

After a minute's rest the two boys took a pliable iron bar the thickness of a ski pole and in a series of twists and spins and shiftings of weight they succeeded in wrapping it tightly three times around the little boy's neck. The veins in his forehead and neck bulged, his eyes watered, the breath rasped out of him in spurts. He was strangling. Quickly his partner picked up a plastic bowl, put it in the boy's hand, and guided him around the edge of the circle to collect contributions from the crowd. A few people tossed a penny or two into the bowl, but mostly what they offered was blank stares or sneers.

When it was clear the boys had collected all the money they could, they worked together to twist the bar free. They gathered up their belongings and stood in the middle of the square, looking down Yanan Road as if they had no idea where they were or where they would go next.

SHANGHAI

At 7:00 A.M. on a rainy Saturday Christina and I met Huang Zhiye outside the gate to our building and set off on our weekend trip to Shanghai. Huang carried a large wicker basket full of ripe, red persimmons. "A gift I am carrying for my friend to a friend of his," he explained.

The Chinese thought nothing of asking a person to carry heavy and awkward bundles long distances for them. Often it was the only way they could transport goods without going to great expense. A Hangzhou tailor once asked a foreign student in the university to bring a television back from Hong Kong for her, and other foreigners I knew had been presented with similar requests: If I give you the money, will you bring me a VCR, a small refrigerator, a tape player? To the Chinese such requests were not inordinate; they were simply a way of life.

We squeezed into the crowded bus that would carry us to the train station. Huang looked worried, glancing at his watch and hugging his wet umbrella, balancing the basket of persimmons on the back of the conductor's seat while she made her rounds. The conductors on these city buses were usually women. They were young and thin and incredibly icy, and their voices reached supernatural pitches. They wore metal ticket machines on straps across their chests and belts of change at their waists and they staggered up and down the heaving buses shrieking, "Buy a ticket!" If you asked them a question at the wrong moment, they snapped, "I don't know!" or crossed their arms and stared stonily out the window. They had control of the bus's electric doors and could shut them with a punishing snap.

On city buses passengers never paid at the door; instead they rushed on and settled in until the conductor confronted them. It was an inefficient system in the face of such overwhelming crowds, so it was no wonder the conductors were always bad-tempered—all day struggling through a sea of white shirts and irritability, nailing fare dodgers and putting up with their squawking and shouting.

We reached the train station at exactly 7:30, by Huang Zhiye's watch. The boarding gate had already been closed, and Huang banged on it until the gatekeeper ambled over in her slippers and let us in.

Most Chinese passenger trains are old and green and very long, made up of hard-seat cars for common Chinese, a few soft-seat or first-class cars for foreigners and the more privileged Chinese, and cargo and dining cars. Because Huang had bought the tickets for this trip, we were sitting in a hard-seat car; soft seats were over twice the price of the hard ones and they would have been difficult for Huang to get.

The seats were straight-backed benches facing each other across tiny tables, like booths along each wall. One car could seat approximately 130 people, but there were many more than that aboard this car. In the aisles and on the platform between the cars, people stood or else sat on their luggage on the filthy floor. Much of the luggage was homemade, rigged up out of cardboard, newspapers, and a pink raffialike string that appeared everywhere in China and had a myriad of uses. Because of the heat many of the men had rolled their pants legs above their knees, baring their hairless white shins, and several people draped wet towels over their heads like veils. Some had stripped down to their T-shirts, and all of them but Huang smoked with determination, though smoking was forbidden in this car. Overhead, tiny fans in wire cages rotated on the ceiling, and music and news blared from loudspeakers tucked into the walls. The news was shrill and the music was sentimental and unlikely, tunes like "Red River Valley" and "Auld Lang Syne."

The passengers had brought white tin mugs or glass jars for tea, and several minutes after the train left the station, an attendant struggled up the aisle carrying a long-spouted copper kettle, expertly filling the mugs and jars the eager passengers held up to her.

We shared our booth with a silent young husband and wife who had spread provisions enough for six on the table between us. They had jars of tea, a bag of water crackers, pears, pumpkin seeds, sunflower seeds, a bag of buns, and a bag of rice balls wrapped in lotus leaves. The husband held a small silver pocket knife in his hand, and as he listened to the mesmerizing clatter of the train, he flipped the knife from side to side, endlessly and mechanically. His face was long and thin. He wore a digital watch with a smashed crystal. His wife—between him and the window—had a wide, porous face and long fingernails filed down to threatening points. She wore a golden tin ring on her finger—a cheap, dented thing like a child's prize from a bubblegum machine. The lace window curtain fluttered persistently into the side of her head and across her face, but she made no effort to restrain it. She and her husband remained silent all the way to Shanghai and never touched the food before them. They were happy just to have a seat. They stared dreamily out the window. Here it seemed all their problems had subsided; they had nothing to accomplish and no responsibilities; a few hours on the train were a relief.

The rain had stopped, and the scene outside the window was at times soft and pretty, at other times fiercely geometric. The arrangement of the small farms seemed the model of tidiness and efficiency, with room enough for the essential and little more. The parts fit together like pieces of a puzzle: hayrick against the toolshed, toolshed against the pigpen, pigpen against the mud wall, mud wall against the house, house fronted by a tiny duck pond. Beyond this lay a sea of fields: cabbages and turnips and endless miles of swaying green hemp that flashed and rippled like water. Some fields were divided by lines of poplars or oaks, others by grassy earth walls and morning glories. To the west lay short blue mountains. The houses were red brick or white-washed cement with black pantiled roofs. Now and then we crossed over a narrow canal crowded with long wooden boats, some with dogs on their decks. In the distance a figure squatted so low in a field that only his straw hat was visible above the long grass. A farmer watered his garden by scooping water from a pond with a long-handled wooden bowl, a device shaped something like a giant spoon. With the ease of a man ladling gravy on his dinner, he dipped the bowl into the pond and flipped it swiftly over his head, propelling the water in a jagged arc onto the field behind him, complementing the morning's rain.

Two hours out of Hangzhou we passed a field bristling with bamboo poles sticking deeply into it at intervals. Tied to the top of each pole was a rectangle of white cloth starched stiff as a shirt collar. From a distance the cloths looked like sheets of typing paper caught up in a wind. Huang thought the poles were erected to scare birds but didn't know for sure. "I am not a farmer," he reminded me.

Across the aisle and one booth down from us a big woman in a black dress sat sighing with her small, bespectacled husband wedged in beside her. He was an old army figure in an unconvincing uniform two sizes too big for him. He had dry, cracked lips and silvery stubble on his chin. He read a pamphlet all the way to Shanghai, holding his glasses to his face with one hand and the pamphlet up before him with the other. From time to time he drifted off to sleep with his mouth open and the pamphlet drooping into his lap. The wife had a mannish face, and her thin gray hair was tousled and matted, as though earlier in the day she'd been wearing a tight woolen ski hat. A book titled

Learn to Type English lay on the table before her, but she didn't open it. Instead she ate: peanuts and pumpkin seeds, two tangerines, half a loaf of bread, an apple, dried plums; she slept a little, woke up, ate some dried dofu, another tangerine, spit the seeds into her hand and tossed them on the floor. She looked bored and annoyed. When her husband nudged her arm to draw her attention to something he'd read in the pamphlet, something he thought was humorous, she grimaced over her shoulder at him and nudged him back and barked a few short words to the effect that he should leave her alone already. Her sighs were loud and full of disgust, and her pained expression clearly announced her opinion that a proper army couple such as they ought to be sitting nicely in first class, instead of here among the riffraff.

Huang Zhiye had fallen deep into conversation with a pair of teachers from Zhejiang University and from the looks of it was immensely entertained by the exchange. His joy was satisfying to watch. His face lit up with great intensity; his eyes watered behind their glasses; he giggled uncontrollably in rising, wheezing, three-toned spurts, holding his hand to his mouth, trying to maintain a modicum of restraint, as though he felt his mirth had surpassed that of his comrades and that this was shameful. Each time the laughter subsided, he let out a heavy sigh, shook his head, and rubbed his thighs, beseeching himself to remain calm. There was something adolescent about Huang's mannerisms, which added to his appeal.

Suddenly, in the middle of a field, the train stopped short, the passengers fell silent, the little fans whirred to a halt, and immediately the car grew close and hot. Only the radio persevered with a Chinese approximation of "It's So Easy to Fall in Love," as if to distract us from the inconvenience, the tedium, the heat. The passengers stared blankly at the mugs and jars on the tables. Within minutes the ground outside the train became strewn with garbage; banana peels, apple cores, tin cans, papers, half-eaten buns, rice, the chewed remains of sugarcane. Trash sailed freely out of windows. I could hear the tinkle of bottles as they smashed against the railroad ties and the slap of watermelon rinds against the trunks of trees. When I put my head out and looked forward toward the front of the train, I saw an endless column of bare elbows jutting gaily into the air and a delicate, long-fingered hand dropping an empty fruit tin onto the tracks.

With the train stopped, I grew more conscious of the people who had been standing for two hours now. They were peasants, their faces were brown, their hands were rough, their teeth were solid and white, and their coarse black hair was cut jaggedly, as though with a dull steak knife, with no thought for style or appearance. To them a haircut was merely a means of keeping the hair out of the eyes. Set into their dark faces, their eyes had a strange clarity and brightness, which gave them a disengaged look, as though they were operating in another dimension. They carried string bags and baskets, and when one passenger vacated his seat for a moment, two or three peasants sat down in it, spitting and smoking, staring unabashedly at other passengers until the seat's lucky owner returned and shooed them away.

"Mr. Huang," I said softly. "Why has the train stopped?"

Huang considered the question carefully, then opened his mouth and raised his hands before him, preparing to explain. "Mmm. You know, in China there are several kinds of trains: slow-fast, medium-fast, and most fast. When another train approaches from the opposite direction, in order to avoid colliding, slower trains are obliged to pull aside into a byway and let the faster train go through."

"You mean there's only one track for trains going in either direction?" I said.

"That's right!" Huang nodded gleefully at how quickly I understood the concept. "And we are on the slow train!"

The big woman across the aisle hoisted herself higher in her seat and squinted skeptically at Huang, doubtful of the sound of English tumbling out of this excitable man's mouth.

I considered this temerarious railway system until another passenger train rumbled past us toward Hangzhou, a long string of open windows flashing by like the frames of an old black-and-white film, a jerky blur of dark heads, white shirts, and tin mugs.

As the train began to move again, Huang turned to us and said, "What about your lunch?" We shrugged—we hadn't thought to bring lunch.

"For me," Huang said, "lunch is essential," but, like us, he didn't seem to know what he would eat. The only edible thing in our party was the persimmons, and they didn't belong to us. There was the silent couple's untouched picnic, but that, too, was out of the question. Huang said, "We could go to the dining car," but the grimace on his face indicated that this was something we should not, under any circumstances, want to do. A few minutes later a worker came up the aisle pushing a cart filled with boxes of steamed rice and vegetables; Huang gazed longingly at it as it approached. The food was damp and unappetizing, and when Christina and I said we weren't interested in it, Huang frowned at it and said quickly, "No, and I would not eat it either." Several times the cart passed by our seats, and each time Huang tried to peek at the food.

As the train pulled into Shanghai's old railway station, the younger, more nimble passengers tossed their luggage through the windows and leapt out after it, while boarding passengers climbed in, hoisting their possessions after them, pushing and shouting, scrambling for vacant seats. As individuals the Chinese were calm and rather deferential; in a large crowd they became frenzied. I was astonished at the numbers of people surging off the train and down the unlit platform, pushing to get out to the street. In all their hurry they still had time to gawk at Christina and me, to chatter about us between tugs of the green duffel bags and cardboard cases they dragged along the ground. I felt a wave of panic as I saw Huang being swept into the crowd ahead of me and had to struggle to keep myself from hooking my finger into the belt loop of his trousers.

Outside the station Huang turned to us and said again, "What about your lunch? We could go into this restaurant across the street."

Like many of the small state-run restaurants in China's cities, this one had all the atmosphere of a two-car garage. The cement floors were bare and coated with a film of spit and soup and mud; the pale green walls were cracked and peeling, and the nude bulb in the ceiling cast down an intrusive light. The wooden tables and chairs were greasy and unsteady. Orders for food were taken by a stolid, red-cheeked matron in a filthy white apron and skullcap. The patrons in these restaurants were always working men, often loud and sometimes drunk on beer and *baijiu*.

At Huang's suggestion we ate *baozi*, or steamed buns, the same thing I had had for breakfast that day, and we drank warm beer out of plastic mugs. Huang refused beer because of the ulcer he suffered. He had told me one day as we walked home from school together that the ulcer had forced him to forgo some of life's greatest pleasures. "I used to love wine," he said, "Now I cannot sustain even a sip, for it encourages the bleeding attack." During the Cultural Revolution he had been sent to work with peasants in a small village in the countryside. The food there was bad, and he became very ill and never quite recovered. He told me that the previous year an acute case of bleeding had sent him to the hospital for a week.

As we prepared to leave the restaurant, Christina and I offered to pay for our lunch, but Huang waved his hands before him to ward our money off; he wouldn't hear of it.

The Number 66 bus to the Shanghai Foreign Language School was so full of people, I couldn't imagine how Huang thought we would get on, but when the deciding moment came, we had no choice in the matter, for the surging masses simply swept us in, settling things in an instant. I found myself in the middle of the bus with my cheek pressed hard against the shoulder blade of the man in front of me and my arm pinned between us. I couldn't see anything, but I could feel the bus sweeping and swaying along the narrow, twisting streets. I realized that my heart was racing, that I was extremely afraid. Each time the bus made a sharp turn, I lost my balance, but it didn't matter; anchored entirely to the man in front of me, I couldn't fall. With all the shifting of people and bucking of the bus, I ended up in the arms of a middle-aged man. He looked at me, stricken and horrified, and tried to shake me off.

When we were safely on the sidewalk again, Huang noticed our fear and amazement and laughed. "In China, on the bus and everywhere else, you must push very hard. No one will mind. They will push back. It is the only way to accomplish your task."

Only a few weeks later I would read in the *China Daily* that fifteen workers had been trampled to death by a frantic mob on a dock in Shanghai. The crowd had been waiting for the ferry to take them to their factories on the other side of the river, but the ferry was delayed because of fog, and the people grew anxious; if they came late to work, they would be penalized and would not receive their full bonus at the end of the year. Naturally when the ferry finally arrived, the people began to run, hoping to make it on the first trip across. In their zeal they trampled their co-workers. At rush hour in Shanghai special traffic police cordon off lines at the major bus stops to prevent just such calamities.

The Shanghai Foreign Language School was a brutal concrete compound built beside a railroad track on the northern outskirts of Shanghai, in the Hong Kou district. The school's guest house had beige linoleum floors and the muffled, isolated feel of a boarding-school infirmary. On the table in the foyer a television with a monotonously rolling black-and-white picture had been turned up to full volume, and four older men in slippers and pajamas stared absently at it, smoking and talking, spitting into a brimming spitoon on the floor at their feet.

At the reception desk Huang devoted a great deal of time and energy to persuading the manager that Christina and I were foreign teachers at Hangzhou University and as such should be allowed to pay the Chinese rates of ten yuan per night per piece, instead of the thirty or forty yuan required of foreigners. The formidable manager placed his reading glasses on his flat nose and pored painstakingly over our work cards, checked our faces with the photos therein, conferred with a man in another room, and returned to tell Huang that we would be permitted to pay ten yuan, but that it would have to be in Foreign Exchange Certificates, the hard currency we were officially exempted from using. Embarrassed by the man's obvious attempt to take advantage of us, Huang persisted quietly. Eventually the manager gave in, wrote up an elaborate receipt, stamped it with a rubber seal, and tossed three keys onto the counter. His unspeaking, unsmiling, ponytailed assistant led Christina and me to our room, plunked two thermoses of hot water down on the floor, and shut the door behind us.

The room was small, with two narrow beds, two washbasins, two pairs of plastic shower slippers, and an ancient television on a three-legged table. As soon as we had washed our faces and put away our things, Huang knocked on our door and asked, "What is your plan?" We were forced to confess we didn't have a plan. We knew only that we wanted to see what was interesting about Shanghai, and whatever it took to accomplish that we were ready to do.

Huang seemed skeptical. "Shanghai is China's biggest city. Ten million people are here. What part would you like to see?" We didn't have an informed answer; we made a few suggestions, but we had expected Huang, with his great knowledge of the city, to act as our guide. We asked him to suggest something. He said, "I am your host. It is not my decision. It is your decision. You are the guests. I must do as you wish." He sounded trapped, and his face was twisted into a smile that could have been taken for a grimace. No matter how we urged him, Huang refused to make suggestions about what we might find interesting in Shanghai. To him hospitality had a formula that could not be tinkered with, and the formula required letting the ignorant guest decide what course the weekend would take. It was politeness pressed to the point of perversity. Our wish, Huang assured us, was his command. But even when we suggested a walk into the city, he wasn't enthusiastic. He drew the gauze curtains aside, peered anxiously out the window, and declared, "The city is quite far! It seems as if it will rain!"

We told him we were undaunted by rain and that if he wanted to stay inside, we would be willing to take a walk without him. Huang laughed a long time at this.

"You know, Shanghai is a very, very big city. Even a Chinese can get lost here. Neither of you can speak much Chinese. You would have great trouble finding your way. I must accompany you." With that he picked up his umbrella and marched to the door. "Let's go, then," he said hopelessly.

Many of Shanghai's smaller streets are narrow and follow a gentle curve, like an archer's bow, bending just enough that I never had a clear idea of what we were approaching or what was around the bend, and as we walked along these streets, with their similar strangeness and their uniformity of houses and shops, I had the odd sensation that we were making no progress, that we were passing again the very scene we had passed only moments before, as if on a tread-mill. I felt I was experiencing a mere illusion of movement, and I appreciated that—it gave me the reassuring feeling that I would miss nothing these streets had to offer.

Everywhere I saw people occupied with chores or games, cooking on coal stoves in doorways, emptying basins of dirty water into the street, beating wet laundry against a stone slab, and boldly stringing perilous, throat-level clotheslines directly across the sidewalk. In the doorway of her one-room apartment an old woman set up shop with a large potful of eggs boiled in spice and tea. On a corner another woman sold slices of watermelon, the crowd dense around her, eating hurriedly, their plastic handbags dangling from the crooks of their elbows. They spat the glistening seeds into the gutter and threw the rinds down happily after them, and when they were satisfied, they mopped their faces with hankies and moved on. In the middle of the sidewalks men sat on stools and played chess or cards while their pet birds sang in cages hung from branches above their heads. A man and his son hawked matchboxes on a table in front of their house, selling them at twice the usual price because of a recent shortage of matches. As we walked by them, the son hit me gently on the chest with his price card to get my attention, then laughed nervously when he saw my dismay.

Our walk was not leisurely; merely stopping to look in a window was hazardous. When I tried it, a bag in my hand got knocked to the ground by passersby, my feet were re-peatedly stepped on, and so many bodies passed between me and the window that I never saw clearly what I was look-ing at.

Built up close to the street, the old shops and houses formed a kind of wall on either side of it. They seemed somehow medieval. Most had two floors—the second floor usually had a facade of dark wood—balconies that overhung the street, and dark wooden interiors with cement floors. A glimpse through a door revealed that the inhabitants made ingenious use of every inch of their space. Kitchen utensils and clothing hung neatly on walls; bunk beds acted as storage shelves during the day; five people—young and old—sat on low bamboo stools eating from bowls they held in their hands.

The larger streets were crowded with buses, bicycles, tiny Japanese taxis, and the sidewalks were choked with people, making it difficult to proceed. There were fewer bicycles on the streets of Shanghai than on Hangzhou's streets, and the motorized traffic was much heavier and far more threatening. As in most Chinese cities, Hangzhou's streets had designated lanes for bicyclists—in Shanghai these lanes were clogged with pedestrians. Conductors leaned out bus windows and rapped sharply on the sides of buses to warn pedestrians that the bus was nearing the sidewalk to stop or make a turn, and this clacking rang out like the tick of a metronome trying to keep up with the frantic pace of the city. To spare him the dangers of a conventional exit through a bus door, a woman disembarking passed her baby through the window to a stranger on the sidewalk below.

Tinny music blared from clothing shops newly opened by young entrepreneurs, and the city air was thick with soot and the smells of vinegar and garlic, coal, automobile exhaust, and chemicals. When I wiped my forehead with my bare hand, my fingers came down black.

Presently it began to rain, and Huang said nervously, "I am afraid you will both catch cold." He held his umbrella over our heads. "I think you did not bring your umbrellas because you are young. It is my fault. If I had only known where your umbrella was, I would have brought it."

Christina and I tried to assure Huang that we were all right, that we had chosen not to bring our umbrellas, and that he could relax, but he could not accept this. He shook his head and said somberly, "It is my duty to guard against the rain." All the way down Sichuan Bei Road he darted from one edge of the sidewalk to the other, his little black umbrella held high in an attempt to keep the rain off both of us at once. Finally, at the intersection of Hai Ning Road, he cried in exasperation, "How can I keep you both dry if you stand so far apart from each other?!" The rain had formed a dark, wet yoke across the chest and shoulders of his blue T-shirt. His hair was slick and flattened. Pedestrians jostled him. He looked terribly distressed. As he peered grimly into the sky, the rain dripped down his pudgy face and splattered against his glasses.

"Mr. Huang," I said as gently as I could, "we're wet because we were stupid enough not to have brought our umbrellas when the sky was overcast. It isn't your fault."

Huang stared through me sadly—my statement, true as it was, did not relieve him of his responsibility as host. "Just look at your feet!" he cried. My bare feet in their flimsy flip-flops were covered in mud, and the backs of my legs were speckled too. I had no way to explain to Huang how little this affected me.

After several more minutes of walking, Huang said, "And where will we go now? What is your opinion? Walk and walk endlessly? Shanghai is nothing but one shop after the next, one street turning into another street. There is nothing in Shanghai for you but shopping for food and clothes." His tone was full of disdain for Shanghai and disparagement for us, as though the best thing we could do under the circumstances was to catch the next train back to Hangzhou. This puzzled and irritated me. I wanted to ask him why, if there was nothing in Shanghai, did he bring us here? Why did he invite us to visit such a terrible place? I wanted to say it seemed entirely irrational, but instead I told him not to worry. I told him that we were interested in the very streets of the city, in the smell of them, the people on them, and the buildings and shops. I told him we could stop, but if he was concerned about us, we were very happy.

We walked silently then, Huang three steps behind us with his head slightly bowed. He had abandoned the effort to keep us dry, but the pained expression on his face persisted to remind us that there was nothing in Shanghai for us.

Despite Huang's many protests and warnings I had detected that afternoon something in his voice that mystified me, a tone beneath a tone that hinted there was something else here, something better we could have been doing, if only we could guess what it might be. He had asked us here for a reason, but I had the feeling he would keep it a secret until we hit on it. And if we didn't hit on it, *tant pis*.

Huang stepped into the shelter of a doorway, looking extremely anxious now. "And how will we solve the problem of dinner?" he asked.

Just as at lunchtime, Christina and I had difficulty guessing what the question meant. Its tone suggested there was no solution. At a loss, we listed all the possible foods we could eat, and after each one Huang said either "Too far" or "Not good" or "It is impossible." When I said, "Fish," Huang said, "There is no fish."

As we continued up the messy, beleaguered street, I thought, In all of Shanghai there is no fish.

Huang led us to a large wooden two-storied restaurant, where noodles and *baodzi*, or steamed buns, were being served through a window that opened into a steamy kitchen. Every wooden stool and table in the restaurant was occupied, and many people ate standing against the wall. Huang studied the blackboard menu propped up next to the window and said absently, "What will you have?" Christina shot him a withering glance. We had no idea what it was possible to have—we couldn't read the blackboard.

"What do they serve?"

"Noodles and *baodzi*," Huang replied.

"Nothing else?"

"There is nothing else."

I wanted to say, Impossible! for the blackboard was a tangle of characters that surely reached beyond the realm of noodles and *baodzi*.

Without realizing it, Huang was making us feel like children, stupid, stubborn ones at that. Even I could make out a character on the board that I was certain meant "chicken," but how could I dispute what Huang had said without calling him a liar? And in the end how could I actually be sure what the board said? How would I apologize if it said, "There is nothing in Shanghai, including chicken and fish"? I wasn't prepared to make a fool of myself by challenging Huang.

We sat at a sticky round table with a group of watery-eyed workmen, and for the third time that day, I ate *baodzi*. We spoke very little. Huang raised his shoulders and leaned into his bowl of noodles, shutting us out. From time to time he tapped his tiny foot on the gritty floor, cleared his throat, and looked up and out the open door into the rain, and dove back into his bowl. The workers plucked at their noodles and turned their faces toward us, trying from under their blue caps to determine what our relationship was to Huang. People at other tables also turned to stare. It was impossible to eat.

Huang again refused our offer to pay for the meal, saying, "I am the host, the man, it is my duty."

In that moment I realized Huang's predicament: He was the man and the host, and as a result of those considerable burdens he felt it was his responsibility to pay our way that weekend. This was why he had discouraged chicken and fish, the dining car in the train, visits to museums, and why, when we went into the Friendship Store, he never ventured farther than the first-floor lobby, looking ill and frightened, as though we might ask him to buy us things.

Like most Chinese professors, Huang made very little

money. The irony of this was that as foreign teachers Christina and I made at least four times the money Huang made, money that had no value for exchange outside of China. It was money we would eventually either have to spend in China or give away. In light of these facts the thought of Huang trying to pay our way was absurd. But we were compelled to defer to his pride. He would not allow us to pay for things, and he would not allow us to get lost, and all three of us were having a terrible time because of it.

That night, back at the Foreign Language School, Christina and I sat on our sagging beds and listened to the other guests padding up and down the dim hallway to the bathroom in their pajamas and plastic slippers. They were middle-aged Chinese men, somber and quiet, with baggy, fatigued eyes and shaved necks. They smoked incessantly, and the sound of their hacking and spitting echoed mightily off the bathroom walls.

While we were out, someone had come into the room and turned our television on, and now through the snow, we could see several Chinese actors in elaborate ancient costumes sweeping in and out of the stone rooms of a dungeon. We were both starving. Christina had had the forethought to buy a bag of White Rabbit toffee, which we split between us as we discussed how we could spend the next day out of Huang's company. We wanted to see the city freely and without feeling that a simple walk was a foolish waste of time. But how would we propose this to Huang without hurting his feelings? We would have to be kind but firm. We would have to be diplomatic. While we plotted, Huang himself knocked on the door and came in, dressed in slippers and blue pajamas. He sat in a desk chair and smiled stiffly at the television. He had the face of an infant. Before long his smile softened and his mouth fell open. He leaned forward in his chair to get a better look at the young woman hiding her painted face behind a paper fan; she wore a colorful headdress of silver and feathers and paper flowers, and each time she made a gesture, Huang unconsciously made it too. When she leaned forward to give her father a kiss on the cheek, Huang puckered his lips and leaned with her. When she danced across the room, Huang tapped his feet, and when she smiled with delight, he tilted his head dreamily and mimicked the smile. He was transfixed—he was there in the dungeon with the woman—and I was as fascinated watching him as he was watching her.

Eventually Huang sobered up. He stretched in his chair and said, "Anyhow, and what is your opinion about tomorrow?"

We asked him if perhaps he would like to spend tomorrow without us. We said we didn't want to be a nuisance, didn't want him to be bored, but that we hoped to spend the day walking and that this might be tedious for him. He laughed loudly. It was clear he hated the idea. He was sure we would get lost, and not know the buses, and possibly get hurt, and miss the train back to Hangzhou tomorrow night, and what about our lunch?

At that moment, in his pajamas and sweater, Huang looked more dejected than he had all day.

What we had told him was not untrue; he seemed so tortured in our company that we thought he'd be relieved to be rid of us, but there was no way to deny what must have been obvious to him: We didn't want him, and furthermore he had failed as our guide. We assured him there was no reason to worry, that we could take care of ourselves. Hadn't we come halfway across the world without him?

Huang's face was twisted with fear and failure, and his hands hung limply at his sides. The very thought of letting us loose in this city must have terrified him. "As you wish," he said softly and slipped out of the room.

By eight o'clock I was insane with boredom. While Christina, whose capacity for books was enviable, read *Selected Readings from the Works of Mao Zedong*, I walked up and down the hallway, peering recklessly through the little windows in the various doorways. In the largest dorm room eight men lay on cots, some of them sleeping, others reading books or papers by the dim ceiling light. The air was blue with cigarette smoke. I could see Huang lying on a cot with the bedsheet pulled up to his chin and one arm draped across his eyes. He looked dead. If he was still awake, I wondered, what was he thinking? Was he cursing our foreignness and our stubbornness? Cursing the day his wife got it into her head to go to America?

I went into the bathroom, where a large and comforting water heater, like a space capsule, stood in the corner. I filled a basin with water, carried it over to the sink, and was startled by my own appearance in the mirror; my eyes were shot with red, my face was filthy, and my hair was matted and tangled. I realized the only thing I had had to drink that day was an orange soda and the cupful of beer at lunch. I felt crazy and giddy, and for the first time I wondered if this extended visit to China wasn't a ridiculous mistake.

I slept poorly that night. The room was hot, and bedbugs bit me silly and raised enormous red welts on my legs and arms. I looked over at Christina, sleeping soundly in the other bed. Why weren't the bugs biting her? I fell asleep and had a dream that, without being invited and without knowing who lived there, I walked into a little shingled house in the woods, hoping I could go quickly out the back door and find a beach on the other side of the house. In the hallway I met two young Chinese children, who were terrified that their father would come downstairs and find me there. When I put my hand on the handle of a door, the kids screamed, "Don't open that door! Our father doesn't want that door used, ever!" I asked if I could go through another door instead, and they screamed, "Don't go through any door!" I turned around to go out the door I had come in through, but trees had grown up across it and I couldn't get out.

The next morning, while Christina was in the shower, Huang came to our room, tidy and washed, with his hands folded at his waist and said softly and as if it were an extension of a dialogue he'd been having all night with himself, "But I only wonder if I have offended you in some way." He seemed so confused and sad that I was afraid to speak, afraid that whatever I might say would wound him further. I insisted that he hadn't offended us at all, that it was exactly as we had told him the night before, and that everything would be fine.

After breakfast we said good-bye to Huang, and as he walked away from us down a narrow alley, I felt cruel, as though I had tipped an unfledged sparrow out of its nest and onto the hard ground.

Christina and I walked at a leisurely pace around the city, and that afternoon, when we decided to split up for an hour or two, I went into Xiang Yang Park, bought a map, and sat down on a bench to study it. On a bench opposite mine two wizened, windblown grandparents sat with their tiny grandchild between them. Instead of diapers Chinese children often wore pants with the crotch slit back to front, and when they needed to relieve themselves, they simply squatted anywhere, freely, like dogs. At one point in my study of the map I glanced up to see the grandchild, thus liberated, peeing happily and noisily through the slats of the bench while his oblivious grandparents smiled at me.

I got up and walked around the park. There were tall plane trees here with yellowish-green leaves that glowed in the sunlight, and carefully tended flower beds, and elderly men and women in blue doing calisthenics in small groups. Couples strolled aimlessly in their Sunday clothes, watching other couples or corralling tiny children. Teenagers sat on newspapers on the ground, laughing and talking.

As I walked around the edge of the park, a short, shoeless man came up quietly behind me and said in English, "Hello! How are you? Thank you!" I jumped. His voice was soft and high, and these six English words he spoke perfectly. He didn't have a cane but needed one badly, for his right knee was twisted grotesquely around until it faced backward and his right ankle was collapsed so that he walked on the bone. He was hydrocephalic and bug-eyed, and his fingers and feet were stubby and fat. And he was irresistible. His eyes were bright with mischief, and there was cleverness in his laugh. He followed me fearlessly around the park in his tattered clothes calling out, "Hello! How are you? Thank you!" in the same gentle voice.

Several times I said hello to him, told him I was fine, and said, "You're welcome."

He tittered at my replies and said, "Hello! How are you? Thank you."

I looked at his face, trying to figure what he could possibly want from me and realized he wanted nothing but for me to hear his English. He laughed when I stared at him. He was wall-eyed. He had a runny nose and a wet-mouthed grin that engaged his whole face. He snickered and covered his crooked teeth with a clubbed hand. I carried on through the trees, and he followed after me, devoted. "Thank you!" he said. "You're welcome!" I said.

I was growing self-conscious, and he sensed that, which seemed to amuse him further. He knew exactly what he was doing. He knew he sounded ridiculous and wanted to see how long I would let him go on. I couldn't help laughing too, and eventually, walking at a fast pace, I shook him.

Farther into the park I saw, in an open space between

two large trees, an old man in simple cotton clothes performing tricks with a pretty little bird, a *huamei*, or "painted brow." The bird was the size of a robin, light brown with a yellow beak and bright white rings around its eyes that tapered off to sharp lines at the sides of its head, forming a kind of mask.

The man held the bird in one hand and a flexible bamboo switch, like a riding crop, in the other. At the end of the switch was a tiny cup no bigger than a thimble, into which the man dropped a peanut. He held the switch by the handle and catapulted the peanut high into the air, above the tops of the trees. At his signal the bird took off after the peanut. The man flung a second peanut into the sky. The bird caught the first peanut in its shiny yellow beak, turned around, and on its way back down caught the second peanut, and without deviating an inch off course or hesitating a moment it swooped down and landed gently in the waiting hands of its master. Over and over the pair performed this trick, and each time I was more delighted by it than the last.

The man seemed unimpressed by his own skill and unaware of the crowd that had gathered at the edge of the park to watch him. Forty minutes later when he put the bird back in its cage and began to pack up his things, I wandered away, awestruck. I had had birds as pets before, including canaries as devoted and smart and obedient as dogs, but I had never seen an able-bodied bird like this one that, once released from its cage, did not choose to fly away to freedom.

I went out of the park, walked east up Huai Hai Road, and stared openly at the sea of racing faces. I felt completely removed from anything I had ever known, and for a few minutes my own insignificance thrilled me.

That night the train that took us back to Hangzhou was so crowded that the aisles were blocked with bodies. The train traveled painfully slowly, stopping every half hour, and as it grew late, the passengers began to lie down on the muddy floor, in the aisles, and under the seats. Some fell into a snoring sleep. Huang was sick with physical and psychological discomfort, and he clutched at his knees and tapped his fingernails on the table all the way back to Hangzhou.

After Shanghai, Hangzhou at midnight was mercifully quiet. At the train station hundreds of people were camped out on the ground waiting for a train that wasn't scheduled to arrive until 6:00 the next morning. It was a startling sight, like an emergency evacuation scene, and the stillness of the people was mysterious. I expected Huang to explain this phenomenon or at least to remark upon it, but he simply picked his way through the crowd and carried on to the bus stop. Later I learned that this was a common sight at the train station, that such crowds were there almost every night.

Because we were too late to catch the last bus back to the university, we took a bus that let us off behind the exhibition hall, two-thirds of the way home. We walked the rest of the way along the dark, empty streets, silent and exhausted, listening to the flapping of our own feet. Near the university an army truck roared out of the darkness, passed us, then screeched to a halt. A young driver jumped out of the truck and shouted something to Huang. Huang waved his hand toward the south and shouted, "It's very far." To us he explained, "He has lost his way. He is looking for the bridge that will carry him over the river, but it's far and the road is not clear."

"WAKE UP FROM NIGHTMARE"

As part of a national effort to foster working friendships with foreign lands, the city of Hangzhou invited its foreign residents on a tour of the Hangzhou Women's Prison. Later in the year there would be trips to a silk factory, and a home for the elderly. It was carefully orchestrated tourism, which the authorities encouraged with great force and no subtlety. As with almost every concerted gesture the Chinese bureaucracy made toward foreigners, the tours had a decided propagandistic purpose: China needed foreign currency. If foreigners saw for themselves that the Chinese society was happy, tranquil, productive, and just, they would be willing to invest in it with visits and business ventures. With these tours the Chinese seemed to be saying, "We have nothing to hide," but the actual proceedings were so formal, so tightly scripted and constrained, that they inspired the opposite effect, and the visitor was left wondering what, exactly, was being hidden here.

On a sunny afternoon more than a hundred foreign students and teachers from the Agricultural College, Zhejiang University, the Medical College, the School of Fine Arts, and the Business College gathered at the university gates, boarded four Japanese buses, and roared over the dusty road to the prison just north of the university.

Mitsuko Tokutomi, the Japanese woman, sat beside me on the bus and talked and laughed and made comments about the other foreigners.

Though she was thirty-three years old, Mitsuko had a teenager's enthusiasm and curiosity. She talked about Japan:

It was clean and efficient and crazed by its own desire for perfection. She talked about her childhood: She used to play with the son of Mr. Honda—the Honda of motor vehicles—who lived in the same prefecture. "Mr. Honda was a grease monkey," she said. "We laughed at him, see? Because we had no idea how things would turn out for Honda later on."

Mitsuko said Honda was always fiddling with an engine in his dirty little garage. He was dirt poor and had several sons, one of whom had a talent for repairing things, toys that he broke, televisions, radios, lamps. If a bicycle broke in two, the boy could fix it. If his roller skates broke, he could fix them also. Once, the son got an apple crate and hooked it up to wheels and an engine, and before anyone knew what was happening, the crate was running on gasoline.

"I could not believe my eyes," Mitsuko said. "First: apple crate. Next: going around the yard on wheels, such as a car. All kids went down to see him drive it."

Mitsuko paused a moment to let that sink in, then dealt me a conspiratorial little poke in the arm and said, "Much later that son committed suicide. See how it is in Japan?"

The Women's Prison was like a walled-in factory of three or four buildings arranged in a semicircle around a grassless courtyard; they were mournful cement buildings redeemed only by the hundreds of many-paned windows that ran like ribbons around each floor.

Through the kitchen door we shuffled self-consciously into the prison. The room was so vigorously swept I thought I could see the tracks of the broom's bristles in the hard cement floor. Four young inmates dressed in blue tunics, white aprons, and white cotton hats like bathing caps posed rigidly near some neatly stacked rice bags. The guide, a thin-faced youth in a silk necktie, waved a hand at the women and said, "These ones are assigned to the cooking duties." Their tortured smiles obviously reflected the order that they should stand by the rice bags and look happy for the foreigners. In their crisp outfits and lace-up shoes they looked oddly like English housemaids.

Up a flight of stairs were the prisoners' rooms, small chambers like storage closets, where fourteen women slept on bunk beds covered with straw mats. In the corner of the room were a few wooden shelves piled high with washbasins, soap, and hand towels. The guide said, "Prisoners are allowed to buy necessities from the prison store with the money they earn at work in the factory."

Down the hall in the infirmary six shoeless women sat on narrow pallets and stared glumly at us in their doorway. They seemed as puzzled as we about the purpose of our visit. Alone in a neighboring room lay a woman who suffered, according to the guide, "The infectious disease." No one dared cross her threshold, and as we hurried past her door, I caught sight of her lying still in her bed. A blue gauze mosquito net that was draped over her filled the small room with gentle light. There was an enamel pitcher on a bedside table, her window curtains were drawn, and the bedsheets were pulled up to her chin. Her small head was turned to watch us. I had an urge to wave to the woman, to acknowledge her existence, but I stopped myself, thinking, What if she mistook my wave for a taunt?

The dimly lit corridors of the prison were paved with cheap linoleum and decorated with red-and-orange paper banners that said, Welcome You, Foreign Friends! in silver lettering. Through the tall windows I could see the horizontal profile of Hangzhou, a low, sprawling city of two- and three-story buildings, gray, sharp-cornered, symmetrical, with slate roofs and sickly yellow window trim. The city air was a smoky haze that went hot yellow at either end of the day when the sun was low in the sky.

At the guide's request I followed some people into a classroom. Three African students stood at the classroom window watching two young white-capped inmates in the window of a building across the way. The inmates giggled into their palms and twirled self-consciously in place, while the Africans stared, their dark faces reflected in the window-panes, their sweet cologne filling that corner of the room. In their double-breasted suits the Africans had a feline grace.

As a group the African students suffered extreme alien-ation in China. They came here mainly to study agriculture and medicine, and their course of study sometimes lasted four or five years, with the first year devoted to the study of Chinese. They were lonely and unhappy and had, in many Chinese cities, a bad reputation. They were feared and hated, jeered at on the street. My Chinese students had told me openly that they would not talk to an African, should one approach them, because Africans were wild and violent and—the rumor went—attacked Chinese women or lured them to their rooms at the Agricultural College and raped them. While I found that some African students could in-deed be quite forward in their attentions to women, I was alarmed by the bitter strength of my students' conviction over the issue. I asked who, among my students, had ever talked with an African or had ever even come in contact with one. No one had, but they had heard these things from other people. "We have seen some Africans," several stu-dents said. "They look wild." I explained to the students why I thought it was unwise to base such a judgment on what amounted to hearsay, but as soon as I had finished my little speech, I thought how futile and silly it seemed. Xe-nophobia, racism, rumor, and collective mistrust were deeply rooted elements of Chinese society, and in China the African students would be isolated for years to come.

Eventually the prison guide led us up a narrow cement staircase to see the prisoners at work making parts for elec-tric fans and electric blankets in the factory on the fifth floor. The factory, a loftlike sweatshop, was filled with the mesmerizing hum of electric machines. The inmates, in their blue tunics, sat hunched over their work, producing various stages of electrical parts. I watched one young girl working at a machine that wound copper wire efficiently into rec-tangular coils, like napkin rings. The girl was young and pretty, with long eyelashes and a short black braid that stuck out from under the back of her white cap. In one hand she held a spool of wire, in the other a lump of resin. She connected the end of the wire to a spinning part of the machine, switched the machine on with a pedal, and let the wire spin out, pressing it flat with her index finger. Occasionally she touched the resin to the wire, coating it as it spun. Her movements were exact, repetitive, automatic. She stopped the machine, clamped a bit of wire between her teeth, and snipped it clear with a wirecutter. Crumbs of copper fell from her mouth and collected in the blue cotton basin of her lap. I tried to imagine what crime this girl could have committed. As if reading my thoughts, she turned and gazed expressionlessly at me for a long moment, then turned slowly back to her machine.

The purpose of this tour was to help us know China better, but as I went down the stairs to the meeting hall, I felt more baffled and more distant than ever. I was disturbed by the youthfulness of the inmates—some were only in their late teens—and stunned by the personal nature of their crimes. During a brief chat in the factory one young inmate told a German student that she had been sentenced to three years in prison for having engaged in sex with a man before she was married; two others confessed to the crime of adultery. Another had accepted money in exchange for sex "once or twice."

When we gathered in the meeting hall downstairs, I found Xu Ban drinking an orange soda and I asked him if these purported crimes sounded accurate to him. He dabbed busily at his mouth with a handkerchief and said that, indeed, in most cases the criminal offenses here would be illicit sex, fornication, or adultery.

"Of course, there are some other crimes too," he said, and he pointed out a tall, handsome middle-aged woman who with her husband had tried to hijack an air force jet to

Taiwan. The woman had a beautiful fine-boned face and an elegant physical grace. If it was difficult to believe she was a hijacker, it was impossible to believe her prisonmates were here on the grounds of adultery and premarital sex. I asked Xu again if he was sure he had got this right, and he assured me he had.

The meeting hall was a converted basketball gym with a wooden stage set up at one end of it and long wooden tables arranged in rows on the floor. Bright sunlight shone in through the tall windows and bounced off the polished wood floorboards. We sat at the tables and were served boiling tea in covered cups. The prison warden sat before a microphone set up on a table at the front of the room, rolled up the sleeves of his Mao jacket, lit a cigarette, and sipped loudly at his tea; the microphone picked up his sipping and sent it booming across the room. He smoked and plucked spinach-green tea leaves from his tongue and gave us a bland, expressionless, hoarse-voiced monologue punctuated with long pauses, into which the young interpreter inserted an English version.

Officially the crimes the women committed fell roughly into three categories:

1. Acts harmful to societal structure.
2. Acts harmful to marriage and family.
3. Swindle, theft, larceny, fighting in the street.

The primary goal of the prison, the warden said, was to reeducate the women, to help them to become productive members of society, to help them repent and see the folly of their ways, and to teach them a marketable skill. He rattled off a list of statistics detailing the prison's rate of success, the rate of recidivism, the average prison term, the number of prisoners the facility could accommodate, the average age of the prisoner, and the cost to run the prison. It was a typically uninformative talk, and after a minute or two I stopped listening and turned my attention to a group of Japanese students sitting at the next table. They wore intentionally clunky shoes—like policemen's shoes—and expensive cotton clothes in various shades of black. They were young and had the national habit of acting deeply surprised by everything they heard, as though astonishment were a form of politeness, a sure way of avoiding conflict, and when they smiled or laughed, they did it inwardly, buttonhole eyes cast bashfully downward, a hand raised discreetly to the mouth, which, too, was intended as a form of politeness—although whenever I found myself among a group of laughing Japanese, I had the unnerving sensation that the joke was somehow on me. Unlike Mitsuko Tokutomi, the Japanese students were deeply self-conscious. Once, in a Beijing University dormitory, I mistook a Japanese woman for Chinese, and, horrified and insulted, she hurried to a mirror to check her appearance.

The German students, at another table, seemed generally irritated by the warden's talk. Among their ranks were some of the most vociferous and discontented foreign students at Hangzhou. They were fiercely independent, which was, I thought, what made them unhappy here; they thought hard and missed nothing and were appalled by the wile of the Chinese bureaucracy.

I watched one of the Germans, William, smoldering behind his teacup. At twenty-five William seemed to bear the weight of the political world on his thin shoulders. With him no conversation was ever light, and every subject led back to the oppression and abuse men visited upon each other. William had been in Hangzhou for over a year, and with each passing month he grew thinner and visibly more depressed. He had the long, pointed face of a Russian wolfhound, black circles like thumbprints under his eyes, and a razor-thin nose that turned up slightly at the tip, baring two slits for nostrils. The Foreign Affairs Office had labeled William a troublemaker, as one of the instigators of the animosity that, since the previous school year, had been brewing between the Foreign Affairs Office and the German students.

Like most of the foreign students, the Germans were dissatisfied with their Chinese instructors, and many of them had simply stopped going to class altogether, choosing to study on their own instead. They traveled freely and had parties in their rooms, to which they invited Chinese friends, who were officially not allowed to enter the premises. They refused to pay the imposed book fees for books they never bought. They lived on the first floor of a small university residence and complained about the lack of hot water there. They were an enviably colorful group, dressed in a hip hybrid of spiky haircuts and pointed shoes. They bought Chinese silk in wild patterns, had it tailored into fearless new fashions, and went out proudly on the streets of Hangzhou, inspiring shock and disbelief on the Chinese faces. Ming Yu once said to me, "You can always tell Germans from Americans—their eyes are very big and bright." That seemed true, and when the Germans were unhappy with what they saw as infringements of their rights, they said so.

At the end of the warden's presentation ten prisoners, uniformed in red skirts, white blouses, and white high-heeled sneakers, marched onto the stage in pairs, like soldiers. Their faces were made up in an amateurish, rag-doll fashion, and despite their smiles they managed to appear thoroughly mortified. To a taped marching tune they danced across the stage, bending and spinning, moving their arms and heads in pert, flirtatious gestures calculated to draw attention to the face, and though this dance was traditionally Chinese, it seemed an odd sort of entertainment for convicted adultresses and fornicators to be doing as penance.

When the dance was done, the interpreter stood up with his microphone and said, "And now, presenting small numbers, our prison troupe." The troupe—an electric piano, electric guitar, electric bass, flute, drums, and trombone—struck up a song titled "Wake Up from Nightmare." The guitarist and the bassist wore their instruments like millstones around their necks, clawed wretchedly at the strings, and glared at the floor. They resembled their comrades at the spinning machines on the fifth floor: downcast, bored, and depressed, smiling briefly when they remembered they should. Each time the drummer gave her drums a whack, she winced, as though the sound of them irritated her. In the middle of one song the pianist lost her place, and after much hissing and whispering and rustling of sheet music, the entire band had to start the song over again. When that song screeched to a halt, we clapped politely and prepared for the next, a stupefying dirge called "Greeting to Our Team Leader."

The singers who replaced the band were slightly more personable; they smiled cheerfully and skipped across the stage in a lighthearted jig, their voices trembling with emotion. The hijacker was the lead singer, and her rendition of a song called "Please Trust Me" was beautiful and eager.

With a blend of fascination and horror I watched these inmates perform: They had obviously been coaxed or prodded or forced to entertain groups of foreigners an endless number of times per year, and they had to look happy, and like they were having fun, and like they had repented and the prison had corrected whatever was wrong with them, whatever evil streak it was that had got them in there in the first place. I thought there was an edge of hysteria in the cheerfulness of the prison, and some of the more skeptical foreigners, people who had been in China for several years, maintained that the prison was a fraud, that it had been contrived solely to trick the foreign visitors into thinking that the prison system in China, like the factory system, the school system, and the farming system, was a compassionate and successful one. The skeptics claimed that in truth this was not a working prison, that at five o'clock these so-called inmates went home to their families and made dinner, just like the rest of China's paid workers. These women were actresses, not prisoners, and what we had seen was a country club by comparison with a real Chinese prison, which none of us would ever be allowed to set foot in. In a hundred years we could not begin to imagine what prison conditions in China were really like or how real prisoners were treated. William said he had seen China's prisoners from a train window on his way to Xinjiang, that they were chained together, heads shaved, dressed in stripes, and breaking rocks, "Like in a fucking movie."

Someone less indignant suggested that the women truly were prisoners, but well-behaved ones, incarcerated for petty crimes and selected to populate this special model of a prison.

But whether or not this was a real prison seemed less important to me than the fact that prison life—or someone's painstaking contrivance of it—didn't appear much different from the life outside the prison, from the life of the average hardworking, law-abiding Chinese citizen. The work was the same in prison as out, and the living conditions were virtually the same, and there was always someone giving orders.

That night in a rainstorm I walked over to the campus to visit Ming Yu in her room. The door was open and she was alone washing pots and dishes in a basin of cold water on the floor. She had placed her small desk lamp precariously on the windowsill to illuminate the washing project, and its light shone down brightly on the top of her silky head. She wore a white apron and had shoved her shirtsleeves hastily up above her elbows. Her hair was woven into a loose braid that fell forward over her shoulder. She jumped up and greeted me warmly, dried her hands on a towel hanging on a wire across the window, and indicated with a wave of a tin saucer that I should sit on the bed, for the two chairs were draped with drying laundry. She sat down next to me with the wet saucer in her lap. Long strands of hair fell around her face and into her eyes, but she made no move to sweep them away, and sitting there with the apron and the pot, she looked like a Chinese housewife. The only incongruity was the pair of heavy black storm boots she wore on her feet, boots identical to the ones I was wearing. I raised one foot off the floor to draw Ming's attention to the co-incidence. She looked surprised, said she had never seen an-other woman wearing boots like this, said they were men's boots and that Chinese women didn't wear them.

"But you're wearing them," I said.

"That's right, because the quality of the women's boots is not as good."

I was well aware that these boots were men's boots, for when I had tried to purchase them at the department store in the city, the salesgirl refused to sell them to me and kept pointing instead to some white high-heeled boots against another wall, saying, "Those are women's boots. You want those." I explained to the salesgirl that I had no choice but to buy the men's boots, since in China the biggest size for women was two sizes too small for my size-9 foot. The salesgirl gave me a doubtful frown and crossed her arms censoriously over her chest until I put my foot down next to hers as proof. Finally, when the girl realized the truth, she gaped, stricken with wonder, and several other salesgirls, sensing a spectacle, put down their lunch tins and hurried over to ponder the sight of my aberrant feet.

I told Ming the story, and she looked at my feet and said politely, "Yes, they are a slight bit bigger than Chi-nese."

Ming's eyes were bright that night, and it struck me that she always appeared happy and self-confident. I rarely saw anxiety in her face, and she was never self-conscious or coy or affected. She was one of those rare people who are exactly what they seem to be.

We chatted then, and I told Ming about the trip to the women's prison, which seemed both to interest and embar-rass her. I asked her about the crimes the inmates had re-portedly committed, the adultery, the sex, the "acts harmful to societal structure." She listened thoughtfully, and apolo-getically she said, "Chinese men want a virgin for a wife."

Ming told me that traditionally young Chinese women were expected to marry the first man they entered into a serious relationship with, chiefly because if they had more than two boyfriends in their history, they were considered loose, a bad bet for a wife. If the woman was wise, her first boyfriend would later become her husband. There was very little sex before marriage, first because society forbade it and second because girls, aware of the consequences it might have on their eventual marriage, were not often willing to succumb.

When I told Ming how far the institution of marriage had fallen in most Americans' estimation, how superfluous and even ornamental the legal bond was coming to seem to many Americans, how sexual experimentation in American colleges was as common as English courses were here, she said, "Hmm," nodding her head to indicate she was already aware of that. She squinted at the ceiling, her mind turning over images of an oversexed America. With subdued exasperation—or possibly it was disappointment—she said, "Chinese wouldn't do it."

She paused and looked at her bookshelf, as if for assistance. "Tolstoy has said that in body a woman is more faithful than a man. He means in sex of course. Women really hope to guard their virginity and preserve themselves for one whom they can truly love. Do you agree with Tolstoy?"

If Tolstoy really said that, I agreed with him; most of the women I knew were more faithful by nature than the men I knew.

Ming's gaze moved slowly up the bookshelf. Her reference to Tolstoy was neither pedantic nor self-conscious. Tolstoy, Chekhov, Mann, Shakespeare; this was her daily reading, her frame of reference. From these writers she learned how to think, how to behave in the world, and she turned to them for information and confirmation the way American women turned to glossy fashion magazines.

As Ming spoke, a figure appeared in the doorway, a doll-like woman in a librarian's navy-blue pullover and gray skirt. When she realized I was there on the bed, the woman said, "Oh!" startled, and her hands flew up to cover her mouth. An instant later, repossessed of her social grace, she said gaily, "Ha-ha! Hello!" and flung the incriminating hands up into an arc of welcome. "Greetings to our home!" she said desperately, which sounded like an effort to dispel any notion I might have got that she was unaccustomed to the presence of foreigners.

She all but ignored Ming Yu and seemed compelled to explain herself to me. She only wanted to ask Miss Ming if she could borrow a box of matches to light her stove. She lived directly across the hall. Her name was Emily. She was a student of English literature, which she loved.

Emily's speech was crisp and British, and her stiff smile was blinding as she took in the two ugly pairs of boots.

Ming stood up, took a box of matches from her apron pocket, and handed them to Emily.

"How fortunate!" Emily said to me with a little clap of the hands. "I shall not have to venture any farther in my pursuit!" And with that she pranced boldly into the room to shake my hand. She was wearing Minnie Mouse's bulbous buckle-strap high-heels. "I hope I will have the pleasure of your company again, Rosemary," she said.

When Emily was gone, Ming smiled at me. She seemed entertained. "Emily. She calls herself that, even among Chinese, after Emily Dickinson. She is a graduate student in Miss Weston's class, and at times she is rather a nuisance."

"How does she know my name?"

"I should say many people know your name, even people who have not met you. Foreigners cannot go unnoticed."

"Well, anyway, what about you?" I said. "Do you agree with Tolstoy?"

Ming turned the empty pot over in her lap and looked critically at her own reflection. "I think women are more faithful than men, perhaps not so eager for sex for sex's sake.

I worry about marriage. I am afraid that it might not be nice."

It wasn't clear what Ming meant by "not nice," but the remark reminded me of something George had said, though more forcefully, when I asked him if he had ever considered marriage. Occasionally George invited me to his room for tea, and on that particular visit he had been sitting in an armchair in his room with the white morning sun flashing in against the back of his head and forcing his pale face into the shadows. With unexpected anger he had said, "Anyone who marries is a fool! Marriage only ends in unhappiness!" Even in shouting, George's lips were motionless, and his voice seemed to emanate from his beard. He glared at me. "Western women don't like me. I don't know why. Only Asian women seem to like me."

Myself, I had begun to appreciate George for his intelligence, his mordant humor, and his outstanding singularity.

Ming said, "Rosemary, when you have a boyfriend, do you share their interests, or do you develop your own interests?"

I told her that usually I did a little of both, that I didn't like to fake or force an interest, but sometimes I found that a beloved person's enthusiasm could be infectious.

"Yes, that seems the correct way," Ming said. "I am a bit sorry to discover that I am a woman who will change herself to be closer to a man. It is not really a wise thing if one considers the possibility of separation. It seems this happens more with women; they change themselves to suit the man, and rarely the reverse. Also, I find that men can discover ways to escape a drab life, while women are to face and cope with the troubles; as a result I think women age more quickly than men. As time passes, women get worn out and they grow so attached to daily life that they become only another part of the humdrum picture. This is a sad thing."

I asked Ming if she feared the same thing would happen to her. She said that she didn't know, that people in her department had commented on her detachment from reality. "I used to get drawn into trivial arguments with them, and I would feel offended for a while, and then I would return to being myself, by myself. I don't argue now. Mostly I am afraid of being the same as others, bad or good, simply for the sake of preserving myself. I don't want to be involved in the struggles for position and titles just as a show, but reality always wants to involve me.

"I remember a conversation I once had with a university teacher in which he mentioned the theory of Kant. He said it is not of importance how a person exists, but the most important thing is that he exists in his own way. That teacher was unlike the usual kind of Chinese man, and I did not expect his remark to have made such a deep impression on me. Every Chinese I meet advises me to act like a Chinese. People in their thirties and forties laugh at my attempt to go abroad and predict that by the time I reach their age, I will be like them—well tailored to the culture. They say their early years were also full of dreams and fantasies, but look at them now: tempered and quite false, I think."

Ming tossed the pot onto the other bed and leaned back on her elbows, resting her head against the wall. Her apron was stained and worn, and her mind teemed with visions and ideas and inspected every aspect of her predicament. She was unlike any other Chinese person I had met. She had an unusual willingness to say what she thought, and her ideas were so sophisticated and worldly, and so uncommon, that I thought they could only have been inspired by books.

Weeks before, when I asked Ming where she had got so many books, she said she had bought most of them with her student allowance, Y17.50 from the state. She bought psychology books, language books, sociology books, and biographies. Most of the novels foreign friends had given her. She had said, "I don't like to let people borrow my books, because when I read them, I usually make comments in the margins. I don't like people to read what I've written, and I don't like to borrow library books, because I cannot write in them. One time I forgot that I was reading a library book and wrote so many things on the pages that I feared I would be heavily fined."

I realized now that it was half past eleven, already too late for me to get safely back into my building without having to wake the ornery gatekeeper.

"It's late," I said. "Where's Miss Wen?"

Ming looked quizzically at her roommate's bed, as if realizing for the first time that Wen was absent. She glanced at the open door. "Oh, Wen is at a conference of Physical Education in Suzhou. She is judging a gymnastics competition."

When I told Ming I thought I should be going, she began talking about a biography of Camus she was reading and showed me her photo album, obviously trying to keep me there a little longer. There were photographs of Ming at various points in her life, and in some of them she looked quite striking. I told her how nice the photographs were and remarked that she looked different in each one.

"Yes," she said, "other foreigners have noticed the same thing."

"You look pretty."

"Foreigners often say I look pretty, but Chinese do not think so. And when I was a child, I was considered to be rather unattractive. A plain face, not appealing. Perhaps the face has improved a bit."

Ming spoke of her face as though it belonged to a stranger.

When I left Ming's room at 11:40, a soft rain was falling. I was surprised to find the main university gate locked and the lights in the guardhouse off. I could go around to the east gate, wake the guard there, and tell him a lie about where I had been, or I could climb over the eleven-foot cement wall right here. Outside the guardhouse there was a little wooden school desk, which the guard sat at during the day, writing down names and comments about people coming and going; I dragged the desk up to the wall, climbed onto it, and hoisted myself to the top of the wall. I could see all the way down University Road to the luxury hotel ablaze with lights—the only lights around at that hour.

A Public Security Bureau motorcycle and sidecar screeched around a dark corner and roared off down the middle of the wide street in the direction of the hotel. I watched in surprise as—in a rare moment of abandon—the officer shifted his weight and tilted the motorcycle at an acute angle to the pavement, until the sidecar was lifted clean off its wheel and into the air. He rode on this way for forty or fifty yards, shirking his civic responsibilities and seizing the people's motorcycle for his own amusement.

The drop to the other side of the wall was far, but I was so annoyed by the inconvenience that without stopping to consider my actions, or even to muster my courage, I dropped myself over and fell through the air. I landed on my feet with such force that the weight of my own body knocked me forward to my hands and knees into a deep puddle of cold mud, and even then the momentum continued to push me lower, until my forehead was resting against my forearms. I stayed there in the mud for a moment, because I felt suddenly peaceful, and because I was overwhelmed with fatigue. The streets and the sky were dark, and the fine rain was like gauze against my hands and neck.

At the Experts' Building the gate was locked. I banged loudly on the guardhouse door, and presently a light went on in the window, and Zhen, the diligent, pumpkin-headed guard, appeared at the window in his long underwear. Zhen had a fake laugh and kept notes and records on the foreigners. He demanded to know who was at the door.

"Rosemary," I said.

He yanked open the door and looked me up and down, shaking his head at the sight. His short gray hair was mashed flat against the side of his head, and his fat cheek bore the marks of the wrinkles in his bed sheets. "You fell in the mud?" said he.

I ignored the question. "How are you?" I said.

"Not so good." He pointed to the little wind-up clock on the desk. "It's too late."

The guardroom, awash in the sickly light of the bare fluorescent tube on the ceiling, depressed me. Twenty thermoses of boiled water stood on the floor near the door. I took two of them, and as I went up the stairs to my room, I imagined Zhen fishing his grubby booklet out of the desk drawer and, under the heading "Rosemary," making careful note of my appearance, my lateness, my boots, and possibly even of the extra thermos bottle I had taken.

That night I had a dream about traveling through China in an elegant limousine with a Chinese person I was unfamiliar with. I lifted up a velvet seat cushion and found under it a television and a canary. The limousine traveled fast down a narrow mountain road walled with red brick. I was frightened by the speed of the limousine, and when the driver slowed down to take a sharp curve, I jumped out and ran down a footpath that led to a field of cabbages. While running I realized there were thousands of other people on the path with me, all of them Chinese. We were running from a man with a machine gun. The feeling of danger was intense, and in the field below, thousands more waited in fear.

YU
XING

Every afternoon I took a walk around the West Lake. Besides the famous lake with its tidy causeways and man-made islands, there were numerous public parks in Hangzhou, botanical gardens, a mysterious and little known flower nursery, low blue mountains to the west, and to the south the Qiantang River, a wide opaque green plane that flowed slowly, almost imperceptibly, into Hangzhou Bay and out to sea. The Chinese fascination with flowers and trees was demonstrated in full force in Hangzhou, and though each tree was human-planned and prompted, the effect was enchanting. There were temples here, famous self-conscious ones made drab and unholy by the curious masses, and smaller, serious, lesser-known ones in the hills.

Enterprising men and women stood in strategic spots at the lake's edge with wooden canoes tied up to the willows and shouted at each passing person, "Go out on the lake! Ten yuan!" Vendors sold apples, tea, film, and soft drinks. The vendors who knew no English banged things to draw attention to their wares. The ice-cream man banged his wooden ice box with a stick, the photographer rattled his tripod, the trinket vendor clacked two wooden flutes together and blew into them both at once to demonstrate their quality. They made laughable gestures of communication: the motions of eating, drinking, paddling, strumming, dressing. They were excellent at charades, and some days it took a lot of dodging to avoid them.

One bright afternoon I was standing on the square in front of the Young Pioneer Palace watching a group of kite-flying children when I heard a voice behind me saying in an all-too-familiar way, "Are you busy? May I talk with you?"

It was inevitable. I had resigned myself to the fact that wherever I went in China, people would stare at me and try to practice their English on me. When I walked along the streets, they followed me as though my hair were on fire, and they shrieked their hellos and waited nervously for my answer, like titillated children waiting for a snake to spring at the poke of a rake. Their English "Hello!" sometimes sounded mocking and hostile; it was often the badgering, perseverating hello usually reserved for parrots and babies. Other times it was a single wanton shriek, or a shy, almost seductive murmur from a doorway. In the marketplace it didn't mean hello at all but meant, "Come over and buy these oranges!" When I responded to the greetings, I found that few people listened. When I tried to speak, they yammered excitedly over me—to the average Chinese citizen my presence was little more than an opportunity to try out the few English words they had learned. At times I felt like a walking target, and though English was my language, and though they had to struggle to keep from tying themselves up in their own sentences, the Chinese seemed to hold all the power in these encounters.

One day as I walked alone along a remote road, an old man on a bicycle rode up next to me and declared without preliminary greetings, "Foreign lady, I have read the story 'Rip Van Winkle.' It begins this way, 'Whoever has made a voyage up the Hudson must remember the Catskill Mountains. They are a dismembered branch of the great Appalachian family, and are seen away to the west of the river, swelling up to a noble height and lording it over the surrounding country. . . .' "

And on and on the man rushed, reciting the story in a loud, flat, breathless voice, while his bicycle bounced heavily over the bumps and into the potholes. When I tried to interrupt him, he lowered his eyelids and recited louder, grin-ing ecstatically and gripping the handlebars with his yellow hands.

" 'When the weather is fair and settled, they are clothed in blue and purple, and print their bold outlines on the clear evening sky; . . .' "

He was positively bellowing now.

As we approached the entrance gate to the Zhejiang Flower Nursery, I paid the visitor's fee and hurried in, knowing full well the man wouldn't pay good money to keep my ear.

That same day a persistent, puffy-eyed teenager latched on to me as I walked around the lake, clomping along behind me in his high-heeled sandals, swinging his arms like a young child and casting loudly over my shoulder the standard questions: where was I from, was I married, how much money did I make, did I think the lake was beautiful, did I like Chinese food, was I alone, was I lonely, did I have a car at home, a house, how big a family, did I know how famous the lake was, how famous Hangzhou silk was, had I tried Longjing tea, was I wearing fashionable shoes, could I teach him English, could I speak into a tape recorder for him, if I was American why wasn't my hair blond, could I help him go to America?

Around the lake, people stared at the scene we made, and some followed briefly to listen or even to join in, and when they got tired or when their vocabulary was exhausted, they dropped by the wayside. When I tried to lead the conversation into deeper subjects, the boy strayed back to the niggling questions. After an hour and the fourth mile of my walk, I stopped talking altogether. Still the boy followed stubbornly behind, hoping perhaps that by mere proximity correct English would rub off on him.

Unlike those taxing, blabbering people, the voice behind me at the Young Pioneer Palace was silent, waiting for a response. I turned to find a delicate, nervous young man, whose eyes fluttered with delight when I spoke to him; they were beautiful brownish eyes shaped like apricot pits. His straight hair hung flat on his forehead, and his tattered clothes fit his skinny body like a wetsuit. He wore tight cutoff shorts, a plaid shirt, and carried an army-green book bag over his shoulder. He said, "My name is Yu Xing." His voice was high, and he spoke quickly as if to elude his own miserable pronunciation. He told me he worked in the Hangzhou Machine Factory and had taught himself English with books and tapes and the Voice of America on shortwave radio. The amount he'd learned under those conditions was impressive. He blushed and objected when I told him so. "Not impressive," he said in the typically self-effacing Chinese way, though his very soul was thrilled with the compliment; I thought he would clasp my hand in his and press it to his heart.

As we walked together toward the lake, he said, "Sunday is my holiday, so every holiday I come to West Lake and go to the English Corner on Number-Six Park and can practice my English. Or at the Foreign Language store can see some books or see some tapes. All other days for working in Hangzhou Machine Factory Number Nine."

I asked the boy how many hours he worked every day. He twisted the strap of his bag nervously around his fingers. He said some days he worked ten hours.

In the shade of a willow near the lake Yu Xing and I sat on a bench. Tourists rented dark wooden canoes and paddled them back and forth across the water to the three small islands at the center of the lake. Young families strolled along the lake's edge in their best clothes, stopping to take pictures or to buy bean cakes and pumpkin seeds. The air was cool and clear, and the sharp sunlight struck the water white.

I asked Yu Xing how he liked his work. He smiled and shook his head. "I hate it," he said.

"What would you prefer to be doing?"

He fished through his book bag and pulled out a splayed paperback titled *The West Lake*. "I prefer to do the tours guide of Hangzhou," he said, "But I must study English better for my tourings guide. Now my English is too bad for the nice."

I asked Yu Xing if I could have a look at the other books in his bag—they were an English-Chinese dictionary, English workbooks, and a book of elementary English texts, all of them outdated, worn, and greasy. "Yu Xing, what don't you like about the factory job?"

He blinked his soft brown eyes at me and raised a hand in supplication. "Pardon?"

"Why do you hate the factory?"

Without hesitation Yu Xing unbuttoned his shirt and revealed a collection of angry purple scars—each as thick as a garden slug—across his chest and collarbone, scars left there by the chips of glowing hot metal that flew off the machines he welded. "The pieces are hot," he said with a smile. When I looked at him, he closed his eyes. I couldn't picture him doing that kind of work; he was slight, almost girlish, and I could have knocked him to the ground with a gentle shove.

Yu closed his shirt and told me that some days he worked ten hours, that his work was very hot, and that it wore him out. "I wear the glasses for my eyes. But nothing to protect the rest. I do not talk with the other workers. Not having time. And my money is not a lot."

I asked Yu Xing how old he was. "I am twenty years old," he said. He looked like a boy. He told me he regretted not having had the chance to go to college, that he regretted not having finished middle school. "I had to work instead," he said. "My family are farmers. But each night I teach myself English and some day I will be able to speak it well."

I believed him.

Passersby stopped to watch Yu Xing talking with me. They clutched their shoulder bags to their chests and looked with interest from me to Yu Xing and back again, and when we turned to look at them, they shuffled a few feet away, stopped, and resumed the staring.

After a lull in the conversation Yu Xing smoothed his book bag flat in an absentminded way and stared across the lake at the short mountains. I could see him preparing a question in his head. He turned to me. "May I ask you where you came from in America?"

"Boston," I said.

Yu leaned back against the bench and stared dully at me, with the book bag cradled like a baby in his arms. He turned the word over in his mind, and its shape appeared silently on his lips: "Boston." And then, with a wild surge of energy, he flung himself up out of his seat. The dictionary and the guidebook tumbled to the pavement. "I cannot believe it!" he shrieked, clapping his hands, with the book bag dangling awkwardly from his elbow. He was wild with happiness. He dropped to a crouch, scrambling to gather up his books. He muttered something about a painting exhibit and said, "I must give you to see!" He marched off along the edge of the lake, gesturing at me to come along.

Yu's bare legs were long and thin and smooth, like wooden stilts, and he walked in a prancing, coltish way, as though with each step his knees might give way. Because the straps of his sandals were broken, he had tied them to his feet with pink plastic string. Now and then his book bag dragged along the ground, picking up spittle and bits of ice-cream wrappers and leaves. As we got farther and farther from the Number-Six Park, Yu's English became less intelligible until eventually I understood very little of what he said, although he spoke earnestly and a great deal. Occasionally a clear phrase trailed out of his mouth and over his shoulder like a puff of black smoke: "Very sad," or "Everyone knows," or "Historically speaking." I assumed he was practicing his tour guide's speech.

Finally Yu Xing stopped before the iron gate of a walled compound and said proudly, "The Zhejiang School of Fine Arts. And I will see you next time. Or I am afraid I would have to eat my words."

Off he went under the sycamores, with the bag slung over his bony shoulder.

I went through the art-school gate, baffled. The place looked deserted, but inside to the left of the gate I saw a brick building with its doors flung open, and that looked promising, so I ventured in. At the door a stout girl in sunglasses demanded an entrance fee of thirty cents.

The first floor of the building was a three-room art gallery. One of the rooms was filled with soft and handsome watercolors of Boston by a man named Wang. The various scenes of the city were titled in English: "Paul Gore Street," "Winter of Boston," "Enjoyment of Two Old Men," "Jamaica Pond," "Morning of Little Street, Boston," and "Girl Athlete." There was an impressionistic representation of the Bostongas tank, an obese white bulb that loomed up between the Savin Hill beach and the Southeast Expressway. The tank wore a ragged rainbow of color like a kerchief over its bald head—a design by the artist Corita Kent. Wang had titled his rendering of the tank, "Woman Art Designed Boston Gas Can."

Every Sunday Yu Xing would find me somehow when I took my walk around the city. No matter where I chose to walk, he'd be there waiting for me.

One rainy Sunday a few weeks after we first met, I was sick with a cold and decided to stay home. Yu Xing looked for me around the lake, and when he didn't see me, he grew anxious and stopped another foreign woman in the street and asked her if she knew me and where I was. The woman happened to be a British teacher who lived in the apartment above Christina's and mine. She informed Yu Xing that I was ill, and two days later I received a letter from him advising me to take care of my health. He attributed my illness to the bad weather, which I must surely be unaccustomed to here in China. He assured me that eventually I would "be fitted the weather." He told me that upon hearing of my illness he was eager to come and visit me, but "because we have a different habits," he hesitated to do so, and now he was writing this letter to ask me if I would be offended by a visit from him. "Meanwhile," he wrote, "I should tell you that you are so friendly. You have taught me so much English pronouncation and so on I must thank you." He invited me to come and visit him and his family in their home the following Sunday so that he could "express" his heart. He signed off with: "It's end. and have a nice time. and a well health. Your friend, Yu Xing."

For a boy who had never been formally trained in English, who spent ten hours a day in a factory, the letter seemed a remarkable triumph to me. Like so many Chinese people Yu Xing had positively willed himself to learn English. At the Sunday English Corner at the lake hundreds of people of all ages gathered faithfully to practice English with each other. One Sunday morning during my first month in Hangzhou I happened upon this group, and because I had had no previous knowledge of the English Corner and its purpose, the scene struck me as thoroughly bizarre. I sat on a nearby bench to watch and listen, and gradually people spotted me and came over to chat. Before long the entire crowd had enveloped me and my bench; they stood with their knees touching mine, they peered over each other's shoulders to get a better look at me, they cupped their ears and strained to hear me speak. Eagerly they asked me questions about myself and the world. Every word I spoke appeared to strike them with the force of a revelation. Every scrap of humor sent them into fits of hysterical giggling. I shook a little girl's hand, said, "How do you do?" and the crowd squealed with laughter and repeated after me, "How do you do!"

The people at the English Corner were most curious about my impressions of China. On that morning I was in a bad mood about China. Some things had been made clear to me: I would never be able to go down the street without being followed and talked at. As a foreigner I was generally misconstrued and mistrusted, seen as an opportunity, as a child, and sometimes as a freak. My teaching group didn't make use of me; the city streets were unforgivably dirty; the Foreign Affairs Office was taking advantage of the foreign teachers; indirectness and ambiguity were a way of life here; and the people were bullied and pushed and gypped by their distant government.

Calmly I told the people the things I thought so far about China: I told them how ill maintained the university was, how absurd it seemed that seven adult students slept in one small room, how hazardous things were, how they seemed to be suffocated by rules and regulations and policies. I mentioned the littering and the stinking public bathrooms and anything else I could think of that shocked me or made me angry, and the people smiled. They agreed. Strangest of all, they seemed amused by my assessment, in the way people are amused to learn that they talked aloud in their sleep, and what gibberish they said, and how they said it.

"Yes!" they agreed, "These are old Chinese customs, so what can we do?"

They weren't offended by my views, I supposed because they had so little to compare themselves with. The things I had said were like ancient history, and my little critique, predicated on Western values, had as little impact on that Sunday's English Corner as our celebrated forays into outer space. I could complain, but my complaints would make no difference, and I would only sound mean and hard.

I sat there on my bench expecting the crowd to desert me, but they pressed closer, smiling. "Welcome you to our city!" they said.

"MAKE WAY FOR
MEN WHO LOOK
LIKE MEN"

After hearing Ming Yu talk about the nature of the relationship between teacher and student, I worried that I had done a poor job of keeping an authoritative distance from my students. I found them appealing and lovable in a way I had never imagined twenty-year-olds could be, and it was difficult to balance their childlike image with the reality that they were adults. They laughed so easily and so delightfully that I was never quite able to overcome my urge to joke with them or to tease them in an affectionate way, and they noticed that and teased me back. Outside of class they imitated the way I spoke, the way I walked, and they told me I was "something like a boy," because my hair was short, because of the daring way I rode my bicycle, and because I wore men's rubber boots on rainy days. Some days I wore a brown leather jacket that, with age, had turned the color of dark chocolate. One winter day Karen, a friendly student I had come to know well, approached me after class, scrutinized the jacket, and said, "The jacket is ... well ... I should say that you must wash the jacket. And why not wear a woolen scarf in the cold? And how about a dress?" Karen herself never wore a dress. In fact a dress was an occasional thing for women in the winter, and older Chinese women seemed never to wear dresses at all, choosing instead the timeless baggy blue or gray pants.

Just as there was no escaping the heat in summer, there was no escaping the cold in winter here. It was a biting, stinging cold that pervaded every corner of every building, and it was exhausting in its persistence. There was no central heating in the university and, like all foreign teachers, Christina and I had been given one small heater intended to heat all three of our rooms. The heater was useless and our rooms were always freezing; ice formed on the insides of our windows. At home I rarely took off my jacket and I worked and typed and ate with gloves on. I slept in two sweaters, sweatpants, and a hat. Inside, the Chinese wore fingerless woolen gloves that allowed them to cook, write, and turn the pages of books and still keep their hands relatively warm. In class my students sat at their desks, hunched and paralyzed with cold in their flimsy vinyl jackets and cotton slippers, writing their notes and compositions with these gloves on their hands. The gloves gave them a shady, Faginesque appearance. The windows in our classroom didn't close properly and when the bitter winter wind slapped them open, we simply left them that way; closed windows made no difference in the temperature.

One day after my class with the Chinese Department students, Maria and her roommate Helen approached me as I was going out the door and, blushing, they asked me if I would join them for dinner in their dining hall that night. When I accepted the invitation, they thanked me for my generosity and asked me to meet them in their room in Dormitory Number 12 at 4:00. Dinner, they said, was served at 4:30.

That afternoon I walked through the maze of dormitories on campus until I found Building 12, a place not much different from the building Ming Yu lived in, though it seemed a little more depressed. The hallways were narrower and darker, the floor was wetter, the air was mustier, and the smell of the bathrooms was more sickening.

I went down the hallway and knocked on the wrong door. The girl who answered was so stunned at the sight of my foreign face that she dropped the large book she held in her hand. I smiled at her, apologized for the interruption, and carried on down the hall. When I glanced back over my shoulder at her, she was standing in the middle of the hallway gaping after me with her arms dangling by her sides and the book held limply by one corner of the cover so that it dangled in a reckless fan of pages against her leg. When she saw me looking, the girl hurried back into her room and shut the door.

After knocking on a few more doors and startling a few more students, I found Maria and Helen's room. Their door was open, so I stepped in.

The seven roommates lay on their bunks reading magazines and books and letters from home. One of them sensed my presence and peered at me over the edge of her bed, straightening the eyeglasses on her flat nose. Her face froze in an expression of pure shock. She sat bolt upright and banged her head so hard against the corner of the shelf above her bed that the cups and cassettes stacked on it tumbled into her lap. She had no time to be pained by the little accident. "Hey!" she hissed to the others, "a foreigner has come!"

In an instant the rest of the girls were sliding to the floor and standing at attention against the bunks, straightening their sweaters and smoothing down their tousled hair. Maria and Helen stepped forward to claim me. They led me into the room by my elbows and sat me down on one of the two straight-backed chairs.

The room was unremittingly ugly. It was cold and dreary, a broom closet of a place, illuminated only by the fading light of the one narrow window in the far wall. Though the day was rainy and raw, the window was flung wide, as though all efforts to keep the place warm and dry had long ago been abandoned—I thought I saw mist drifting between me and the girls.

Each girl had her possessions stacked on one shelf above her bed: books, radios, tin mugs, vases of plastic flowers. There were several posters on the walls—a semifocused starry-eyed couple gazing into each other's eyes in the middle of a field of daisies, a golden retriever chasing a butterfly. Two wooden tables were pushed together in the middle of the room, and their sticky tops were cracked and covered with tea jars, spoons, and bowls. Under my feet the cement floor was gritty and damp.

The seven girls looked seedy-eyed and pasty in this room. They wore tight pastel-colored sweaters and dark Dacron pants with slightly flared bottoms, and they all wore glasses. They tucked their hair into place and pushed their feet into plastic slippers and stared at me. Though Maria had told me that some of her roommates argued and didn't get along well, just then they were unanimous in their curiosity. I motioned for them to sit down, and they collapsed in a line on one of the beds across from me. They stared some more. This was probably the first time a foreigner had been to their room. The staring made me uncomfortable. I waved to them and said, "How's it going, everybody?"

Standing beside me, Helen raised her hand in protest and said possessively, "No! No! Those do not speak English! Only Maria and I can speak English!"

"Oh," I said.

Someone had flung a Chinese magazine onto the table, an eight-by-ten newsletter printed on coarse paper. Judging from the line drawings of girls inspecting themselves in hand mirrors, it was a magazine directed at young women. I could see the table of contents and tried to translate some of the titles. Out loud, slowly, I read: "Women, Make Way for Men Who Look Like Men."

At my elbow, Helen guffawed and hid her big face in her hands. "Wrong!" she brayed hysterically, "Ha-ha! Very wrong!" Helen's laugh was deep and unrestrained and made me laugh along with her.

Maria reprimanded Helen with a soft punch in the shoulder; Helen returned the punch and hooted some more. Of all my female students Helen was probably the largest. She was tall, solid, and quite buxom for a Chinese girl, and of all my students she was the most visceral. She laughed the loudest, sighed the deepest, yawned openly, displayed the greatest surprise, and when she was bored, she perspired and her eyelids grew heavy. Helen had pudgy cheeks and thick black hair molded in a page boy around her face. She was clumsy, banged into things, came late to class, and once or twice she had fallen asleep with her head on her desk until I shook her awake, which made her blush and snicker with shame.

Helen had a marked interest in boys. Once I had seen her standing arm-in-arm with a boy from another class on the steps of the department building, and after months of not seeing such a thing among the Chinese students I had to fight an inclination to label Helen as loose.

Helen leaned over my shoulder to point to each character in the title and said instructively, "Rose! You look. It says, 'Women, You Should Make Men Act Like Men.'"

"Well, what does *that* mean, Helen?" I said.

Helen pursed her lips and raised her hands before her and rubbed her fingers in concentration. "Ah . . . it means women should . . . they should, ah . . ." She looked at Maria for help and Maria blurted out, "Boss men around!"

"Men can't boss themselves?" I said.

"Correct!"

"What do you two think of men, anyway?" I asked.

They exchanged knowing looks. "Selfish," Maria said.

"And don't pay attentions to women," Helen added.

I agreed with them and read two more titles; "In Summer, I Wore a Pretty Dress," and "Romance in a Field." Both girls seemed impressed. "You can read Chinese," they said. "No, no," I said, with the proper degree of modesty, "I can't read Chinese at all."

But in truth I was learning Chinese and was taking great pleasure in it. There were times I had felt dumb and faceless in China because I couldn't say in Chinese the things I thought or wanted or needed. I realized how bound up my identity and my personality were to language; because my opinions could not be formed in characters and monosyllabic tones, I sometimes felt as if I had no identity here, and that depressed me. On winter afternoons when I felt cold and dull, I practiced Chinese characters as a distraction. I bought two fountain pens, a notebook, and a primer filled with elementary texts and directions on grammar and on the physical form of the characters. I spent hours practicing the strokes, I made flash cards, did exercises, wrote out whole passages again and again until I could re-create them from memory. *Hand, mouth, ox, home, moon, man. Xiao Wang, please sit down.*

I never thought I would actually learn Chinese. I saw it as a pastime, like stringing beads or weaving baskets. I wrote little stories of my own in Chinese and began to take a genuine interest in the characters. In Chinese my chronically juvenile handwriting was somehow improved, and for once in my life I felt artistic. Each character seemed, to me, an intricate picture that looked, after all, like what it claimed to be, and writing them down was a soothing, gratifying exercise.

And then one day I realized I could read Chinese. Walking along Liberation Road in the city, I saw a sign that said, *Zhi sheng yi ge haizi hao* (To Produce Only One Child Is Good). I was stunned. I stood in the street and read the sign over and over again, persuading myself that it was true, that I had got it right. It was like a miracle. I could actually read the sign. The scratches and lines that I had come across all my life and had thought of as somehow primitive and laughable were clear to me now. I felt I had let myself in on a very old secret and was thrilled with the responsibility it seemed to bring.

Then I was starved for more signs, for more things I could decipher, for more practice and gratification. I sat at my desk every afternoon and drank tea and listened to Strauss—a wildly popular composer in China—and wrote and read Chinese.

A few days before my dinner with Helen and Maria, I had written *mei*, the character for "beautiful" in class on the blackboard, and the students had watched my progress with suspense. I could feel them willing me to get it right, and in my nervousness I had gone about it from all the wrong angles, putting the lower strokes before the upper and the right before the left, and the result was a sprawling, crooked, stick figure, like a child's rendering of an ant. I had expected the students to laugh at me and my feeble effort, but they didn't laugh—instead after a long silence they burst into wild, appreciative applause, grinning and cheering, and their unconditional pride in me, their delight at my success, was so stunning that I had to turn my face back toward the blackboard.

In Helen and Maria's room the light was so bad that I had to hold the little magazine up to my face to read it. In it was a kind of Ann Landers column called, as far as I could make out, "Intimate Older Sister." One of the letters in the column began, "Dear Intimate Older Sister, Last year my boyfriend and I parted ways, and I was extremely unhappy. A couple of times I wrote him letters, but he did not answer me."

I read the letter slowly, starting over again several times. Maria and Helen peered over my shoulder, checking to see that I was getting it right, and the five on the bed looked on, stupefied, as though they were staring at a television screen. They stared unabashedly and made no effort to veil their curiosity.

"You can understand our magazine," Maria said.

"A little bit," I said.

"You have magazines like this in America?"

"Yes."

"Magazines about boys?" Helen said.

"Yes. We have a lot of them." I wished then that I had *Seventeen* or something to show them.

At 4:30 all seven girls jumped up without warning, as though a silent alarm had gone off in their heads, and they grabbed their tin bowls and spoons and headed out the door. Maria shoved a bowl and spoon in my hand. "Please come on," she said, grabbing her jacket. We hurried out of the building and across the courtyard to the dining hall. Students poured out of surrounding buildings in droves, all heading in the same direction, all carrying bowls and spoons. They moved with urgency and purpose, hoping to get a head start on the line.

The dining hall was an enormous open room, like a barn, with a raftered ceiling. Endless rows of tiled tables stretched out across the wet cement floor, and at one end of the room there were small windows in the wall through which food was served. Already hundreds of students stood in swollen lines, waiting for the windows to open. Huge handwritten signs on the wall said, Don't Cut into Lines! but seemed to have no effect whatever on the students, who cut and pushed and elbowed each other relentlessly. Pushing seemed to be one of the most egregious of Chinese characteristics, and its natural consequence was that no Chinese person ever seemed truly offended by another's push or shove, no one took the lack of civility personally. That is not to say the Chinese people did not fight—they did, terribly. In fact I had never seen more riotous, freewheeling street arguments than the ones I saw in China. Once, in Nanjing I watched two women stumbling down Zhongshan Road in a tug-of-war over a child's pair of pants they had both wanted to buy from a sidewalk vendor. Each one got hold of a leg and tugged with all her might, and they screeched and howled and pulled each other's hair and slapped each other's faces, and—best of all—they had a crowd of fifty or sixty delighted onlookers going along with them, now taking this side, now taking that. But such fights were immediately forgotten, in part because they were expected. Pushing was the norm, and, as Huang Zhiye had pointed out to Christina and me, if you didn't push, you would never accomplish anything in China.

I sat down at a table, while Maria and Helen disappeared

into one of the lines. At the end of the table two girls were already eating, spitting bones and gristle onto the table. They had long ponytails, wore athletic suits, and looked as though they'd just come from basketball practice. They ate remarkably fast, with their heads down, as though they were trying to block out their surroundings, and as I glanced around me, I noticed that other students at other tables were eating in the same voracious, defensive manner. From time to time the two girls peered at me from behind their bowls and muttered and giggled to each other. Students went up and down the aisles between the tables looking for places to sit, doing double takes when they saw me. A foreigner in the dining hall was an unexpected surprise. Some of them shouted "Hello!" at me and hurried away. The tables filled up quickly, and the din in this room was deafening.

Maria and Helen returned with five dishes and five bowls of rice and sat down opposite me. The food looked terrible. The dumplings had dried out and turned a chestnut brown, the cabbage was boiled down to a kind of film, floating on the top of the soup, and there was a dish of meat that looked like minced pencil erasers. Only the rice and the bowl of fried peanuts looked edible to me. Helen saw me looking at the peanuts and cheerfully pushed them toward me, and Maria stuck a spoon in my hand and urged me to eat.

I looked at them; with their straight hair and their identical horn-rimmed glasses they were like two scientists. "Why do students always eat with spoons instead of chopsticks?" I asked them.

"With a spoon you can eat faster," Helen said, digging into the dumplings. Helen had a sumptuous way of chewing that made every bite look delicious and satisfying. I scooped up a spoonful of peanuts. Around a mouthful of dumplings Helen said, "Rose, what kind of food do you like?"

I told her I liked a lot of Chinese food. In particular hot-and-sour soup and *xiao long baozi*, or little cage dumplings, and I liked the way the Chinese cooked cuttlefish and noodles with pig's liver and fragrant mushrooms. I said the names of the foods in Chinese, and she and Maria laughed so hard and long at my poor pronunciation that I thought they would choke on their food. Even the hurried, eavesdropping pair of athletes at the end of the table were laughing and covering their mouths.

"And I like apples very much," I said.

Helen halted her chewing and made a face. "Apple is not food!"

"Well, then, what kind of food do *you* like, Helen?" I said.

"All food."

Maria said in her soft, fainting way, "I appreciate the way my mother can cook a duck and also she can cook *jiaozi*. It is very good. Food at home is different from food here." She pointed her spoon in accusation at the loathsome cabbage soup.

I asked them if they had ever eaten dog. "Of course," they said. I told them how strange it seemed never to see any dogs on the streets or even in the hills or around the lake. I asked them if that was because all dogs were slaughtered and eaten. They said, no, the dogs were mostly "sent out into the country." I remembered reading somewhere that in China, dogs and dissidents shared the same fate. Perhaps because they knew I liked dogs, none of my Chinese friends had ever admitted to me that dogs were also systematically rounded up and slaughtered. Weeks before, when I was walking along Guangming Road toward Zhejiang University, I had heard what I was certain was a dog slaughter going on in a little shed set back from the road. It sounded as though people were swinging dogs full-speed against the walls of the shed, a dull, repeated thudding like the muffled thump of snow as it slides from a rooftop to the ground below, and the thudding was accompanied by a cacophony of high-pitched barking, so unaccustomed to me that at first I mistook it for the honking of ducks or some animal I simply didn't recognize. Two young men who had heard the barking came racing down the road on foot with expectant grins on their faces, obviously hoping to catch a glimpse of the slaughter. They ran up into the woods toward the small shed, and I stood in the middle of the dusty road, confused and faintly horrified. Though no one had told me what was going on, I knew. And then, suddenly, the hellish noise stopped, and the two young men, seconds too late for the spectacle, ambled disappointedly back down the lane.

Maria tapped her spoon on the side of one of the bowls and said to me, "You are not eating."

I told her I wasn't really very hungry, that 4:30 was early for me to be eating dinner. "In our building we usually eat dinner at six," I said.

Helen looked askance at me. "Oh, I would starve!"

While we talked, two students from my Geography Department class saw me sitting there and came over with their bowls. They were Ternie and Peggy, an inseparable pair who always sat in the front row of the class, by the windows. Peggy was a tiny girl from Hainan Island in the far south of Guangdong Province. She had suffered a mysterious three-year illness, and because of it had started the semester several weeks late. She was a shy stutterer, and her efforts to speak English often threw her into a red-faced turmoil. Occasionally she missed classes, and Ternie would approach me to apologize for her, to tell me, "You know, Peggy is ill and very delicate and cannot do the same as other students."

Ternie was a mature, sad-faced, long-haired senior from Beijing, who was auditing my class because, like so many others, she wanted desperately to improve her English. Peggy idolized Ternie; she clutched Ternie's hand as they walked around campus, slung her arm around Ternie's shoulders or waist, and in class I often saw her stroking Ternie's hair, tucking it behind her ear for her, like a mother or a lover. In turn Ternie was fiercely protective and careful of her friend, speaking for her in class and carrying her heavy books for her.

In general the affection girls displayed for each other in

China seemed sweet to me; it was spontaneous and free and more natural than the restrained, sometimes fearful way American women approached one another. But in this particular relationship I sensed something more than simple affection. The adoration on Peggy's part seemed obsessive, and I predicted she would suffer a great deal when Ternie graduated that spring and returned to Beijing. Peggy's physical attention to her friend was almost overbearing; while Ternie talked with me, Peggy buried her face in Ternie's arm, hugged her, and gazed up at her. I guessed that the connection between these two girls rested on the fact that they had both come from a great distance to study in Hangzhou—of all my students they were the farthest from home, and they were always homesick and lonely. Now they sat down next to me at the table and together smiled shyly at me. I introduced them to Maria and Helen, explained that they were students from my other class, and as soon as I did, I felt a deep mistrust and resentment well up between the two pairs of girls.

I often felt a vague unfriendliness between my two classes of Chinese students, felt that they were in competition with each other for my approval. I generally found my students to be wary and reserved with each other. Even within classes, unless they had a reason to get to know each other, they didn't try. They had an all-or-nothing way of relating, and among the women this seemed borne of competition. Boys and girls lived in entirely separate spheres. One of my male students once said to me, "You know, Chinese boys and girls seldom do anything together, unless of course they fall in love."

After I introduced the two pairs of girls, there was an awkward silence, and seizing the opportunity, one of the two basketball players at the end of the table called down to me in English, "Hello!" She had a pinched face and modern, plastic-rimmed glasses. "Are you an American teacher?" she said.

My four students turned and looked incredulously at her—what nerve she had to insinuate herself on our party.

"Yes, I am."

"May I ask you something?"

I shrugged, thinking I should be loyal to my bristling students. "Okay."

"Can you give me an English name?"

Helen stared at the stranger as though she had just sprung up out of a hole in the cement floor. I asked the girl her Chinese name, which sounded something like "Lisa," so I called her that. She said, "Lisa," loudly and with elation. "May I talk with you?"

I said, "Okay," surprised at my own discomfort.

The basketball player looked warily at the other girls. "May I talk with you *another* time?"

I told her she could talk with me anytime she saw me, that I always enjoyed talking to Chinese students, and that I would even talk with her friend.

"My friend does not speak English," she cried, summarily dismissing the friend.

Nervously Peggy began to stroke Ternie's hair. Helen carried on with her eating. Maria looked sadly at me through her glasses; I felt as though I had betrayed them all.

I realized we had had nothing to drink with our dinner and I asked the students what they liked to drink. Orange soda and tea came the answer. I asked them if they ever drank alcohol. They said, "Oh, no! We hate that. It makes our faces red and ugly. Only men drink beer and wine."

When I told them that I liked to drink beer, Maria grinned and pointed her spoon at me. "See?" she said. "Like a boy!"

A LIFE IN
THE COUNTRY

One December evening while Christina was at a class and I was in the shower, there came an urgent knocking on the outer door of the apartment, and it persisted long beyond the point at which any reasonable individual would have given up and retreated. Naturally I imagined an emergency. I leapt out of the shower, yanked on my clothes, slung a towel around my head, and opened the door. There was Huang Zhiye in the dirty yellow light of the hallway. He was dressed in a padded blue jacket and had a big brown envelope clutched to his chest.

Huang grinned and said, "Ah," at the sight of me. His plump cheeks were whipped pink by the bitter cold, and in the relative warmth of the house his glasses had misted over.

"You knocked a very, very long time, Mr. Huang," I said.

"Lucky I did!" said he.

"I was taking a shower."

He said expectantly, "Yes."

In my bare feet I was still an inch taller than Huang. He went up on his toes to meet my gaze and dropped immediately down again when he saw my annoyance. He lowered his head and rubbed the envelope with a blue-mittened hand. I thought he would burst with nerves. I invited him to come in and sit down in my room until I was properly dressed.

The multiple layers of clothing Huang wore under his jacket gave him a lumbering, lumpy obesity. He had difficulty bending his elbows and bumped into the doorframe on his way in. He stumbled through the dark foyer and into my room.

The room was a shambles; there were papers and books in piles on the desk and floor, the bed was still unmade, beer bottles and glasses were lined up on the bookshelf, and, as often happened, my plastic desk lamp had tipped spontaneously over the edge of the desk and now shone crazily under the bed, illuminating thick dust, spilled paper clips, and a pair of chopsticks. On my tape player Patsy Cline was singing "Back in Baby's Arms."

I scooped a pile of clothes off the corner chair and motioned for Huang to sit down in it. He sat straight-backed and stiff-legged. With the tail of his scarf he wiped the mist from his glasses and stared out the window at the darkening winter sky, and at the bras and underwear I had hung from the windowlocks to dry.

The soft amber light of the table lamp made Huang look disappointed and sad. I dropped the clothes on the bed and returned to the bathroom to straighten myself out and to persuade myself that I should be gentle with Huang.

When I returned from the bathroom, I offered Huang a cup of tea. He raised a bulky mitten at me. "My ulcer," he said.

"Even tea aggravates it?"

"Too much tea, yes. I have already had my quota of tea for the day." He pressed the raised mitten gently, almost accidentally, to his soft cheek. "You know, because of my ulcer I have had to forgo some of life's greatest pleasures," he said.

"Yes, I know. It must be very frustrating."

"God, terrible," he agreed, shaking his head.

Huang fell silent then and stared around the room in his quizzical way, as though he had no idea why he had come here, and he hemmed and sighed and patted his mittens together. His stomach growled loudly. His thick hair, once so tidy, had grown longish with neglect and crept over his ears and collar, and the bags under his eyes seemed more pronounced that evening. I had an image of Huang tossing and turning sleeplessly in his bed at night.

"How's your wife doing in America?" I said.

"Fine."

"Does she like America?"

Huang shrugged. "She does not say."

"She doesn't tell you what America is like?"

"Not very much."

I stared at Huang; how could it be that Bai expressed no opinions about her American life to her husband, particularly when she had expressed some of her ideas in letters to me? I could only guess that what she had told him about America was not flattering and that Huang didn't want to offend me.

He said, "My wife is lonely and studies too hard. She says it is difficult to make friends in America. Her only American friend is your mother." He paused. "My wife cannot understand why so many Americans drive such long distances for no reason. For amusement. And everyone has a car."

My mother, who often took Bai out in Boston, had told me about Bai's aversion to the auto, how even the shortest of trips nauseated her to the point of vomiting. Bai, I knew, refused to ride even a bicycle in China, so it was no wonder the car unnerved her.

"Do you have a car?" Huang asked.

"A very old one," I said.

"My wife says every person in your family has a car."

This observation made me paranoid; what else, I wondered, did Bai tell Huang about my family? The comment about the cars sounded like a criticism to me, and I felt compelled to excuse my family's decadence. But before I could speak, Huang said, "I did not guess how much I would miss my wife, or how difficult it would be to live without her." He laughed sadly at the difficulty, opening the envelope in his lap. In it were applications for admission to Clark, Brandeis, and Illinois Universities, which Bai Yiping had sent him from Cambridge. She was eager for their daughter, a twenty-year-old student at a university in Beijing, to study in America. As Huang pulled the applications from the envelope, a slick slab of loose pages and brochures flopped from his lap to the floor. With a sigh of resignation Huang pulled off his mittens and lowered his pudgy self to the rug. "I wonder . . ." he said, raking up the papers, "do you think my daughter could possibly get a scholarship to one of these American schools?"

I told Huang I had little knowledge of the opportunities available to foreign students in the United States but that I supposed it was unlikely that an undergraduate from China would be accepted at an American university with a scholarship; a brilliant student of physics, possibly, but of English language and literature, most likely not.

Huang said, "Yes, my wife says the chance of acceptance is one out of ten, but we won't lose anything by trying. Myself, I am worried that my daughter's TOEFL scores may not be high enough. She has only got five hundred ninety. What is your opinion of that score?"

"Five hundred ninety is high. And if she can write a good essay, that should help."

"Perhaps you could give my daughter some advice? Perhaps after she writes her essay, you could look at it?" Huang spoke softly, addressing the rug. He didn't like to ask me for favors.

I found it disconcerting talking to the back of Huang's head, but he seemed reluctant to turn around and look at me. "Of course I will," I said.

At that moment Mitsuko Tokutomi burst into the room in a rush of cold air, laughing and calling my name before she'd even got through the foyer. She stopped short in the doorway with a rice bowl in one hand and a fashion magazine in the other and took in the spectacle of Huang Zhiye on the floor. Her eyes shone with amusement. She waved the magazine at Huang's figure, and with that exaggerated Japanese dismay she gasped, "Oh, my goodness! What has happened here?"

"Nothing serious, Mitsuko," I said, "Mr. Huang has dropped something. You remember Mr. Huang."

Mitsuko sat merrily on the arm of my chair and balanced the rice bowl on her knee. She bared a bright wedge of teeth. "Of course I remember Mr. Huang." She batted her shiny black bangs out of her eyes and tilted her head inquisitively toward Huang. "Huang, Huang," she said, "*Ni hao!* Nice to see you again! Can I ask you one thing? What do you think about Mr. Yang, the head of the Foreign Affairs Office?"

Huang peered cautiously over his shoulder at Mitsuko; her demanding grin and her swinging sneakered foot clearly disturbed him. He lifted himself into his chair and smiled at his lap. "I have heard about Yang."

Yang Shiren was an irksome subject not only with Mitsuko but with the entire foreign community. His most recent exploit had been to charge the foreigners ten yuan for a visit to a silk factory, a visit that was to be provided free by the provincial government. The foreigners from Hangzhou University were the only people out of two hundred who paid for the visit. It was not Yang's dishonesty that insulted us all so, but his supposition that we would not, in natural conversation with our colleagues at other schools, become aware of the truth. In this Yang displayed a thunderous stupidity.

Mitsuko's face was bursting with amusement. "Oh, really? What do you hear about him?!"

Huang shook his head. "Not important to say."

"Mr. Huang, you Chinese never seem to have an opinion. I wonder how come that is."

Huang said, "Opinions. Ha-ha."

Mitsuko said, "No opinions. Ha-ha. It's not so funny."

Huang peered at her. "We are different from you," he said. "Everything is different here."

Mitsuko opened her mouth to speak, and I interrupted her. "I think what Mitsuko means is that sometimes the Chinese seem hesitant to speak what's on their minds."

Mitsuko gave me a nudge of encouragement.

"Not hesitant," Huang protested.

"If not hesitant, how come no complaints?" Mitsuko demanded.

"You must understand, we have the Party, we have so many official committees, so much bureaucracy. We can bring trouble to ourselves."

"Party!" Mitsuko cried with laughter, "Foreign Affairs Office is no Party!"

Though Mitsuko displayed the standard nationalistic disdain for the Chinese, she managed to find endless humor in her life in China. At the beginning of the semester, in her apartment, she had told me that the people who lived in the building beyond the wall had a habit of peering through their windows at her when she was changing her clothes at night. "I got tired of that trick," she said, "so now what I do? I lift up my shirt and show my titties to them, on purpose," and to my dismay she went to the window, lifted her sweater, and demonstrated for me this brazen flashing. She turned her fugitive grin on me. "See how I do? And after that they run away! They don't know my face, so I don't care what they think. All they know is my body. Maybe they think I am a crazy Chinese!" Mitsuko laughed so hard at that idea that she had to lie down on the bed, and she kicked her heels in time with the laughter, like a child. Her laugh was a soulful, infectious gasping. She rolled from side to side and screeched at the ceiling; the idea of mixing up her identity with the Chinese! Preposterous!

The similarities between the Japanese and Chinese did not seem to frighten or annoy Mitsuko the way it did other Japanese, partly because she found numerous things to ridicule in her own country and partly because, beneath her contempt, she had a sort of admiration for the Chinese—for their artistic and musical ability, for their cuisine, and I sensed in her a low-grade envy for the hapless, unbuckled Chinese way of life.

Mitsuko raised the rice bowl from her knee and offered Huang some of the kelp that was in it. He turned it down with a polite wave of his hand, and Mitsuko's face fell. "You don't *like* it? Oh. Okay. But has vitamins and iron." She offered me some.

"No, thanks, Mitsuko," I said.

She shrugged and looked curiously around my room. "*Jintian wanshang nide fangjian bu ganjing,* huh?" she said. Your room's a mess tonight.

Huang laughed agreeably at Mitsuko's attempt at Chinese. "You speak Chinese," he said.

She laughed back at him. "Of course."

Mitsuko rose to her feet. "I can see you two are at business, so I will leave you alone." She put the bowl of kelp on my desk, pointed to my tape player, said to me, "When I hear this music, I really, really like your country," and went crashing out of the room.

Huang looked overjoyed to see her go. He asked me why I had never mentioned our trouble with Yang before. I told him I assumed he wouldn't be interested, that I guessed there was probably little he could do about it.

Huang looked wounded. "Of course I would be interested. I am your friend. And we have trouble with Yang too."

"Who has?"

"My wife and I, and our colleagues."

"What kind of trouble?"

"Inconvenient for me to say."

A nod seemed the only suitable response.

Huang continued, "You cannot understand what it is like for us. I am a Chinese, so I have to live like a Chinese and think like a Chinese." He looked anxiously at the ceiling. "This is not a good topic. We should discuss something else."

I supposed it would be fruitless for me to say I thought it was an excellent topic, so I suggested instead that we look over the applications. Huang looked anxiously around the room, twisting his fingers into a web. "You know," he said, as though he hadn't heard my suggestion, "I and many people have got into trouble for supposedly being too outspoken."

"Outspoken about what?"

Huang closed his eyes. "It is not something you should be burdened with."

"But we're friends."

Huang looked silently at me, drawn face-to-face with the essence of our friendship: it was a conditional friendship, one that distant political forces imposed limits on. He sighed. "Some professors get denounced for uttering a word against the Communist Party. Others get denounced for supposedly uttering words they have never said. If someone in the department doesn't like you, they can make trouble by spreading rumors of this sort."

Huang unbuttoned his collar, wiped the sweat from his forehead with the cuff of his jacket. "You Americans can protest if you are dissatisfied. We cannot."

"Why not?"

"Because we fear we will be sent out to a life in the country, to a place that would be bleak and backward and dreary. Our government has the power to do this. If a man does something they don't like, they can send him out. You know, every Saturday we must meet with our departments for political discussion meetings. But it is not a discussion. It is a lecture on Party decisions and policies. If I don't go, I will look bad, so I go."

Huang said that people his age felt they could not afford to disagree. There was too much to be lost. Younger people felt differently. They felt freer. "You may not see it in your students, because they like you, and you are a foreigner, but everywhere there is a new refusal among the young Chinese."

Huang said that sometimes it seemed that defiance for amusement was their main goal. If you told them something, they disagreed, just to disagree. If you said, "This music is good to listen to," they said, "It is not good. I will listen to another kind!" They were strictly reactionary.

Huang was on a downward roll. Thoughts raced out of him. He and his wife had been trying for years to get a better apartment in the university, but each year they were denied. They had even asked to be transferred to another university, but were denied that also. They had no choice but to accept the lot they had been given here at Hangzhou. Bai Yiping was Cantonese and had never wanted to come to Hangzhou, but she had been assigned to this university and this was where she had spent the past twenty years of her life. All year Huang had been defending her against people who claimed she did not deserve to be chosen for the Radcliffe exchange. They claimed she had had unfair connections, that she was not the best candidate for the scholarship, and that there were others who were better qualified. "No one is better qualified than my wife," Huang said, and with such conviction that I could not doubt him. "They are only people who also wanted the opportunity to go. Quarrelsome people."

Huang said that the kind of fighting and spying that went on his department was dangerous. It was the kind of thing that made people want to commit suicide. No one wanted to be out of favor with the bureaucrats and no one wanted to give up their desires.

Huang waved his hand feebly at me. "It's not something you should have to think about. You are far from your home. You have your own worries. And these are things we had best keep in our hearts."

"I'm sorry your wife is lonely."

"Thank you. I think she should get a job and save some money, but she is too busy about the studies. When I was in New Zealand, I got a job on my second day."

"Doing what?"

"Putting books back on the shelves in the library."

In the silence that followed, Huang and I stared at the now-black window. I thought of the ever-present construction sight across the yard. I said, "Mr. Huang, there seems to be so much construction going on in Hangzhou these days."

He said, "Yes, everything is getting much better since Mao died."

JAPAN

Mitsuko Tokutomi invited me to travel to Japan with her during the winter break; I accepted her invitation.

During our first few days in Japan Mitsuko and I stayed at her parents' house in a small town south of Tokyo. Mitsuko's parents owned a small hardware store, which fronted their house, and which Mitsuko described as being simply a hobby for her retired father. The family's real money was made by Mitsuko's mother, a stooped, mild-mannered woman in her late seventies, who happened to have an extraordinary aptitude for buying and selling stocks and bonds. Each morning as we sat cross-legged at the breakfast table eating vegetable stew and a shockingly expensive smoked salmon that Mitsuko's father drove sixty miles each week to purchase, Mitsuko's mother switched on the television, folded her thin arms up into the sleeves of her kimono, and watched the morning's trading activity. Her face assumed beatific poise as she listened to the quotations, the way another woman's would at the sound of a favorite old song on the radio. Eventually, with one eye on the television, Mrs. Tokutomi went to the telephone, dialed her broker, and told him what to buy and sell.

Mitsuko was proud of her mother's genius for money and told me that, long before it happened, her mother had predicted with stunning accuracy the Wall Street crash in October.

The Tokutomis had a small safe built into the wall of their living room, and one evening Mitsuko's father opened it to show me the hundreds of dollar bills he had stashed there; he had picked them up on one of his vacation trips to America and had saved them as a memento, the way I saved train-ticket stubs to remind me where I had been. That winter the dollar was at a record low in Japan, and when Mr. Tokutomi took the bright green bills out of the safe, Mitsuko laughed, *"Kodomo ginko!* Play money!"

We had arrived at Mitsuko's parents' house in the middle of a cold night; Mr. Tokutomi had met us at the airport and had driven us the two hours back to his house. On the flight from Hong Kong to Tokyo Mitsuko and I drank too much in celebration of my birthday, and now that I had sobered up a bit, I had a nauseating headache. The trip was long, and all I could see from the windows of the car was the wide and perfectly smooth highway, the bright blue Esso and Mobil signs, and the 7-Eleven stores along the way. I said to Mitsuko, "This could be Ohio."

She looked back at me from the front seat. "Right, but in Japan you never see cars broken down on the side of the highway, like in Ohio. Here all cars are new. No one breaks down." Mitsuko laughed so loudly that her father leaned away from her. Her face was bathed in the eerie green glow of lights on the control panel of the car; her teeth were like tiny green tiles.

When we arrived at Mitsuko's parents' house, I was exhausted and dazed. To get to the house, we had to walk through the hardware store, and in the darkness I hadn't noticed that everyone had taken off their shoes before they went into the house. In my winter boots I stepped over the threshold, but before I could do any damage, Mitsuko's mother, directly behind me, grabbed the hem of my coat and tugged me backward out again. Mortified by the slip, I asked Mitsuko to apologize to her mother for me.

"Never mind," said Mitsuko, delighting in my little gauchery. "We expect you will make many mistakes while you are here."

The tiny two-story house was all sharp angles and sliding paper doors, painted screens and tatamis. The floors were waxed wood, the furniture dark mahogany. Everything was pretty and so delicate I was afraid to lean on anything. We sat on pillows on the floor, and as we drank a midnight tea, Mitsuko and her mother kept pointing at the father's teeth and laughing at him. Mitsuko explained to me that the new set of false teeth her father had bought was much too big for his mouth and that to anyone who knew him he looked positively ridiculous. The father, a big, gentle, sheepish, gray-haired man in corduroy pants and a cashmere pullover laughed along with Mitsuko and covered his mouth with his hand.

Mitsuko's mother kept referring to me as "Roosevelt," because that was one of the few American names she was familiar with and because to her it sounded enough like Rosemary. She avoided looking too long at me, to be polite, but every time I turned around, I sensed she was watching me. And I watched her. She moved slowly and gracefully and was quiet. She had a kind face and the elegant, powdered, pampered look many older Japanese women shared. I had no idea what she was saying, but I could nevertheless see she had a sardonic sense of humor. She said things under her breath that sent her husband and Mitsuko into fits of laughter, though her own expression never changed. Her soft eyes had a slightly downward slant, and her voice was beguiling.

By the time I left Japan, I thought the most beautiful sound in the world was the voice of the older Japanese women; it was a quavering, undulant purring that reminded me of high notes softly blown through a wooden flute. I would hear that voice often, coming across public address systems in Tokyo, gently interrupting the silence on subways and buses to announce the stops and to welcome the people aboard. It had a deeply reassuring quality, like the voice of a grandmother consoling an anxious child. It was the absolute antithesis of the Chinese screech.

Mitsuko and I slept upstairs on futons on the floor. The room was comfortable, with soft lights and original calligraphy by Prime Minister Nakasone on the wall. The entire house was warmed by a complex central heating system. There was a Jacuzzi in this house, and a microwave oven, and futuristic toilets that pumped fresh water through a thin pipe above the back of the toilet so that the conservation-minded could wash their hands with the same water that went to fill the tank.

The next day Mitsuko and I had our hair cut at the barbershop next door. The barbers were Mr. and Mrs. Endo, an older couple who wore their hair in almost identical crew cuts—shorn to within a half inch of the scalp, their heads resembled cantaloupes. I pictured them spending all their free time cutting each other's hair, washing and snipping and going at each other with the electric shears. They were both very short and wore identical brown smocks with "Endo" embroidered over their hearts in cursive white stitching. Their small shop was cluttered but clean and warm on this bright but bitter-cold day, and the whole place smelled sweetly of pomade and shampoo. The sun came through the window and struck the tall jars of Barbasol a brilliant turquoise blue. The walls were sparkling mirrors.

The husband cut my hair and the wife cut Mitsuko's, and as they worked, they discussed Mitsuko's father's ridiculous new teeth, and Mitsuko laughed so hard the tears ran down her cheeks, and she pinched her eyes shut and rubbed her face with her hand. She howled and stomped her running shoes on the polished chrome footrest of her chair. Mrs. Endo smiled indulgently and held the scissors and comb over her head, away from Mitsuko, as if to keep her from flailing into them and hurting herself. Mitsuko seemed to enjoy every single moment of her life.

Mr. Endo fastened a vinyl bib around my neck and washed my hair gently and for a long time. He was silent. His short, blunt fingers were surprisingly soothing against my scalp; that and the fragrant shampoo had a mesmerizing effect on me. I stared at Endo's head, hovering just above mine in the mirror. His face was a study of crags and lines and shadows, his eyes were puffy slits. A face like that didn't belong in a beauty salon. It belonged in the boiler room of a fish cannery. He asked Mitsuko to tell me that he had concocted this nice shampoo himself and was just beginning to market it. He held up a plastic bottle that said *Endo* and turned it so that I could see the label. He touched my hair as though it were spun gold, studying it in the light, combing it carefully. His silver scissors whispered around my head. He said to Mitsuko, "Your friend's hair is very soft."

The last haircut I had had took place in a ramshackle windowless shed on a street in Hangzhou. The woman there had stuffed dirty towels into the collar of my shirt and used what looked like gardening shears to cut my hair, dry. The only light in that shop was the light that fell in through the open door.

At one point in the cutting I looked in the mirror and realized that Mrs. Endo had lathered Mitsuko's entire face and was shaving it with a straight-edged razor. She shaved the chin, the cheeks, the forehead, and all but a sharp line of the eyebrows. She wiped the razor on her smock with a couple of quick flicks of her wrist, then moved on to the throat, the nose, the temples, the neck. She shaved right up to the edge of Mitsuko's large dark lips.

"Mitsuko," I said, "you shave your *face*?!"

Mitsuko murmured sleepily behind Mrs. Endo's hand. "Of course. You don't shave yours?"

"Never. We don't do that."

"Wow. Too bad. You should try it. It feels beautiful. We do it. Japanese think the smooth face is the most beautiful face."

Mrs. Endo held Mitsuko's head still, with her fingers spread over Mitsuko's forehead, as though she were palming a basketball, and she scraped gently with the razor, inching down the ridge of Mitsuko's nose.

"In a hundred years I wouldn't do that," I said. But though it horrified me a little, I was enthralled by the practice, even envious. Confronted with this exotic Japanese practice, I felt provincial and deprived. I imagined this was how Ming Yu sometimes felt when she stared admiringly at my bracelets and earrings, then said, "It's not for intellectuals."

When the shaving was done, Mrs. Endo draped a steaming white cloth over Mitsuko's face, and Mitsuko let out a deep sigh. As we stepped out of the shop and into the bright sunlight, Mitsuko glowed.

We walked back to the house. A group of schoolboys in navy-blue uniforms and striped neckties rode past us on shiny new bicycles. The town, with its clean narrow streets, small white shops, and sparkling windows reminded me of a village in Switzerland.

That evening Mrs. Tokutomi showed me her collection of kimonos. She had scores of them laid out in tall, custom-made shallow-drawered cedar bureaus. The kimonos were unspeakably beautiful, more like art than clothing, and were made of heavy silk and satin, with elaborate designs embroidered into them in gold and silver threads. They were olive, salmon, magenta, puce, and silver, and there was a funeral kimono all of black but for a brightly colored dragon that snaked around the knees. Mitsuko said some of the kimonos were worth over ten thousand dollars each.

"My mother wants to know if you would like to have one," she said.

I was stunned. "Of course not," I said.

"Why not?"

I couldn't think of a good reason why not, but the offer embarrassed me.

Mitsuko said, "My mother always remembers how generous the Americans were with the Japanese after the war. And she remembers how nice was General MacArthur, and now she feels sorry for the Americans. She thinks America is sliding downhill."

All the more reason not to accept a kimono, I thought.

Mitsuko and I left her parents' house and spent a few days in Mitsuko's tiny apartment in Tokyo. One of the first things Mitsuko told me about Tokyo was that suicide was very popular there; in the past year or two there had been five suicides in her building alone. She also expressed the Tokyoite's opinion that Tokyo was the only place in the world that mattered, and she laughed, as if she, for one, knew better. She said the people in Tokyo were the most obsessively self-conscious people in the world; in public bathrooms the women flushed the toilet twice, once to cover up the sound of their pee, and a second time to get rid of it. "If they get a run in their stocking, they leave work immediately to buy another pair." Tokyo housewives, as prim and repressed as they seemed, had affairs with their children's tutors, or even took up "high-class" prostitution as a second job while the children were at school. Many women who had engaged in premarital sex rushed to have their hymens surgically reconstructed before they were married "so that their husband will think he is getting a fresh wife."

At a large temple in the city Mitsuko led me up to the edge of a bin of burning incense and said, "The smoke from this incense is supposed to be like special medicine. They say if you rub it on your head, it makes you smart. Rub it on your face, you will be beautiful. Rub it on your arm, arm gets strong. Rub it on your breasts, your breasts get bigger."

She looked critically at my chest, gave me a nudge, and said, "Maybe *you* need to try that!"

Mitsuko had told me a lot of things about Tokyo, but none of what she said could match the stunning efficiency or cleanliness of the place, and neither of us could have guessed how alienated I would feel there. In Tokyo there were no apparent struggles, no fights or strife. People waited in orderly lines and begged each other to go first. Everything was mechanized, sparkling, and humming hypnotically. On Tokyo's streets all the cars were white, the fashion that year. On the subway the people sat straight in their expensive clothes, knees together, hands folded neatly in their laps, not looking at each other and trying not to touch. No one pushed to get off the subway, no one ran or shouted, and they apologized—compulsively—for bumping into each other. I caught myself staring in dumbfounded fascination at the sparkling linoleum subway floor, cleaner possibly than the dinner plates in our dining room in Hangzhou. It stunned me when the Japanese shopgirls came out to the front of the store to greet me with a smile and a bow, and I watched in disbelief at the way they packaged a purchase: They wrapped it in colored tissue paper, boxed it, wrapped the box, tied it with satin ribbon, and placed it carefully in a bag within a glossy bag. They did everything quickly and politely. They bowed from the waist whenever I turned toward them. They looked wealthy and clean in their designer clothes. Their long black hair was like satin.

The discomfort I felt in Tokyo was directly related to the five months I had just spent in China; it unnerved me that though they lay side-by-side, and though they had shared a written language, China and Japan seemed like the two most dissimilar places in the world. While the Chinese had a reckless kind of curiosity about me, the Japanese, for all their politeness, seemed wary and even disdainful. When they saw me approaching on the street, a shock flashed for a millisecond across their faces, and then they looked fiercely away. They were no less aware of my presence than the Chinese were, but they chose to pretend I wasn't there. That seemed, to me, like a very Western thing to do, and it had a bad effect on me. I wanted to rush out into the middle of the street and shout, "I'm right here!"

I never thought I would miss the gasping, pointing Chinese hordes, but in Tokyo I missed them. I asked Mitsuko why the people seemed so uptight about me. "They are actually very curious," she said. "If you could not see them, they would stare at you a lot." She also told me that blue-jeaned, backpacking young Western travelers sometimes settled in her neighborhood for periods of time and that her neighbors referred to them as "white trash."

I left Tokyo alone. I was sick with a bad cold and a rattling cough that had plagued me for three weeks and seemed to be getting worse. I spent two days in Hong Kong, then returned to China by train to Guangzhou. Chinese New Year was fast approaching, and everyone in China was traveling to visit relatives and friends, carrying huge bundles and bags of gifts. Xu Ban had told me, "Rose, traveling in China is not traveling at all; it is suffering," and that was truer now than at any other time of the year. This was the first time I had traveled alone in China, and I felt excited about that—and nervous. Though I never worried about crime in China, never thought twice about being mugged, I had a vague, floating fear of China's enormous bureaucratic forces and of that unfathomable population, the very idea of which could paralyze me in the rare moments I allowed myself to think about it, and I feared the recklessness, the freakish Chinese accidents that seemed to happen with startling frequency. Only ten days before, Mitsuko and I had read in the Hong Kong papers about a bad train accident in Yunnan. According to the report, ninety-four people had been killed.

The first person I saw when I passed through the customs check was a middle-aged Chinese woman dressed in conservative Western clothes—a tweed skirt, a pink blouse and sweater, an expensive raincoat, and black high heels. Her hair was held back in a loose ponytail with a polka-dot ribbon. She had a black umbrella hooked on her arm. She looked like a housewife from Connecticut. She marched up to me amid the throngs of travelers and said in friendly, flawless English, "May I help you in some way?"

It made me wary when Chinese strangers wanted to help me, for their need always seemed greater than my own. "In what way can you help me?" I said to the woman, without interrupting my advance on the front door.

"I can help you buy a train ticket," the woman said sweetly, grabbing my small bag out of my hands and hurrying it out to the front of the station and into a soft rain.

"It's very kind of you," I said, catching up to the woman, "but I think I can get the train ticket myself."

The woman laughed dismissively, puffed up her umbrella with a tidy whoosh and snap, and positioned it over my head. "No!" she said with a tight smile. "Just look over there. They have been trying for three days to get tickets."

I looked at the huge parking lot in front of the Guangzhou station: It was a nightmare of confusion and chaos. Thousands of peasants with mountains of luggage were camped out on the wet ground in front of the station, sleeping, eating, arguing and playing cards, and hoping against hope that they would be able to buy a ticket. Some of them were sick and vomiting on the ground, some had live chickens and ducks with them. It was a gray-blue sea of cotton clothing and luggage.

I stared at the woman; her eyes were hard as marbles. "Even foreigners are not getting tickets easily!" she said.

"If that's true, how do you think you can help me to get a ticket?"

She leaned toward me, widened her eyes for emphasis. "I know someone inside." She pointed in the direction of the station ticket office and leaned back on her high heels and gave me a knowing look that said, And don't you think for a minute I don't! Then, girlishly, with a hand raised to her mouth, she giggled into my shoulder, "Of course, there will only be a small handling fee. . . ."

I snatched my bag out of the woman's hand and put an abrupt end to her assistance. I was determined to get a ticket by myself.

Wary of the reckless, avaricious Guangzhou taxi drivers, I bought a map and walked the mile to the Medical College, where my status as a foreign teacher would allow me to spend the night cheaply. Most of the medical students had gone home for the holiday, and the college, with its wet palm trees and gray rock gardens, looked dead. But for two young maids I was the only person in the grim guest house. My room was a stark cell with nothing in it but an armchair and a double bed shoved into a corner. The sheets on the bed were pink nylon. The curtains seemed to be made from scraps of mosquito netting and old cotton trousers.

I sat in the chair and stared out the window at a squalid tenement across a muddy lot. This was probably the most insignificant spot in the world, and in my entire life I never imagined myself in a place like it. My head was pounding and my sinuses were bursting.

I left my bag in the room and walked back to the China International Travel Service office, next door to the train station. Inside, fifteen foreigners sat on benches along the wall, thumbing through guidebooks and biting their nails. At the long ticket counter a lone young woman sat on a stool with a newspaper raised before her face; I could see her visored cap and the tops of her ears just above the paper's masthead. It worried me that nobody was doing business with her, nevertheless I approached the counter and told her I wanted to buy a ticket to Hangzhou. She ignored me. As she turned a page of the newspaper, I caught a glimpse of her narrow shoulders and one side of her face; she was fashion-model pretty, had large eyes, dark eyebrows, a dark red mouth. The big cap looked ridiculous on her, like part of a costume for a school play.

I asked the woman again, a little more loudly this time, about a ticket. She turned another page, continued to ignore me. I wanted to bat the newspaper out of her tiny little hands with my umbrella. "Hangzhou," I said. The woman shifted in her seat, turned another page. The people on the bench looked on with fading interest. A huge, Swedish-looking man with a blond beard down to his sternum said, "She is not speaking today."

I could feel myself stumbling into a familiar anger, a tangle of frustration and humiliation that Chinese officials inspired in me. I borrowed a pencil and paper from the Swede and wrote in carefully fashioned Chinese characters, "I want to buy a ticket to Hangzhou," and I folded the paper up into a tiny square and tossed it over the top of the *People's Daily*, half-hoping it would knock the girl on the nose on its way into her lap.

In a rush of air the newspaper crashed down onto the counter. The woman put her palms flat on top of it. Her glare met mine. "What do you want?" she snapped in Chinese.

"I wrote you a note," I said.

She brushed the note off her lap without looking at it and said there were no more tickets to Hangzhou, or to anywhere else for that matter, and that if I wanted a ticket, I would have to go into the main ticket room in the station and get the ticket myself "just like everybody else."

That was very bad news, and it was why the other foreign people were sitting there doing nothing: it could take days to get a ticket that way, and even under the most favorable of conditions the public ticket rooms in China could be a terrifying experience.

I stomped out of the CITS office and headed across the parking lot toward the station. I was lightheaded with determination. The sky was the color of a brand-new ax blade, and though the rain had stopped, ominous thunder grumbled overhead, racing from north to south in an echoing arc. I picked my way through the sleeping people, the luggage, and straw baskets, the shoulder poles, and the squawking ducks, and stepped into the ticket room in the station.

My heart sank as I stood in the doorway; the vast, hot, high-ceilinged room was a riot of people pushing and arguing, and the room was so smoky and dim I could hardly make out the features of the faces that rushed around me. The people were packed in hip-to-hip, and they shifted and swayed against each other like seaweed in a gentle current. I was afraid to submit myself to it, feared I might never come out again, but what was the alternative? Days spent waiting at the Medical College while my money ran out and I got sicker and sicker? Through the haze I could make out some of the place-names above the numerous barred-in ticket windows along the far wall. I headed for Window 8 and stood in what I thought was a line, but the lines were blending and crossing, and people who thought they were in one line ended up standing in an entirely other one, and yet another. It was impossible to stay on course. Everyone around me seemed puzzled as to which line they were actually in, and they shrugged and inched forward, hoping for the best. From time to time a little fight would break out somewhere in the room, and like a wave the entire crowd would begin to shift toward one wall, everyone leaning against everyone else, trying to regain their balance. My whole body was tensed in defense. Sweat ran down my back, down the backs of my knees. I saw an elderly woman not far from me slapping the head of a young man in front of her; he in his heavy leather boots was standing on her foot. Again and again she slapped; she was nearly hysterical. Oblivious—or obdurate—the man didn't move.

For four hours I stood in that room; sometimes I even seemed to be losing ground, slipping backward toward the door. I asked several people who seemed to be waiting with me whether this was the correct line for Hangzhou; one person said it was; another told me with great authority to go to Window 7; and a third said Window 12. I stayed where I was, partly because I doubted their advice and partly because moving through that crowd seemed an impossible feat. The faces around me were ashen and veiled in a pall of anxiety.

When I got to within five people of a ticket window, I saw there were iron barriers set up there to force people into some semblance of a line. And I saw a station official in a green uniform standing at the head of my line and realized, to my horror, that he was allowing people to cut in front of us in return for small gifts, cigarettes, and money, and that people who had made it to the window were stuffing cartons of cigarettes through the bars to coax the worker into giving them a good ticket. I knew this was the way things worked in China, but this was the first time it affected me personally. I felt desperate. The Chinese people were breaking their backs to survive, and people in positions of power were only making life more difficult.

Heads and hands beat against the bars of the window, trying to get the ticket seller to turn his attention to them. And there were shouts from within the ticket room, and curses, and then the window slammed shut until the people backed off, and when it reopened, the heads went banging up against it again. I dreaded my own turn at the window, feared I'd forget the little Chinese I knew, or that I'd be injured in the crush. My heart was racing wildly, my eyes were dry and throbbing in my head. Shoulders and faces crashed roughly into me again and again. When I got up near the window, a man, waved on by the attendant, tried to step in front of me, and before I had time to think about it, my hand was flat against his chest, pushing. The man backed away, frightened by the look of disgust I gave him.

When I reached the ticket window, the man behind the bars gave me a bored look and said, "Give me your work card."

My heart skipped a beat in hope. I handed him the little red booklet. He opened it, looked at my picture, read my name, looked at my face, and sat there for a moment, as if trying to decide how he felt about me. He frowned and pushed the book back to me. "No more tickets to Hangzhou. Come back at nine o'clock."

Grubby hands full of money shot past my face and through the bars, and a screeching woman pressed her hot ear to mine, trying to see the man's face. She shouted so loudly that I seemed to feel her voice in my own lungs. Nine o'clock was three hours from now, which meant I would have to go back to the beginning of the line immediately and start all over again.

"What about to Shanghai?" I said, voice trembling.

"Wrong window for Shanghai! Plus, no tickets for Shanghai!" The man seemed to be gloating. All I could see of him were his large, perfect teeth, and behind him I could see greenish walls and bright lights. I didn't believe there were no tickets to Hangzhou, and in my feeble Chinese I tried to tell him so. "This is not good" and "You cheat me" were the harshest epithets I could come up with.

The man shrugged and shut the window in my face.

I made my way outside, heartbroken and furious, and sat on a low stone wall beneath a tree. The decorative purple-and-green cabbages planted at the base of the tree seemed hateful and absurd. Why plant pretty cabbages to look at when you couldn't get the people from one place to the next?

It was dark now. Raindrops fell softly on the leaves

above my head. I was starving and dehydrated, my clothes were damp with sweat, and in the hot room my cough had worked itself up to a constant, racking wheeze. My forehead and cheeks were burning. All around me people moved in a frenzy through the rain. Guangzhou's public buses roared up to the curb, spewed out hundreds of people, and roared off again. Taxis cut each other off, their windshield wipers thumping madly askew, their headlights illuminating the slashing raindrops and the city's garish billboards advertising televisions and refrigerators. Many of the people who'd been sleeping on the ground had moved across the street and were taking shelter under an overpass. I coughed so hard I had to lean over my knees. There was lightning then, and thunder, and for a brief moment I imagined having to stay in Guangzhou for the rest of my life.

"You know what it is?" I heard a woman's voice say behind me. "It's the damn Mao Zedong."

I turned around; an impossibly tall woman was speaking to me from the other side of the cabbage patch. She had straight black hair down to her shoulders and scholarly wire-rim glasses and a big leather bag on her shoulder. She came over to me with a striding gait and sat down next to me on the wall. She pointed angrily at the train station and said, "It's the damn Mao Zedong. All his fault." Her face was damp and angry. She had sharp green eyes. Her name was Bettina Klein, she was from Germany, was in her late thirties, and for three years had been a student at Beijing University, and never in her entire time in China had she seen anything as disorganized as this scene right here. Since morning she had been trying to get a ticket back to Beijing.

"I vow to get a ticket!" she said, wielding her own fist.

"I do too," I said, impressed by this stranger's energy.

"But I don't think we will get a ticket!"

I shook my head. "Me neither."

That night I walked all the way back to the Medical College through the dark, tumbled into the bed, and tumbled immediately out again when I realized the bed was sodden with water. Lying in it was like lying in a puddle. Water—somehow related to the bathroom upstairs—had leaked down the wall and onto the bed. I wrapped myself up in my jacket and lay crosswise at the very foot of the bed, the only place still dry. I shivered and coughed all night and thought how I would thank God if I got through the rest of this year alive.

I woke at dawn the next day. My feet were black and blue from being stepped on the day before. I sat in the armchair and ate some peanuts and an apple I had in my bag, and at nine o'clock I headed, full of dread, back to the train station.

As I passed by the CITS office, I saw some foreigners waiting outside. They seemed hopeful that there might be tickets that day, and I decided to wait around with them on the chance that something might happen. Anything to put off going back into the hellish ticket room. Standing there I fell into conversation with a woman from New York, Ruth Dinerman, who was teaching that year in the north of China and was traveling now with a kind of guide from her university, a Chinese teacher named Wang, who had been assigned to accompany her on her travels. Ruth was small and had curly black hair and a pretty, impish face. She seemed thoughtful and self-reliant, and I could not imagine why she would want to saddle herself with a guide. She told me she was debating where to go next on her trip—it had come down to wherever she could get tickets to. She decided to try Hangzhou, which may have been lucky for me, for when we went inside to buy our tickets, very quickly, almost as a matter of course, a CITS worker—not the wretch from the day before—had put Ruth and Wang and me together on one ticket to Hangzhou. I didn't mind that this meant I had to travel on the train with Ruth and Wang.

I was elated to have got a ticket, ecstatic beyond all proportion.

When I mentioned to the worker that I had suffered
hours in the train station the day before, he said, "Why did
you do that? We had tickets here."

Our train was to leave at 6:30 the next morning. Ruth
suggested I stay that night in her hotel room with her in
order to make our early departure easier. We arranged to
meet at the hotel at dinnertime, and I left Ruth and Wang
and spent the rest of that day wandering around the streets
of Guangzhou. I ran into Bettina Klein again, and when I
told her of my luck with the ticket, she flew into a fury;
she had checked into an expensive hotel simply for the privilege of using their private ticket office and, having no luck,
had bought a plane ticket back to Beijing. All together she
had spent five hundred yuan.

That day I met several foreign people who had arrived
in Guangzhou from Hong Kong but were leaving immediately because they hadn't been able to get tickets to anywhere else in China. For a country so eager for foreign
tourism and trade, this seemed like a pathetic state of affairs.

I wandered around the city that afternoon, through the
gardens and back streets. I walked over the river and back
again and bought four works of art from a sidewalk calligra-
pher. Though the day had started out clear and sunny, by
the time I went into the New China bookstore in the late
afternoon, the sky was nearly black with clouds and I was
feeling feverish and tired.

In the bookstore I found two more photographic Chinese history books and two old propaganda posters of Mao
and his associates. The posters so fascinated me that I asked
the salesman to give me five of each of them. He counted
the posters out, rolled them up, and wrapped them in brown
paper. "Why?" he said, handing them to me.

"Why what?"

"Why buy these pictures?"

"I think they're interesting," I said.

"What's interesting about them?"

The salesman had a friendly, crooked smile and rotting teeth. His hair was twisted into a shaggy permanent, and he wore tight jeans and a blue pullover sweater with *OK!* woven into it in red threads. His question was sincere. He couldn't see what I saw in those posters, and I had to think carefully about my answer. I thought it might even be a kind of perverse interest, because in fact there was something slightly hideous about the posters. They were at least twelve years old. They were photographs, but they had been tinted and treated and touched up so much they looked like paintings. One of the posters depicted Mao and five other leaders standing at a table after what had obviously been a very successful meeting in the Great Hall of the People. Behind them I could make out less significant Party members milling about before a red velvet curtain. The title of the poster, written in red characters, was "Comrade Mao Zedong, Comrade Zhou Enlai, Comrade Liu Shaoqi, Comrade Zhu De, Comrade Deng Xiaoping, and Comrade Chen Yun together." The comrades' faces were the warm colors of ripe peaches and apricots, they appeared to be wearing bronze lipstick, and their short hair bristled and shone with a reassuring gray around the ears. They were dressed in identical Mao suits in various shades of blue and brown, and everyone was turned smiling toward Mao in a congratulatory way, as though he had said some unbelievably pithy thing just before the breakup of the meeting. Chen Yun had his hand raised toward Mao, as if to shake, and Liu Shaoqi, who had no idea what misery was in store for him, smiled at Mao in an almost doting way. Deng Xiaoping, the only one among them still alive, stood at Mao's right, grinning and tiny, like an eager little schoolboy with a whiffle haircut and streaks of gray blown into the hair around his ears. How happy they looked! The insignificant Party members lurking in the background were hidden in a shade of brownish light. They had blurred features. They looked like Chinese ghosts. The contrast between them and the principal players was stark and further emphasized the idolatrous slant of the poster. The whole thing seemed shamelessly false to me, and that was why I could not stop staring at it.

I realized I didn't have the vocabulary to tell the man what I felt when I saw these posters. "It's history," I said finally.

"But why buy so many?"

"My friends would like to have them too."

"American friends?"

I nodded. "We don't have these pictures in America." As far as I could see, the Chinese didn't really have them around much either. I had been in six or seven different Chinese bookstores and had never seen posters quite like these. In fact it seemed particularly strange to find them in Guangzhou, China's most Westernized, capitalistic city.

The salesman shook his head at me.

"You don't think they're interesting?" I asked.

He pointed to a poster of Madonna in black lace farther down the wall. "She is interesting."

"Who is she?"

The man's face seemed to crack in two. He rocked back and forth on his heels; he had never heard anything so funny. "I don't think you are American at all!" said he, taking my money and turning away.

On my way out of the bookstore I saw a large crowd of people gathered at a counter near the door scrambling to get copies of some new book kept in stacks behind the counter. The salesgirls were practically flinging the books over people's heads into their upheld hands. Three people grabbed onto one copy at once, and a bitter battle ensued over who should take it. I tried to see what the book was, but with all the struggle it was impossible for me to make out the characters in the title.

Through the store window I could see the rain falling again and people bicycling by in their plastic ponchos. I tucked the posters and the two photography books inside my jacket and went out onto the street. The rain had turned the already filthy street into a river of mud and pebbles.

Just outside the door a middle-aged woman stood, holding a copy of that book in her hands; in the fray the paper cover had been ripped almost completely off the front of the book. With a look of deep concern the woman inspected the tear, smoothing her hand over the cover and fitting the jagged pieces together again, and again and again, as if by sheer hope she might restore it to its proper form. The rain fell hard on her bare head and dragged the curls of her perm down flat into her eyes. She had an ugly face with thick lips and a flat nose and glasses. She wore a baggy blue jacket, baggy gray pants, and muddy cotton slippers on her feet. I guessed at her life, her depressed husband in his T-shirt, her dingy cold-water kitchen, the damp bed, the sheets she washed by hand, the vase of plastic flowers on a rickety bureau, the moss on the walls of her tiny apartment, the nosy neighbors, a numbing job threading bobbins in a silk factory, political-education meetings, the second child she couldn't have.

The woman's face seemed to swell up with sorrow as she looked at the precious spoiled book. Her disappointment was so strong I couldn't stand to watch her anymore, and I turned around until I was facing the bookstore window. There was a dusty stack of dictionaries for a display there. I heard myself sob, felt hot tears running down my cheeks. I put my hand to my mouth, and the tears rolled over my fingers. I pulled my umbrella down close to my head to hide myself. I closed my eyes and thought I might howl. The history books and posters, so heavy and awkward under my jacket, seemed, in that moment, as absurd as the decorative cabbages, and I wanted to be rid of them, to let them drop from my waist to the sidewalk. A sound escaped my mouth. In a minute I felt someone standing beside me; the woman with the book, peering up under the edge of the umbrella, curls snaking into her eyes like black noodles. She looked anxiously at me, and when she saw my foreign features, her anxiety seemed to increase, as though she felt it was part of her civic duty to make everything right with me.

"Miss," the woman said softly, "what's the problem? Are you sad?"

"I am not sad," I said. I told the woman that I would be fine, and smiled to show I was already on my way to recovering. She nodded her head and retreated, shuffling through the mud in her soggy slippers, clutching the wrecked book, satisfied that what I had said was true.

What I had said *was* true—it was not sadness that made me cry but relief. I was relieved to be back in China after the rigidity and coldness of Japan. Try though they might, the Chinese could not hide that they were human. Their struggles were always right out here on the street for everyone to see, and I felt grateful for that, and for their vitality, and was remorseful for whatever criticisms I had had of them.

A NEW
COAT

On our two-day train trip to Hangzhou I got to know Ruth Dinerman and her guide, Wang, a bit better. I liked Ruth, but Wang was an overbearing know-it-all, and prideful. Ruth paid for his hotels, meals, and train tickets in return for his minimal and sometimes annoying services as translator and guide. Ruth told me that in her Chinese university that was the way things were done; foreigners were not considered capable of traveling alone, and the prescribed procedure was to take a Chinese person with you wherever you went.

Since Ruth and Wang planned to spend a few days in Hangzhou, I invited Ruth to stay in my room, which might be nicer than a hotel and would at least save her some money. Ruth accepted the invitation, and Wang stayed in a Chinese hotel, an arrangement that seemed to please them both.

On our second evening back in Hangzhou Ruth and I ran into George Greatorex on the street. He had a blue Mao cap on his head and a scarf wrapped around the lower part of his face, and through the mist I at first mistook him for a Chinese man. George was one of the few people in the university who hadn't gone traveling during the winter break; he said he was planning to leave China in a few days and needed time to gather his things together. At that moment he was on his way to see Ming Yu, who would be leaving Hangzhou that night to spend the New Year with her parents in Wuxi. George and Ming were going to make dinner in Ming's room, and George invited us to join them.

This was to be the last time George would see Ming Yu before he left China, so it seemed odd that he would want me and a complete stranger to spend the evening with them. I told George I thought our presence might be an imposition, but he insisted that we come, said he had a special bottle of wine that we could help him drink, and as if to tempt us, he lifted the bottle halfway out from within the folds of his jacket.

"Well, maybe we'll come later," I said. "After you've had your dinner."

"Fine," George said.

When Ruth and I arrived at Ming Yu's room, she was putting pots and dishes away in the makeshift closet and getting her bags together for her trip. Dressed in a soft white sweater, she looked tiny and fragile and surprisingly happy. "You came back," she said when she saw me. Her eyes burned with excitement.

George, too, seemed happy, though he was unusually quiet. He sat in the desk chair, and with his thin legs crossed and the scarf around his neck and the glass of wine cupped in his hands he looked like an aging priest. I introduced Ruth to Ming, and we sat on the bed and chatted and drank George's wine.

Ming talked about what it would be like being home in Wuxi, seeing her brothers and her parents, the gifts that would be given, the food they would eat, and the old friends she would see. At eight o'clock she said, "I had better prepare to catch the bus now." She put on a handsome new coat I had never seen her in before, a reefer of thick green wool, with a straight cut and narrow lapels. I admired the coat and asked Ming where she got it.

"I had a tailor make it."

"Where did you get the pattern?"

"I had no pattern. I asked the tailor to copy it from a

magazine photograph I found of President John Kennedy's sister. She had a coat like this."

I could believe that. "It looks nice," I said.

"It has a silk lining," George said almost proudly, and Ming showed us all the lining. Her long black hair hung around her face as she looked down at herself.

George, Ming, Ruth, and I went out of the building and walked through the campus to the university gate. Ruth and I were on our way into the city to have dinner and would accompany Ming on the bus. At the gate the guard stopped Ming and asked her to show him the contents of the pack on her back. When I asked her why he was doing that, she said, "When we leave for holiday, we have to do it. They want to be sure students and teachers do not take anything belonging to the university when they go home for vacation."

"Like in a prison," George said.

As we stood at the curb waiting for the bus that would take us into the city, Ming said happily, "I hate for people to see me off, and at the same time I love it."

The long double bus roared up the street through the darkness and into the misty yellow circle of light thrown down from the streetlight. Ruth and I climbed onto the bus, and George and Ming said good-bye briefly. Ming got on the bus, and we all looked out the window at George in his cap, standing under the streetlight holding his bicycle by its handles.

As Ruth and I prepared to get off the bus at our stop, Ming stood up, kissed me on the cheek, and said cheerfully, "I will see you in a few weeks!"

We jumped off the bus, and Ruth said, "George paid for that coat."

"What makes you think that?"

Ruth shrugged. "I just know."

———

A few days later George left Hangzhou virtually without notice. I said good-bye to him standing in the hallway outside his room. He gave me a shoebox full of things to give to Ming Yu when she returned, things he had had in his room that he wasn't taking with him: a bottle of ink, some strong light bulbs, some paper, postage stamps, envelopes, a book about the Japanese invasion of Nanjing, a Baltimore Orioles baseball cap, and a photograph of himself that I had taken. Before I went back to my room, George gave me his address and said, "Write to me in England."

"I will," I said, though I knew in my heart I probably wouldn't. I had spent a lot of time talking with George that semester and had found many of our conversations enjoyable. I sometimes had dinner with him in the restaurant across the street from the Experts' Building, and when I felt depressed or cynical about China, George's commiserating company was oddly comforting. But there was a dark side of George I didn't know. There was something tragic about him, and his bitterness sometimes made him seem cruel.

That night I was correcting some old commentaries my students had written in response to an essay on the problems of homeless women in New York City. I had finished one or two papers when I heard a knock on my door, and before I had a chance to get up and answer it, the visitor opened the door and walked into the foyer. I thought what an unnerving Chinese habit that was, and it seemed very odd to me that while walls were all-important in China, a door could mean so little.

The visitor was Xu Ban. He walked into my room and stood before me and said seriously, "Rose, the train crash in Yunnan."

"Yes, the train crash in Yunnan," I said.

"You have heard of it?"

"Yes, I have. I heard it was very bad."

Xu looked intently at me, nodding his head. "I am afraid Christina was on that train."

The hair at the back of my neck prickled up. "She was?"

"I am afraid she was," Xu said sadly.

I stared at Xu in horror, waiting for the next sentence, but he said nothing, wrapped his arms around himself. I thought of Christina's parents. *"Well?"* I said. My voice sounded loud in my ears.

Xu smiled broadly. "Wonder of wonders, Christina is fine! We had a phone call from her, and some people saw her on the television news in the hospital in Kunming. She has traveled to Hong Kong now for the rest of her holiday. She will be back in Hangzhou in a few days. Though many people were killed, Christina has not been killed at all. Beginner's luck! Ha-ha!"

A few nights later Christina returned from her travels looking pale and thin. We sat on her bed, and she told me about the train crash. She had been sharing a cabin with a Swede, a Chinese man, and her Hong Kongese friend, Zhang Bin, who was a student that year at Hangzhou University. In the middle of the night Christina was awakened by a heavy bump. "It felt like the train had gone over a rock on the tracks," she said, and the next thing she found herself on her hands and knees on the floor of the cabin in the pitch dark. The floor, she later realized, was actually the ceiling, for the car had turned over. She heard a breath rasping heavily in the darkness near her and thought it was her friend, Zhang Bin, dying. She crawled around until her hand struck another hand—Bin's hand, she thought—and she held on to that hand until eventually the breathing stopped completely. As she tried to get out of the car, through the window, she came upon her watch, which she had hung on a hook above the berth. When she went out the window, she met Zhang

Bin there. His face had been slammed into the edge of the little table in the cabin and his lips were bleeding and his front teeth were cracked in half. It was one-thirty in the morning and completely dark. Christina and Bin and some other people sat on the ground, and eventually they saw people, other passengers, searching in the darkness with cigarette lighters. Someone led them to the mail car, where they sat until morning. Christina said she saw headless people. Some of the cars had gone over the edge of a steep cliff, and others were completely flattened. They shivered in the mail car, with people bleeding to death all around them. At daylight local peasants came to gawk, or to help out in whatever small way they could, but it was seven hours before real help came in the form of soldiers, who pointed a gun at Christina and ordered her to take the film out of her camera and give it to them, as though she might have had the presence of mind to take photographs of the carnage.

At the hospital Christina and Bin waited hours for help. A doctor told Christina that 158 people had been killed in the crash, then officials showed up and ordered the doctors not to reveal any more numbers, and officially the number of dead was reduced to 94, the number I had read in the Hong Kong paper. The cause of the accident was speed; the train had been traveling too fast on a downgrade and as it went around a bend the end cars got caught in a whiplash and went over the edge of the cliff, pulling the rest of the train onto its side.

Christina was comparatively unscathed by the crash— some of her fingers were black and blue and for days she had difficulty moving them—but for weeks afterward she had trouble sleeping.

Weeks later I heard rumors that the actual number of people killed in the train crash was closer to four hundred. True or not, manipulation of the facts was a common practice in the Chinese media and was part of an effort to make China seem like a safe place for tourism.

PROFESSOR LI

New Year is China's most important holiday. Its date changes slightly from year to year, like Easter and Thanksgiving. Even two weeks before it was to happen, many people I spoke with didn't know exactly what day the new year would be arriving. I looked it up in a book of Chinese customs and discovered that "New Year falls on the first new moon after the sun has entered Aquarius, which will never happen before January 21st, nor after February 19th." When finally it did come, in the third week of February, for three or four days the streets of Hangzhou became dangerous for walking: Fireworks flew incessantly out of doors and windows, exploding at my feet and whizzing by my ear. On sidewalks groups of celebrants shot off rockets, which landed in balconies and knocked potted plants off window ledges; some of them were powerful explosives, with the deafening ring of dynamite. Indeed, on the television and in the newspapers there were pleas from the city to the people to curb the use of fireworks at home and to supervise their use by children. It was announced that this year the city would not sponsor a public fireworks display, ostensibly because such an event was too costly. Despite the antifireworks campaign, my neighbors enjoyed tying long strings of firecrackers to sticks, lighting them, and dangling them over their balconies late into the night. On New Year's Eve I rode my bicycle slowly through the streets and listened to the firecrackers in the distance; it was an inviting sound, like hailstones rattling down on the roof of a car.

At his request I had planned to spend New Year's Eve with Huang Zhiye and his children, but that morning Huang's daughter, Xue Mei, who was home from university, appeared at my door, pale and trembling, to tell me that her father was ill again with his bleeding ulcer and that the dinner would have to be canceled.

When I went to see Huang later that day, he was lying in bed looking miserable and depressed, with his hair sticking up in tufts and the beginning of a beard sprouting on his chin. I thought he would cry when he apologized for the canceled dinner. He said this time he was afraid he had stomach cancer. He was pale with worry, and his apartment was freezing. He said, "I cannot die. I cannot leave my wife. The doctors told me I should go into the hospital to stay until I get better. I refuse. What about my children?"

Because I was occupying the only chair in the bedroom, Huang's son and daughter stood in the doorway. Huang passed me a piece of paper, a prescription the doctor had given him, and I stared at the unintelligible characters until Xue Mei softly reminded both of us, "She can't read that." It was true. At that time none of the characters I had learned except "doctor" and "hospital," was remotely medical. Too, the Chinese cursive script was nothing like the printed characters I was learning. The one thing I could make out in this scrawl was, "Drink only milk."

The next day I went to the Bank of China to pick up some money that had been wired to me from New York. I had been to the bank several times before and liked going there. There was something of the thirties in the bank's decor, though the building was only a few years old. The small reception area was occupied by two black vinyl couches placed back-to-back in the middle of the floor and was separated from the body of the bank by a smudged wall of tellers' windows. The bank itself was a vast, warm, low-ceilinged room, littered with desks and workers. On each desk an orange gooseneck lamp cast out a comforting golden light. The mood was always relaxed, and there were as many abacuses here as there were electric adding machines. Tellers dressed in simple clothes and moved slowly, with no apparent superior.

While I stood in line this day, I saw a man in slippers shuffle in from a side door carrying a white laundry bag on his back. He dropped the bag on the floor and shuffled out again. A worker took bundles of foreign currency from the bag and stacked them like bricks on his desk, pausing now and then to take a mouthful of rice from a tin box he kept in his desk drawer. Next to his desk a portable safe the size of a mini-refrigerator stood with its door recklessly ajar, revealing more bundles of money and a pair of basketball shoes.

Two coatless young women entered the lobby in high heels and velvet dresses, giggling and carrying a small suitcase awkwardly between them. They skittered up to the couch and flopped down heavily on it, chattering and peering through their bangs to see if anything in this bank was as interesting as they were. Eventually they snapped the suitcase open and spilled a pile of Foreign Exchange Certificates onto the cushions between them. Halfheartedly they sorted the money; blue notes went with blue notes, pink with pink, green with green. They approached their task with stunning indifference, oblivious of the notes that fluttered to the floor or that slipped between the cushions of the couch.

As far as I could determine, there were no guards in the bank, and certainly no guns, which made me anxious for the women. Only a year before it was my job to count the cash income of a large company in Boston, an income daily into the thousands. I did my work in a locked, bullet-proof room, was instructed to turn every bill face-up, noses pointed in one direction, to wrap the bills in a prescribed fashion, to lock the money in a steel-reinforced bag, and when I delivered the money to the bank, I was accompanied by an armed guard. Above all, I was never allowed to open the bags out of the presence of the exceedingly cautious bank agent.

None of the other people with me in line seemed to share my concern for the women; none even noticed them.

A man behind me in line tapped me on the shoulder and asked in Chinese to borrow a pen. I passed one back to him, and several minutes later when he returned it, I murmured my thanks, absentmindedly, in English. In an instant the man stepped up beside me, briefcase in hand, and stared in disbelief at my face. "Forgive me," he said. "Your face is something like a Chinese, so earlier I have spoken Chinese to you."

In his leather bomber jacket this middle-aged man had a rather Occidental appearance himself; he was tall and big-boned with a square jaw, a long nose, slightly rounded brown eyes, and ruddy skin. His hair was unusually wavy for a Chinese man. He was handsome. I told him that I, in turn, might have mistaken him for an American. "You are American, then!" he said, his interest growing. "Are you visiting here?" When I told him I was teaching here, he shifted the briefcase to his other hand, leaned back on his heels, and inhaled deeply, preparing to speak. "My daughter is in San Francisco. She is a student there. Works part time. Has a car of her own. She has been there two years. Has sent me some money, so I am here in the bank today to receive it. My English is not good, because I studied it many years ago and now do not use it often. Only have to read it for my work. I am a professor of biology at Zhejiang Medical School. I am also the Chairman of several committees. My wife is a professor of mathematics. I think perhaps you are lonesome here in Hangzhou. You have been here a long time. My wife and I would like to invite you to our home for dinner one evening."

The man's speech was studied, not, it seemed, because

English was difficult for him but because he understood so well the subtleties of the words and took great care in choosing them. He spoke softly and with dignity.

I thanked him for the invitation and wrote my address on a slip of paper. He took it and shook my hand a long time, staring doubtfully at me, as though still not convinced of my nationality, as though at any moment I might disappear. Finally he said, "I am called Li."

Several nights later Li called me on the telephone to invite me to dinner at his apartment that night, and I didn't remember who he was until he said shyly, "I am the person you said resembled an American." He offered to pick me up at the Foreign Experts' Building and take me to his home on the Zhejiang Medical School campus, a mile or two away.

That night, while I put my coat on and gathered my things, Li stood in the middle of my room with his cap in his hands and studied my possessions. He pointed to a colorful set of small Chinese-character blocks I had lined up on my bookshelf and said, "Forgive me, but I am sure this is a child's game."

"I know," I said. "It helps me to remember the characters."

"You know what they mean?"

"I know most of them."

"You have studied Chinese?"

"Some." I told him how I'd been studying spoken Chinese a little at the university and learning the characters on my own.

Li went to the shelf and pointed to the first block in the row. "This one is what?" he asked, testing me.

"*Dao*. It means 'knife.' "

"That is correct. And this one?"

"*Tian* means 'field.' "

Li seemed pleased. "And the next?"

"*Yue.* 'Moon.' "

" 'Moon,' yes," Li said with amusement, "but it has another meaning."

" 'Month.' "

"Very correct." Li nodded, but seemed perplexed. "Why do you study Chinese?"

I had been asked this question before by curious Chinese and usually in the same skeptical tone, a tone that meant, "Useless!" Only my students truly seemed to encourage my studies. "It's interesting to me."

"But you will have no chance to speak it when you return to America. No one wants to learn Chinese. You cannot use it anywhere but in China. Across the world English is the language to speak. Even Chinese want to speak English, sometimes even among themselves. You have come across our English corner at the lake?"

"Yes. I don't have a better answer. It's interesting to me. While I'm here, it helps me to understand things."

Li nodded thoughtfully. He stared at the photographs of my family on my wall. "Who are these people?"

"My brothers and sisters."

"So many! And what does your father do?" I told Li my father was dead but that he had been a hematologist.

"Hematology is the science of the blood, correct?" I nodded. "This is very good," Li said. "My other daughter is also a medical doctor. She is in Wuhan." Li pointed again to the pictures. "This building is what?"

"My mother's house."

"She lives there with your brothers and sisters?"

"No, she lives there alone."

Li stepped forward and touched the edge of the photo, examining it, slowly nodding his curly head. He seemed to be saying, I *knew* it. He was entranced. He murmured, "It is yellow. It is wooden. So big, so much grass, trees, and a big garden. She lives there alone. It is like a museum in a state park."

On our bicycles we rode to Li's apartment building, the faculty residence at the medical school, a building distinguished from its drab neighbors only by the number 14 painted on its ends in red. Li's apartment was a large place on the fifth and top floor. Here the top floors of most apartment buildings were reserved for the privileged; the higher the floor, the higher the station of the individual. The reasoning for this was difficult to discern. In my opinion these top-floor apartments were colder in winter, hotter in summer, and it was tiring and inconvenient to walk up all those narrow, cluttered stairs. And certainly no one would claim the view as the attraction, since from these apartments there was usually nothing to see but other gray buildings with laundry—and sometimes fish, or plucked chickens or ducks—hanging from their windows.

Li's wife, Hei Jie, a stout woman with a dark round face and slick hair twisted into a permanent wave greeted me casually at the door, the way one might greet an old friend, one hand on the small of my back and the other on my shoulder, smiling deeply and steering me silently into the apartment. The top of her head, I couldn't help but notice, was level with my chin. Her hair was smooth and wavy, like icing on a cake, and shiny as her quilted silk jacket.

Professor Li's son, Li Xinhua, who had been studying in a side room in gloves and a jacket identical to his father's, appeared in the hallway and shook my hand shyly. He was an extremely tall boy of seventeen with thick glasses and a severe overbite. He towered over his mother. He seemed embarrassed when I spoke to him, and made unexpected snorting noises, like a pig's, when I said something he thought was humorous. Despite his shyness, Li Xinhua's English was quite good, much better in fact than his mother's.

The jackets the Lis wore were not the common ones I'd seen in shops. They were heavy brown leather lined with thick fleece. When I asked, Li told me they were air-force jackets, could be got only in Beijing, and that they cost two hundred yuan, approximately twice the average Chinese person's monthly salary. Li had obviously had no trouble affording them.

Like most apartments in China, Professor Li's rooms were cement and stark, painted a pale hospital green, and intolerably cold at that time of year. This apartment, however, with its two bedrooms, living room, small study, and kitchen, was considerably larger than others I had seen. Li urged me to sit in the living room, which was furnished with a glass-topped table, a bookshelf, a desk, and a coffee table. On the wall hung a West German photo calendar and Christmas cards from Canada and America, scenes of snowy forests, sleighs, red bows, and blond-headed choirboys. On the desk was a large Panda-brand cassette player, which I commented on.

"Do you like music?" Li asked.

I told him I did.

"Then, perhaps you would like to hear the waltz music of Johann Strauss." I said I would. Li slipped a cassette into place, fiddled eagerly with the machine for a minute or so, and then, giving it a friendly punch in the speaker, he said without irony, "This machine does not often work. It is Chinese."

Li's wife put tea and peanuts, dried fruit and chocolate, apples and watermelon seeds, on the table before me, then stood smiling and staring at me with her hands clasped neatly at her waist. I could see her inspecting the cut of my hair, and when she had come to a private conclusion about it, she touched her own hair in response. I held my teacup with both hands to warm my fingers, and smiled back at her. After a minute she said hopefully, "Are you married?" She had difficulty concealing her disappointment when I told her I wasn't. She excused herself and disappeared into the kitchen.

Professor Li sat on one side of me on the couch, and his son sat on the other. They put a photo album in my lap and turned its pages for me. All the photos were of Chinese people posed in the usual Chinese way, stiffly in front of monuments or flowering trees or at points of interest to Chinese tourists: The Forbidden City, the top of Huang Shan, the Ming Tombs, the mountains and cliffs of Guilin. There was one photo of Li sitting on the Great Wall. And several at a convention of biologists that took place on an elegant boat, a kind of floating meeting hall; all the biologists in their white short-sleeved shirts crowded into one corner of the room, smiling for the camera. There was another photo at the Lis' own dinner table with a blond-haired man and a young Chinese woman. I asked Li about the man. "He is an Australian married to a young friend of ours. She was very fortunate to meet him. Now they are in America."

By my right ear Li Xinhua let out an inexplicable howl of delight. I turned to look at him; he had big ears and fencepost teeth—a caricature of a hayseed. He wriggled in his seat and grinned at me, and I grinned back at him.

Li showed me a photograph of his wife's brother's family sitting on the carpeted stairway in their house in Canada. "My brother-in-law has been in Canada since before Liberation. See what a big house he has, and five children. First he went to Taiwan, then he had the opportunity to go to Canada. He did not return. He is a real estate expert and often travels. His life is very comfortable. He has even come here to visit once." Li studied the picture and repeated, "Very comfortable." There was another picture of Professor Li surrounded by complicated equipment in his laboratory, and out of one of the machines at his side I could see a glowing beam of green light shooting mysteriously across the room.

Li closed the album and told me about his work, about his laboratory and his dependency on foreign research. He said he loved to read the work of American physicists and also the work of Jack London. He asked me about Japan, and when I told him my impression of Tokyo, he seemed overjoyed and called his wife into the room to tell her what I had said, as if my experience proved something he had long suspected. Right away I regretted saying anything at all; I had no desire to add fuel to the flaming animosity between the Chinese and Japanese.

At one point in our conversation Hei Jie brought an elderly couple into the room on what was obviously a surprise visit. The man in the couple had the patched dress and dull mannerisms of a farmer, but the woman had a beautiful smile and the charming presence of a film star. Her clothes were stylish in an old-fashioned way. I thought she resembled Soong Ching-ling, the patriot and wife of Sun Yatsen, whose photographs I had seen in Chinese history books. When I mentioned the resemblance, everyone in the room shrieked with laughter, but the farmer laughed longest and loudest, nodding his head, alternately clapping his heavy hands, and clutching the film star's elbow. She beamed and bowed her head and toyed with the colorful silk scarf around her neck.

The new visitors sat on the edge of their chairs, giving the impression they would only stay a moment. The farmer left his hat on. He seemed self-conscious and uncomfortable with my presence and smiled stiffly at me between statements to the Lis. He would say something to them and then turn immediately to me with a loud laugh and an exaggerated shrug, as if to say, "We are fools! Ignore us!" He seemed to fear that I might understand what they were discussing, but in fact he had nothing to worry about: Their Chinese was not only too fast for me but also Hangzhou dialect, a combination that put them utterly out of my range; I had been studying *Putonghua*, the standard Mandarin. At one point in their conversation the farmer began to whisper to Hei Jie, leaning toward her and pointing out the window with his crooked finger.

Li and Hei had little to say. They listened diligently to what their visitors had to tell them, nodding their heads and saying, "Ah," at the appropriate points. When the visitors had gone, I asked Li who they were. He thought a while, looking at the ceiling for the right words. "Critics," he said.

"Critics? What does that mean?"

Li thought again. "Well," he began, "it means critics." He seemed doubtful about his own explanation and clenched his teeth in concentration and stared at the Christmas cards on the wall.

I told him this didn't make sense to me, which he already seemed to know.

"Well, you could say, they are two people in charge of the Housing Committee at the university. They are the people who decide what apartment teachers will live in. They came to tell us that soon we will be allowed to move to a professor's apartment."

"This is not a professor's apartment?" I said.

"No."

I couldn't imagine a Chinese apartment bigger than the one we were in, and I began to see how privileged the Lis were, which I should have suspected back in the bank when I first learned they had a daughter in America. "That must be good news."

Li smiled. "You may say it is good news."

"You don't seem very happy about it."

Hei Jie interjected quickly, "We are happy about it, but we have already heard this news before."

Their answers didn't satisfy me, and it was clear that there was more to this meeting than they cared to share.

Presently we sat down to the thirteen dishes Li had prepared. During the meal Li Xinhua giggled and snorted in embarrassment while his mother struggled to ask me questions in fragments of English. If I wasn't married, did I at least have a boyfriend, and if so, what was the boyfriend's profession? The way she glanced at me when she thought I wasn't looking was disconcerting. At first I had thought she was simple and retiring, but I was beginning to see a curious current running beneath her broken English. I could see her taking notes in her head, calculating my statements before she commented on them, testing my responses to facts and ideas.

She talked about her daughter in America, her daughter's car, and job, and how she herself would like to retire from her job at the university, because it was too wearing now to an old woman. She told me that soon they would like to send their son to study in America. When I asked why they wanted to do that, Professor Li said, "I believe the educational system in America is best. Maybe our system is out of date, not practical. It is also best for students to leave the home. And I think it is good to work part-time and to study part-time. Our son can do that in America."

Almost as if in explanation for the retarded Chinese educational system, Hei began to discuss the Cultural Revolution. "Everything stopped then. Nothing was in order in the university. No one had control. All the students refused to go to classes. Sometimes they went out and marched around the city. Senior professors were forced to wear the . . . the hat of stupidity." With her finger Hei drew a dunce cap on the tablecloth. She said some days in the university she could hear the sounds of the academics committing suicide by jumping off the roof of the library. She could hear their screams as they fell and the dull thud of the bodies as they hit the ground. She said fifty people in the university alone died this way. "Some jumped, and some . . ."—she put a hand around her throat to indicate that some had hanged themselves.

"I had particular trouble because back then I was employed as the secretary to the president of the medical school," she said. "At that time many large posters with large characters painted across them were put up all over everywhere denouncing the intellectuals, beating people down. My name was put in huge black characters in the train station and in the university. They said, 'Hei Jie is a running dog! A capitalist roader! An imperialist! She works for the president of the university! Down with her!' "

Hei laughed loudly, then covered her mouth as if to keep from screaming. "I was sent out to the countryside with my two young daughters to work as a cook in a camp. I didn't mind it. I thought this work was interesting. It was different. And at that time it was safer than being in the city."

Professor Li said he had been sent somewhere else at the time, also undergoing what was known as "reeducation." He was forced to work on a farm, which he, too, said he found interesting. He said, "It was like a rest for me. Eventually I found the work less strenuous than research, and it was more healthy."

Hei said that for many months all the buses and trains and hotels were free to the people so that the Red Guards and people could travel to Beijing and be reviewed by Chairman Mao. "Sometimes it was like vacation, and sometimes I saw people being beaten and dragged out of their homes, and then it was not vacation." When I said I thought this was terrible, Hei smiled and her son snickered.

Their reactions were strange, though not uncommon in discussions of the Cultural Revolution. Several other people I had talked with about it had also appeared to find the recounting of these horrors somehow funny. But their laughter was always strained and nervous, possibly less an expression of mirth than an effort to seem unaffected by the upheaval. The more I talked with people about the Cultural Revolution, the more I thought the Chinese were still too overwhelmed to discuss their pain and resentment openly, so they discussed it casually, the way they discussed Ping-Pong and the rising price of pork.

Eventually, after many dishes and much talk, Hei turned to me in her seat and said gravely, "Now I hope you can help me." She stood up from her chair and ceremoniously revealed a thick folder of papers she had been sitting on throughout the meal. She presented them proudly to me, still warm. They were official documents from the United States Immigration and Naturalization Service, documents needed to obtain an I-20 form required before an F-1, or foreign-student, visa could be issued. Hei told me she needed an American citizen to sign an affidavit promising that he or she would support their son in case the son should need financial assistance while he was in America.

"You would help us by signing this and telling them how much money you have. You will need to have at least twenty thousand dollars and a letter from your bank to prove that." Hei spoke confidently and cheerfully, as though the deal had already been made.

I looked at Professor Li; he looked silently back at me, waiting for my reaction. I was baffled by the suddenness of this, like the spider's pounce on the unwitting fly. I told them I was sure I couldn't help them, mainly because I didn't have twenty thousand dollars.

"Maybe you know someone who does? Maybe your mother? Or your brother? You will not actually have to give us money, just say that if our son ever needs money for some reason, you will see to it that he gets it. In an emergency," Hei said.

I had heard that this kind of sponsorship was rather serious, in a sense an absentee adoption, and I had no idea how to respond. Too, the request was wildly inappropriate for a first meeting. It was also impossible. I told them as gently as I could that it seemed peculiar for them to be asking a stranger for this kind of help. I asked why they couldn't get help from an American teacher they knew at the medical school; surely they had some American acquaintances there—every Chinese professor seemed to have an American acquaintance in China. And I knew there were Americans teaching at this school, knew some of them personally.

"American teachers at this university might talk to other Chinese teachers here, and the other teachers who know us would be jealous if they knew we wanted our son to go to America. They would be jealous, or they would think it was not our son's turn, or that we were getting special treatment. He is so young, you see."

It was true, Li Xinhua was very young, and that was precisely what confounded me. I couldn't understand his parents' purpose and urgency. It was extremely rare that young Chinese students were allowed to leave the country to study at the undergraduate level, and only a brave and well-connected or outstanding few ever bothered to try. At Harvard College that year there were only eleven undergraduates from the People's Republic of China as compared with one hundred fifteen graduate students. "If your son is so young, why do you want to send him now?" I asked.

"It would help his career," Li ventured.

I told him I thought it might indeed help his outlook, help to broaden his mind, but that once he returned to China, it might not actually help his career very much. I told him of the stories I'd heard about Chinese people with doctorates from American schools who'd returned to China only to take up jobs as mail clerks or kindergarten teachers, computer experts who, once back in China, had inadequate computers to work with. There was a chance that their son's knowledge and experience might not be exercised or fully appreciated when he returned to China. "How did your daughter get to America?" I asked.

"A friend of my brother helped her," Hei said.

"Maybe the friend could also help your son."

"No. He has helped others also and now he feels he has helped too many."

"Can your son get a passport?" I asked, hoping they'd forgotten how difficult that could be.

Yes, yes, they said, for them the passport was not a problem. They looked dolefully at me. Either they didn't actually know why they wanted their son to go to America, or they couldn't articulate it in a way that would sound reasonable or justified, and they knew this. They had said they wanted their son to go so that he would learn to be an independant man, but in the same breath Hei told me she wanted to go to Los Angeles to work for a year to get enough money to help her son financially. She made little white fists of her hands and leaned over the table and whispered, "I would go to America on a three-month visa, but then I would stay for a year. I seize all opportunity! I am always working. I would go to America and sew to make money to help my son. I can sew. I have a machine. I made this jacket, these trousers."

I found the aspiration of seamstress amazing coming from a professor of mathematics. They seemed to believe that somehow it would improve their lives for their son to go to America, that perhaps it would bring them all financial gain.

Like the vendors on the streets of Hangzhou, who hurried to show me their wares before I passed them by, Hei Jie began to show me her son's transcript from middle school; all the grades he had ever received, all the honors he had ever won. "You will see that his marks in mathematics and science are excellent!" She showed me the awards she and her husband had earned during their years at the medical school, certificates saying what upstanding people they were, what excellent teachers. She leaned closer to me. Her determination was fierce. "My husband is the chairman of many committees. You can see what kind of people we are, what kind of boy our son is. You can support us. We have a nice home. Nice people. If your mother comes to China, we can give her a place to stay. We can help her if she comes here."

It was cold; in my coat and scarf and gloves I still wasn't dressed warmly enough for this apartment, and my feet in their black rubber boots were numb and heavy. I had nothing to say. The chance that my mother might travel to China was slim indeed. I couldn't help them, and it was disappointingly clear to me that they had invited me here simply because they thought I could be of use to them. I knew enough by now to expect this kind of treatment—it was part of being a foreigner in China—but this was a particular disappointment because I liked Professor Li. I liked his gentleness and his curiosity, and I had hoped we would become friends.

Like many Chinese this family was proud, that much was obvious, but they were proud in an ancient way and for ancient reasons; it was an inherited pride, and certainly not a pride in the present. What disturbed me most was the revelation that even they, apparently well off, had so little confidence in their future and so little hope for change in China's structure. They couldn't depend on their own country for what they needed; things here were difficult, shoddy, second rate, and conspicuously corrupt. When it came to major improvements in their lives, the Lis were without resources and without opportunity, and I could not know what that was like. My time in China was a gift, enriching in a strictly intellectual sense, and in my life such gifts had seemed somehow guaranteed. My luck was unbelievable; theirs—in many ways—was unbelievably bad. And if that was true, what of the others like Huang Zhiye and Ming Yu, who were not even half so fortunate as the Li family?

I told them that I would think about their request and get back to them within the next few days. Li insisted on riding the mile back to Hangzhou University with me. I protested. He said, "But the road will be dark, and there are many holes in it. You will need company."

I said good-bye to Hei Jie and shook Li Xinhua's gloved hand, and Professor Li and I walked down the five flights of stairs, our footsteps echoing spookily in the utter darkness. I put out my hand and touched the wall to guide myself down. "Are the lights in this stairway broken?" I asked Li.

"There are no lights."

"Have there ever been lights?"

"No."

"Will there ever be?"

"I guess not."

Li was right, the road that took us back to my university was impossibly dark and there were many holes in it. One or two riders passed us, weaving blindly and ringing their bicycle bells; in all my time here I had yet to see a bicycle with a light on it for night riding, and this seemed like only one more way the Chinese invited disaster on the road. I realized halfway home that I had a flat tire, which made the potholes and bumps in the road the more unbearable, but I was determined not to tell Li this or to ask him to stop. I knew that if I revealed the flat, he would insist that I ride his bicycle while he walked the rest of the way and that then, according to custom, I would have to repay him somehow. Knowing what kind of repayment he might request, I preferred not to set myself up for it.

The next morning I felt mildly depressed, so I went to visit Huang Zhiye, who looked awful, still sick in bed, himself depressed. I told him about what had happened the night before, and he agreed that the Lis were tactless, too hasty. "Behavior like that is not the Chinese way," he said, sighing and shaking his head on the pillow. "You should simply tell them that you will ask your mother if she can help them, then don't ask your mother anything at all."

"Is that the Chinese way?" I asked.

Huang smiled appreciatively at my attempt at a joke. "It is one way," he said weakly.

When I came home, I found a message on my door from Professor Li saying he would come to see me at 3:00 P.M. That afternoon he arrived with a gift of peanuts and tangerines for me and an envelope of papers, including a typed description of his family, a kind of family resume. Most Chinese found English typing extremely difficult, but these papers had been typed and worded with great care. Among them was an invitation to my mother and my oldest brother to come and stay in the Lis' apartment "for free." My heart sank as I read this. Not only could I not help him, but I wasn't inspired to, and I knew my mother and brother wouldn't be either. I told him I didn't think I would get a favorable response from my family over such a request, that they would think it was too much of me to ask, that it was awkward, and that he was probably expecting too much. I held the papers out to him. He looked away from me. He stared out the window at the construction workers in their blue uniforms on the ledge of the building beyond the wall of our courtyard. He brushed his lips with his fingertips and said in a fatigued way, "Perhaps you are right. Perhaps you are correct." Reluctantly he took the papers back and slipped them into his shoulder bag. He pointed to the typewriter on my desk and asked if he could see a page of what I was writing. I was taken aback by the request and said he couldn't, that it was nothing but a letter.

He cleared his throat and shifted in his chair. "I hope that you will not write about us and what we have asked you to do," he said.

"Why?" I asked.

"Maybe some people would read it and think what we have done was bad."

"Do you think it was bad?"

Li thought a moment. "I don't think it's bad. Relations

in China are very complicated. It may be difficult for you to understand them."

I had heard this explanation countless times before, and at first I had thought it was only a convenient excuse in a moment of discomfort with a foreigner. Now I was beginning to believe it was true. "Despite your decision not to help me, I hope we will remain friends," Li said.

I wanted to tell him we hadn't had a chance yet to become friends, but I said nothing; it seemed foolish for me to try to correct a man whose definition of friendship was undoubtedly less complicated and ultimately, somehow, far deeper than mine.

Eventually, after sitting and staring a painfully long time at the character blocks on my bookshelf, Li stood up and said sadly, "I want to go back."

RED
NOISE

As soon as I heard Ming Yu had returned from Wuxi, I went to her room to visit her and to bring her the box of things George had left for her. She was alone when I arrived, practicing her handwriting again. She stood up and shook my hand warmly and held on to it for a long time. Her hand was rough, but surprisingly warm, even though the room was freezing. I realized that all the useful things here were gifts from George; a heater, a lamp, strong light bulbs, and some beautifully bound English books. I was struck again by the number of English dictionaries and language workbooks Ming had on her shelves.

Ming and I discussed her handwriting a bit—it looked fine to me, far more legible than my own—and I asked her how her father was. The room was so cold I could see my own breath when I spoke.

"It is the same," Ming answered. "We argue and disagree and don't understand each other."

"What exactly do you argue about?"

"The Party, the country." Ming waved her hand indicating she didn't want to talk about it. I told her the story of Professor Li and his family, and she seemed riveted by it, by the discomfort of it. She watched my face as I talked, and her eyes widened and narrowed. She said nothing until the very end of the story, at which point she said, "Desperate."

I gave Ming the box of things from George, and she

sorted through them silently, her fingers gently turning the objects over but not removing any. She plucked out the photograph of George, stared at it, and put it into her photo album.

Ming and I discussed George. We imagined what he was doing back in England now, and as the conversation progressed, I gathered up my nerve and said, "You know, I think George loves you."

Ming spread her hands over the album in her lap, as if to hide the photographs. "How do you know that? Did he tell you?"

"No, he didn't tell me, but I could see it. I could tell from the way he talked about you. I guess it seemed obvious."

Ming nodded. "I love him also."

After a long silence Ming began to talk about George. He had come to Hangzhou in the winter of 1986 with the intention of staying no longer than one term. His main intent was not to teach but to study *taiji* and *wushu*. He and Ming met and became friendly. She was impressed with his devotion to *taiji*, and he was impressed with the way she spoke English. He encouraged her to write something in English, so she wrote a few poems. "He told me he thought the poems were quite good," she said. "We spent time discussing them, and then eventually I began to love him."

At the end of that semester, after Ming had been told by the University Security Bureau that she should stop going to visit George, he asked her if it would make things easier for her if he didn't come to see her here either. She said, "George must have seen on my face that I was unhappy with that prospect. That I could not have borne his absence, and from that time on we both knew."

"Knew what?"

"We were in love."

I asked her whether she had considered marrying

George, but didn't mention my thought that such a marriage would also be a way for Ming to get out of China, if that was what she really wanted.

Ming laughed. "I am afraid of marriage. Also, I think George would not marry."

"Why not?"

"He says he likes his life."

That seemed like a poor excuse to me, and besides, George didn't seem to like his life at all.

Ming said, "He once told me you were the only person in the building he could talk to, the only person who shared a sense of humor with him."

The revelation gave me a strange feeling. I remembered him telling me once that I was the only person he had ever met who was weirder than himself. I must have looked offended by his comment, for he added quite sincerely, "I mean that as a compliment."

I asked Ming why George had invited Ruth and me to come to the room the night she was leaving.

"He thought it would make our good-bye easier."

"Did it?"

"Yes. George even wrote me a letter and said he thought so too."

"My friend Ruth saw there was something between you and thought it was very sad that you had to say good-bye to each other."

Ming looked at her swollen hands and began to cry. Her mouth fell slightly open and her chin quivered. Tears fell onto the pages of the photo album until she closed it. She cried silently. I had never seen her cry, and watching her now was painful. I felt her vulnerability and the weariness she must have experienced every day of her life, a weariness she rarely revealed and never complained about.

I told Ming how sorry I was, that I could imagine how hard this must be for her.

She said, "I think it is possible to live with someone in

the mind as well as in the flesh. In China, people like to have the body of the person they love in the same room with them. They are not satisfied if the husband or the wife or lover is away. But it happens often here that loved ones are separated, and they endure." Her eyelashes grew spiky with the crying and her cheeks went red. Ming wiped her eyes and smiled and said what we both already knew, "He likes his life. He does not want to settle down."

We drank some tea, and I asked Ming what she was reading now. "Hemingway," she said, and jumped out of her chair, reminded of something. "Have you found a copy of the book you have been looking for?" she asked excitedly.

Since November I had been looking for a second copy of a book I had bought in Wuxi, which was titled *Dictionary of Modern American Slang with Bilingual Explanations*. The book, published in Sichuan in 1983, was a list of strange English slang words and phrases, many of which I had never heard before. Some of the entries were so absurd and so amusing that I wanted to share the book with a friend of mine at home. There was a seamy slant to many of the words included in this book, and some seemed to have thoroughly contrived meanings, as though the Chinese person who compiled the dictionary had gone on a binge of invention. *Red noise* was "a bowl of tomato soup"; *wear a hat* meant "to have a girlfriend, to be married"; *ice cream* was defined as "any of certain habit-forming narcotics in crystal form," and *illuminated* meant "drunk." *A harlot's hello* was "something that doesn't exist; nothing; zero as in, 'The silver ore left in our pits isn't worth a harlot's hello.' " *Frail job* was "a sexually attractive woman or one known to be promiscuous." *Fried egg* was "the flag of Japan." *Metallurgist*: "a person who plays heavy metal." *Rough* meant "an automobile that has been in at least one collision." *Onion* meant "a stupid or boring person." *Horses* were "a pair of dishonest or loaded dice."

I told Ming I hadn't found the book anywhere else.

"Then it is lucky," she said, "for I found one when I went home to Wuxi." She took a copy of the little book down from her shelf and handed it to me, smiling. "I have even bought one for myself."

I was delighted to have a copy, thanked her for it, and when I tried to give her money for it, she protested and said, "Some other time you may do something for me."

"THE SHAMEFUL
END OF HITLER"

One rainy morning in March I woke up late and realized
I had ten minutes to make it to my class. I jumped
onto my bike and pedaled furiously through the rain to
campus. The wet streets were clogged with grim-faced bicyclists in their plastic ponchos. Bicycle traffic was always
slower in the rain, and accidents were more frequent; nevertheless, I stood up on my pedals and pumped hard along
an opening between the curb and the crowd. A man cursed
at my temerity and cranked the bell on his handlebars, a
jingling little bell with all the authority of a party favor.
"Fuck your mother," he said.

I smiled and raced on.

For safety's sake bicyclists were expected to dismount
as they passed through the university gate, and most people
learned to do this without ever really slowing down. If you
swung your leg over the back, hopped to the ground, and
ran alongside the bike until you passed the guard, you could
swing yourself back on without losing any momentum at
all. Some people never even touched the ground, but glided
through the entrance standing up on one pedal, like clowns
in the circus. That morning I did this and was stopped by
the guard and scolded. I asked the guard to excuse me, promising never to do it again.

Just inside the university gate I passed by Tatiana Petrova, the Lithuanian teacher, also on her way to class. She
wore a brown trenchcoat and carried her books in a leather
bag on her shoulder. She saw me and called out in her deep

voice, "Rosemary, how are you?" I slowed down to tell her I was late.

Without breaking her loping stride Tatiana said, "What means 'late'?"

I made a circle around her on the path so that I could talk without having to get off the bicycle. "It means my class is beginning and I'm not there to teach it."

Tatiana raised a hand and nodded her understanding. "I also am late."

I could see she had just woken up; her eyes were puffy and her uncombed auburn hair was like soft wool around her face. She smiled warmly at me.

Tatiana Petrova was beautiful to look at. She had a long straight nose and creaseless olive-colored skin. Her mouth was small and even, her cheeks plump, her eyes a brilliant green. Though she was a large woman, she had a delicate physical grace, was almost dainty in the way only some large women can be. Because she spoke no Chinese and very little English, and because the Chinese were wary of Eastern Europeans—and she in turn was wary of the Chinese—Tatiana was lonely and depressed here.

I complimented her on her colorful knee socks, visible below the hem of her raincoat. She listened attentively to me, straining to catch the meaning of my words, then peered down at the socks. "It's Lithuanian," she said. "You don't have some socks?"

I told her I had socks, but none so pretty as these. She nodded, pleased by the compliment, and we said good-bye.

That day I had two visitors in my class. One was a friend of the class monitor, but the other, a young woman, sitting at the back of the room, was obviously alone. She seemed a bit older and more serious than my students, and I was surprised to see her there. I couldn't help suspecting that this visitor was a spy sent to check on me. Before the class began, I asked the girl some questions about herself and asked her to write her name at the end of my roster. My request clearly worried her. She hesitated before writing her name and stared at the back of the student in front of her and said, "Hm," which only increased my fears. Finally she wrote two nearly illegible characters at the bottom of the list. She had a solid face and a large mouth and she spoke very clearly.

I went to the podium and found a note for me there, written in a sprawling hand unaccustomed to writing in English. It said:

Master Rosemary,

I have to say sorry to you for that. My father and mother, they are all farmer in the coutryside and haven't never seen the surface of any city. And they now come here that is from my housetown very far. Want me to lead they to look round the city. I'm very sorry to you. But I can't choice another way. It is actually that I have to choice this. Please believe me! I will learn this lesson from cold, and catch up with others. I will do it. I promise to you.

Your student, Peter

Peter was shy and diligent, and though he had started out in my class as one of the least competent students, he was learning quickly and would eventually come to be one of the best. The note, with all its sincerity and angst, touched me. Without ever mentioning it outright, Peter had found a way to convey the embarrassing message that he was not coming to class that day.

This semester we had no electricity in our classroom, and when days were overcast, the window light was dim and the room was gloomy and cold. The students took out their books and pencils and turned their faces to me. They seemed thin and underdressed for this sort of weather, their damp hair was plastered to their foreheads, and their shoes were soaking wet. On rainy days whole sections of the university's pathways were flooded shin-deep, and students would simply fold their pant legs up above their knees and wade through them. On a bike, you could get through the puddles safely and fast, lifting your feet up onto the crossbar and sailing through on momentum, but most of my students didn't have bicycles.

I called the roll. When I called, "Corinne," there was no answer. Corinne's seat was empty. Judy, a friend of Corinne's stood up and said sadly, "Corinne has gone to hospital."

"Oh," I said. "Is she ill?"

"Not ill," Judy said. She looked at Corinne's empty seat and searched for the right words. "Corinne has fallen down."

"Corinne has fallen down?"

"Yes. And hit her head. Now she is in hospital."

Corinne was a small, flat-faced girl and just about the shyest student I had in both of my classes combined. She found it impossible to speak and buried her head in her arm whenever I asked her a question. "Is she all right?" I asked Judy.

"Yes, but she has cut her head."

I asked Judy what had made Corinne fall down. Arlene, an eager, fluent student in a pink jacket, stood up and said brightly in Judy's stead, "It is that Corinne swooned."

"Why did she swoon? Is she sick?"

Arlene grinned and wagged her head. "No, no, no. Not sick. Only maybe did not eat enough food."

"I see. So she fainted and fell down."

"Yes."

I expressed my sympathy over Corinne's mishap and asked Judy to send her my greetings.

For homework that week the students had read two

short pieces in their textbooks. The first piece, titled "The Shameful End of Hitler," was an excerpt from William Shirer's *The Rise and Fall of the Third Reich*. The second was a piece by George Orwell called "Why Do We Believe That the Earth Is Round?" Since we had already begun discussing it in our last class, I decided to begin with the Hitler piece, which recounts Hitler's last day alive, the day in the infamous bunker with Eva Braun and a group of his associates. Mussolini has very recently met his demise, and in the face of the imminent arrival of the Russians Hitler is preparing to do away with himself. He requests a delivery of two hundred liters of gasoline to set the place ablaze, has his dog killed, and kindly offers poison capsules to his two notably faithful secretaries. At 2:30 in the morning Hitler emerges from his room to say good-bye to his followers, then returns to his bedroom, where he shoots himself and Eva takes poison. End of story.

Though there was no direct mention in the piece about Hitler's particular crimes, the students clearly understood Hitler's aims and ideals and were fully aware of the horrors the Nazis practiced. After each essay in our workbook there was a cloze passage, a kind of fill-in-the-blanks exercise popular in Chinese-language courses; for "The Shameful End of Hitler" the cloze passage was "an eyewitness report of how a comparatively minor mass execution was carried out upon Hitler's order at Dubno in the Ukraine on October 5, 1942":

> The People who had *got* off the trucks—men, women and children *of* all ages—were *forced* to undress themselves by *an* S.S. man *who* carried a dog whip. They had to put down their *clothes* in fixed places.
>
> Without screaming or weeping *the* people undressed, stood around in family groups, kissed each other, *said* farewells and waited *for* a sign from another S.S. man, who stood near a small hill, also

with a whip in his hand. During the fifteen minutes _that_ I stood here I _heard_ no complaint or plea for mercy. . . .

An old woman with snow-white _hair_ was holding _a_ one-year-old child in her arms and singing to _it_. The child was smiling with _pleasure_. The parents were looking on with _tears_ in their eyes.

_At_ that moment the S.S. man near the hill counted off about twenty persons and _ordered_ them to go behind it. Then from there I heard rifle _shots_ in quick succession.

A few minutes _later_ I walked around the hill and _found_ myself confronted by a tremendous grave—an execution pit. People were closely wedged together and lying _on_ top of each other. Nearly all had blood running _over_ their shoulders from their heads. Some of _them_ were _still_ moving. Some were _lifting_ their arms and turning their heads _to_ show that they were still _alive_. The _pit_ was already two-thirds full. I estimated that it _contained_ about a thousand people. I looked for the Fascist soldier who _did_ the shooting. He was an S.S. man who sat _at_ the edge of the pit, his _legs_ dangling into the pit. He had a gun _on_, [sic] his knees and was _smoking_ a cigarette.

I walked among the rows of seats while the students took turns reading this exercise aloud, filling in the blanks as they went, and as it dawned on them what the passage was about, their expressions changed dramatically from boredom to horror, and they grew very still in their seats.

When the exercise was finished, I returned to the front of the room. The students stared silently at me, with their dark heads slightly lowered. They seemed frightened. I asked them what they thought about the passage. "Bad," they said. "Terrible." A few of them murmured their alarm in Chinese, and one boy raised his hand and said bitterly, "Japanese had done similar things to the Chinese. In Nanjing they had dug a huge hole in the ground and pushed a thousand Chinese people into the hole and buried them, still alive."

The horror of this and of the Nazis was obviously real to them. But when I asked them, "What do you *think* about Hitler?" they answered unanimously and without hesitation, "Hitler was a great man!"

A powerful shock passed through me when I heard that, and I remember very clearly the baffled look on the students' pale faces as they watched my mouth fall open. For a full minute I could think of no response. I stood there in dismay, staring at the students, and they stared back at me, and when the silence became overbearing, they stared at their desks, the way they had the first day they met me.

I closed my book and asked the class how they could say Hitler was a great man after what they knew about him. What exactly were they talking about? They stared blankly at me. During the long silence that followed, I felt like a stranger to this room, and I realized how tenuous and incomplete was my understanding of these students.

The monitor stood up. "Hitler was a great leader," he said.

"What do you mean?" I said.

Another boy stood. "So many of the German people followed Hitler."

"True," I said, "but was Hitler right or wrong in what he did?"

The students answered together, and with great conviction, that Hitler was wrong.

"So how can you say he was a great leader?"

"He was successful with his people," the monitor said.

I understood, with some relief and no less dismay, that the students were making a distinction between morality and might, and that to their way of thinking might of whatever sort deserved recognition. A murderer was a murderer, there were no two ways about that, but if he succeeded in persuading an entire nation to murder along with him, he could still be called a great man.

For our academic purposes the problem lay in their choice of the word *great*. I explained that *great* carried with it connotations of moral rectitude, of generosity and humaneness, of constructive acts and superior character. I stressed that, in general, only the truly admirable were called "great," and that a man invested with the mantle of greatness would not usually be considered, at the same time, to be a criminal of momentous proportion. One might safely say, "Hitler was a great villain," and that particular use of the word *great* would indicate the depth of his villainy. And so on. If the students were bent on isolating Hitler's amazing popularity with his people from the rest of his characteristics, then they should consider calling him simply a "powerful man." Whatever they decided to call him, *great* was emphatically not the word to apply to Hitler. I told the students that if they walked around any Western city and said, "Hitler was a great man!" they might get a punch in the nose. They laughed; that much they understood; even the spy in the back row laughed behind her hand at the idea.

The class seemed to accept my qualification, but I wondered how long it would take them to break this particular habit. Once or twice in future months I would hear, elsewhere, the Chinese proclamation that Hitler was a great man, and each time it had the same unsettling effect on me and I hurried to edit the claim.

During the five-minute break, while most of the students got up and wandered noisily up and down the dark hallway or chatted or stared dreamily out the classroom windows at the rain, the spy stayed put in her seat and watched me talking to a group of students. She stared at me, arms folded over her chest, a contemplative look on her face.

When the class reconvened, we moved on to the Orwell

piece, which had some relation to the Hitler piece and, I thought, some instructive application for Chinese society. The premise of Orwell's essay is that due to the vast amount of knowledge we now have, modern man has become necessarily credulous of, and dependent on, authority. To prove this point, Orwell uses the example of the way in which we know the earth to be round. He maintains that anyone standing on a beach can see with his own eyes that the earth is not flat, for sometimes the only thing visible of ships passing along the horizon are their masts. But although this phenomenon indicates a curve, it does not prove roundness. Since that and several other tests fail, says Orwell, consider the astronomer royal, who claims the earth is round; he should be believed, for he can also give an accurate forecast of an eclipse—but then so could the ancient Egyptians, who misunderstood the orbital relationship of the earth and sun and who knew nothing of the earth's roundness. Consider, then, celestial navigation, which depends partly on the assumption that the earth is round; accurate navigational calculations never fail.

In summary Orwell says,

> It will be seen that my reasons for thinking the earth is round are rather precarious ones. Yet this is an exceptionally elementary piece of information. On most other questions I should have to fall back on the expert much earlier, and would be less able to test his pronouncements. And much the greater part of our knowledge is at this level. It does not rest on reasoning or experiment, but on authority.

The idea being, then, that we are forced to put our trust in those who know more than we do, in those who wield the power that knowledge affords.

Because of the elevated language of the Orwell piece the students had difficulty following its logic. After trying in vain to work through it with them, I took a different approach; I asked them if Mao Zedong was dead.

They looked incredulous. "Of course!" they cried.

"How do you know that?"

They gave me suspicious looks. "Everyone knows!"

They knew Mao was dead the way they knew China was bordered on the north by Mongolia and the Great Wall was visible from outer space. The room buzzed with defensive pronouncements. "We read it," they said, or, "We heard it on the radio when we were children," or "Our parents told us."

I asked them if they believed what they heard and read about Mao or about anything else for that matter?

They frowned: Newspapers and parents wouldn't lie.

"Are you *sure*?" I said.

All eyes stared at me now, and their minds turned over the significance of my insinuation. I could see, here and there, some of them picturing Mao alive somewhere in northern China, thinking his thoughts and writing his poetry, and others picturing their parents lying to them. They shifted in their seats, giggled nervously, looked sidelong at each other. They shook their heads at my preposterous questions.

A brilliant girl, Karen, stood up and said, "Of course we are sure! Why would they lie to us?" Though Karen was usually a humorous, lighthearted person, there was no trace of humor in her question; she was worried, and possibly insulted.

"Well, I'm sure they wouldn't," I said. "But you realize that only a few people ever really saw Mao dead, or touched his body and knew for sure that it was Mao. They had all the power over that information, and what if, for some weird reason, they lied and Mao wasn't really dead?"

Just as I expected her to, the spy at the back of the room raised her hand. She cleared her throat authoritatively and with great satisfaction she said, "I have been to Mao's mausoleum in Beijing! *I* have seen his body there!"

Not at all what I expected her to say. She was drawn in. "A lot of people have seen Mao's body there," I said, "but it could be made from wax." (In fact months later when I went to Beijing and saw Mao in repose under glass, I thought he looked, for all the world, like a wax figure.)

"Wax?!" demanded the spy.

"Candles are made from wax. The body in Mao Zedong Memorial Hall might be wax, a doll, a dummy. Not really Mao."

The spy was scandalized. She flipped her hand at me to dismiss the notion. The class was visibly agitated, with the history of the nation on the verge of crashing down on them. I decided it was time to relent. "Okay," I said, "I believe Mao is dead. But still I don't know why I believe it. I only accept what I've been told by the people I'm supposed to trust."

The students thought about that, some of them nodding their understanding, others looking bemused or concerned. I told them how some Americans liked to say that no one ever landed on the moon, that it was just a hoax perpetrated by the government, and that all the pictures we saw on television were made in a desert somewhere. The students laughed uncomfortably. "That's crazy," they said.

At the end of the class I could see the visitor at the back of the room preparing to approach me. I was nervous, ready to be denounced, fired from the university as a troublemaker. I gathered up my books and started for the door. The visitor came up behind me, books in arms, and said, "Excuse me. May I have one word with you?"

I turned to look at her. She blushed. In a trembling voice she said, "I . . . I am a second-year student from the Economics Department. . . . I am sorry I did not ask your permission to come to this class. I have enjoyed this class, and I would like to come here again and listen and practice my English."

If she was really a spy, I couldn't refuse her, and if she wasn't, I didn't want to refuse her. She seemed genuinely relieved when I told her she could join the class, and then the concern returned to her face, and I thought to myself, Here it comes.

She said, "But I would like to ask you one thing. If you would please not tell the department about me, because they would tell my department, and my department would be very angry to know I was here at this time. You see, I should be in mathematics class at this hour, but I know all the material in that class already and I would prefer to spend this time improving my English."

So much for the spy. I told her I wouldn't mention it and asked her her name. She said, "My English name is Rose."

"Mine too," I said.

She smiled shyly. "I know."

That night Tatiana showed up at my door with a pair of the pretty Lithuanian socks for me. I invited her in, and she sat down in a chair and crossed her legs and folded her arms. She smiled as she looked around the room. "Last year this was my room," she said. "I think you have prepared it more comfortably."

For all her ongoing depression, Tatiana often wore an expression of wry amusement.

Tatiana was earning her Ph.D. in linguistics, was an expert in Russian literature, and had been sent to China against her wishes. She spent a lot of time worrying about her two daughters who were living with her mother and whom she hadn't seen in fourteen months. She rarely mentioned her husband except to say that he wanted her to buy new frames for his eyeglasses while she was in China. She had shown me photographs of her husband, or—more accurate—photographs of Lithuania that happened to have her husband in them. The husband looked untrustworthy, with skinny legs and a red beard and a meanish face, like a red fox. In every photograph his eyes were hidden behind dark glasses. Tatiana looked hard at the pictures and seemed to be thinking how little she loved him. Once, I asked Tatiana how old she was when she married her husband, and she rolled her eyes at me and said, "Nineteen! That is the problem!"

Tatiana talked about her friend, Vladimir, whom she sometimes referred to as, "My citizen." She liked Vladimir's company, that was plain, but she also seemed to think him incorrigible, and sometimes even a little crazy. Vladimir was short and solid. His round cheeks were hard, like two beaten biscuits. He was a Foreign Expert sent here by his government, and Like Tatiana he was miserable in China.

One evening Tatiana had cooked dinner in her apartment for me and Vladimir and Bruce Ford, an American student who spoke Russian and was one of Tatiana's few friends here. In the course of that evening Vladimir had drunk an entire bottle of Chinese vodka and put Bulgarian music on loud on the cassette player and danced around Tatiana's room in a stomping way with one hand on his hip and the other waving over his head and a cigarette stuck between his lips. He lit firecrackers off the edge of Tatiana's balcony and kept sliding his arm around her waist until she slapped his wrist and told him to quit it. By the time he left that night Vladimir was so drunk that all three of us had to help him out to the gate and onto his bicycle. Bruce offered to ride home with him to his hotel, to make sure he made it safely there, but Vladimir refused the offer. He kissed us all a sloppy goodnight and rode down the road in a wild zigzag, and Tatiana clapped her hands together once in a way that meant Good riddance!

Now she peered at the photographs on my table, pointed

to one of Ming Yu, and said, "Rosemary, this Chinese girl. Why does she come to visit you so much?"

"She's my friend."

"No. She is a *spy*!"

I laughed. "Why do you think Ming Yu is a spy, Tatiana?"

"All Chinese who come to the building are spies! All Chinese in China are spies!"

"But what makes you say that?"

"I know. They want to find information out."

"Do you think I am a spy?"

It was Tatiana's turn to laugh. "You? Rosemary, ha-ha. You are a nice girl. Not a spy. I bring you socks."

"Maybe you're a spy," I said.

Tatiana clapped her delicate hands to her chest. "I? No! Rosemary, I am not a spy! I don't care about information. I only care about my daughters!"

"Maybe Ming Yu is just like you," I said. "Maybe she doesn't care about information either. I think she's not a spy."

"Hmph!" went Tatiana, as if to say that time would tell.

The one thing Tatiana did seem to trust in here was the Chinese traditional medicine. She was forever taking Chinese remedies for her various ailments, pills for nervousness and depression, for headaches and indigestion and obesity. She bought vials of antiaging serum, and powder and creams. The depression pills were little brown pellets the size of capers; their prescribed dosage was eight pills all at once, two times a day. When I asked Tatiana if the pills and powders worked, she laughed and shrugged and said, "Who knows?"

THE ENGINEERING COLLEGE

Spring came early to Hangzhou, and with the warm weather came the thought that I had only a few months left in Hangzhou. I decided it was time I gave the talk I had promised to give at the Engineering College.

The college administration hadn't asked me to address any particular issue; they didn't seem to care what I talked about, as long as I spoke English. "Just a talk," they said. "English practice." After brief deliberation I made up my mind not to prepare for the talk. I was eager to see how things would go if I spoke extemporaneously, and I was more interested in conversing with the engineering students than I was in lecturing to them.

The campus of the Engineering College was ridden with deep, unfenced pits carved out of the earth to accommodate future foundations. Miles of intricate bamboo-and-rope scaffolding clung to the cement faces of the buildings in support of masons and painters in blue work clothes. To reach the building I was to perform in, I had to walk across a pine gangplank laid over a wide, moatlike trench around the building's foundation.

In a classroom on the third floor of the building twenty-eight engineering students, most of them men in their early thirties, sat cramped at tiny wooden desks awaiting my arrival. The air in the room was heavy with dust, and the afternoon sun shot violently through the long windows and fell hot on the students' heads, making them drowsy. When I opened the door and walked to the front of the room, the heads snapped up, one-by-one, and turned toward me. These students had the same curious expressions my students at Hangzhou had, but there was none of the fear or anxiety that my students had displayed on first meeting me. This group were adults, workers who studied engineering at night and on weekends; they were self-possessed, had a healthy trace of skepticism, and had certainly encountered foreigners before.

I sat at a large desk placed up on a dais—the top of the desk was scarred with Chinese graffiti—and told the students something about myself and how it was that I had come to China. Then I asked them all why they had chosen to study engineering (the answer: "It is necessary for modernization"), why they studied English ("These days English is necessary for modernization"), and what they hoped for themselves in the future ("A better life," or "Compile a family," or "Study in United States"). They seemed excited when they realized I would be addressing them personally, that this was not a lecture. I invited them to ask me questions, which they were reluctant to do until an older woman at the back of the room—the only woman present—raised her long white hand and said, "I would like to ask if it is true that Americans go out of their parents' homes at eighteen years of age to live alone in the society."

The woman wore a blue blazer and a white blouse buttoned up to the throat. The sun illuminated her large face; her gentle eyes and wide mouth. She smiled nervously at me. I told her it wasn't a rule, but that many Americans did indeed leave home at eighteen and that some left at an even younger age.

The woman leaned over her desk. "May I ask how old were you when you went out of your parents' home?"

"I was fourteen."

A murmur of alarm skittered across the room. I hurried to explain my case: I left home at fourteen to go to boarding school but was still dependent on my family, and in summers and on holidays, until I was sixteen, I always returned to my mother's house.

"Boarding school?"

"A high school where the students live, away from their families."

"How far away from their families?"

"My school was a hundred miles away from my home."

The woman raised her hand again, smiling profoundly. "Excuse me," she said, "were you bad?"

"Bad?"

She bowed her head in deference and swept a hand across the top of her desk, as if to wipe away her own impertinence. "Please excuse my question!" she pleaded, and in an imaginative attempt at diplomacy she downshifted abruptly from the second to the third person. "Did the young person live away from her family because she was bad?"

"No, I was good, and I went there because it was a good school and I wanted to go."

"I think the young person must have missed her family very much."

"Yes, I did."

"Then I think it was a bad idea for her to go. What is the use of going away to school as a child? I cannot see the use for her."

"It had advantages over a regular school," I said, "and I also enjoyed it. I learned how to be independent." I spoke briefly then about independence and individuality in America and how important they were to most Americans.

The woman listened carefully. "But fourteen?" she said incredulously. "What was the young girl's hurry?"

Her curious shift in pronouns had exactly the desired effect—I was finding it difficult to remember we were talking about me. "Life is short," I said.

The woman drew her lips back across her strong teeth. "Life is long!"

An impish laughing man with hair the color of caustic

lime raised a finger. "You both are the true examples of American and Chinese thinking." The class roared with laughter at his comment, and that seemed to encourage the woman. She struggled to disentangle herself from her little desk, rose to her feet, and buttoned her jacket protectively over her blouse. She smiled at me the way a Christian missionary might smile at a pagan baby. In a tone more teacherly than challenging she said, "And I have heard that teenage American girls and boys live together before they have become married. Is that true?"

"It's possible among older teenagers, yes. But again it's certainly not a rule. It's a choice some young people make."

"Well, then, they live together in the manner of husband and wife before they are married? Is that it?"

"Some do, yes."

The woman's smile was searing; setting up unsanctioned house was not a Chinese concept. I braced myself, expecting the next question to be, "And did the young girl live together with a boy in this manner?" Thankfully she said instead, "And is it true that there are many unmarried teenage girls with babies in America? Is that also true?"

I said it was.

The woman looked out the window, fingering her chin. "What is your opinion on the sale of U.S. arms to Iran and the relationship between the two countries?"

A rough-looking man in the front row asked a long, multifaceted question, the only intelligible facet of which was, "Have you ever been to the Statue of Liberty?" I confessed I hadn't actually been to the statue, but that I had seen it numerous times from Manhattan and had been very near it in a sailboat. The man's face fell. Forgetting that the Chinese were inveterate tourists of their own country, I tried to console him with the reminder that when you live in a place, you don't always do what tourists do.

"*I* do," he said contritely.

A man sitting next to him said, "But what about the Statue of Liberty?"

"What about it?" I said.

"The source," he said.

After tossing several questions back and forth we established his meaning: Why did the French people present you with such a thing? When I told him the statue was a gift in celebration of America's hundredth birthday, more hilarious laughter ripped through the room. A mere hundred years was nothing to celebrate!

The class was interested to know that the statue had recently been overhauled, that one could walk up into the crown, that one used to be able to walk into the uplifted arm, and they asked if the statue's lips were painted.

A man in the back of the room stood up into a bar of sunlight and shielded his eyes with his hand. "Is it true that in America a person can get in trouble with the law for looking out a bus window?"

"Where did you hear that?" I said.

"I have read it in the *China Daily*," he said, which cleared things up considerably. *China Daily*, the English-language newspaper, had a way of confusing stories, or of hearing them wrong, or of translating them wrong, or—according to other foreigners—of inventing them.

I asked the man if there was more to the bus story. He said this was the extent of it. I told him that, all other things remaining usual, innocent, and in order, looking out a bus window could not be considered a criminal offense. I told him I thought the *China Daily* had either misunderstood the law, had got the facts wrong, or that he had misread the story, otherwise some vital details were missing.

With excellent logic the man said, "You are from Boston in Massachusetts. There are fifty-two states in America. I think there are a lot of laws in the United States, and I understand that some laws are different in different states. So you may not know of the law if it is not in your state."

"But a law against looking out a bus window sounds entirely unreasonable to me, and as I understand it, most state laws are within the range of reasonability."

The sentence had hardly escaped my mouth before examples of unreasonable laws came rushing to mind; we had laws against driving shirtless and shoeless, laws against driving with an open container of any sort of beverage, including bottled water, state laws that gave husbands immediate control of their wife's property and affairs or that forced a woman to assume her husband's surname at the moment of legal marriage; if she didn't want the name, she had to go to court and have it legally changed back to the original. And there were the sodomy and other sex laws. I didn't mention these things, nor reasonability again.

In the back row someone said, "Not only the laws are different in different states, but the laws in America, I think, are different for different people."

"How do you mean?"

"Laws are not the same for rich people as for poor people."

Though I wasn't eager to defend the rich, I also wasn't eager to make America seem any more lopsided and bizarre than it was already coming to seem. I tried to explain. "The laws in America were made to extend to all people of whatever class and means. Under the Constitution the law is the same for all people. To avoid the law with money and power is of course morally wrong. Nevertheless it's true, some wealthy people can avoid the law by hiring important lawyers or by bribing law enforcers to ignore their offenses or by wielding their power and notoriety. The Constitution is solid and clear; it is only the people who try to bend it. Regrettably sometimes they succeed."

From a man with a tape recorder set up on his desk: "Is

it true that some towns in America are called University Towns?"

I thought about that. "I guess some towns are called that."

"Well, in these towns is it true that most of the residents work for the university, but that there are also some unfortunate people who must work for the city?"

"They work for the city if they want to, and I don't think I'd say they were necessarily unfortunate."

"Aha!" said he, unaccountably triumphant.

Another student asked, "How do you think of the Chinese university?"

I didn't think much of the Chinese university itself. The lights in my classroom never worked; the chalk sticks had pebbles embedded in them and scratched the blackboard; the students had the shoddy Shanghai books and ancient, malfunctional audio equipment; their teachers didn't speak English; the lights didn't work; their exam papers were sometimes illegibly printed; exam questions were often senseless or downright wrong; they were cold in the unheated classrooms; the classrooms were dirty; they were pushed and hurried through too much material, and they were tested solely on their powers of memorization.

Too, Chinese teachers had less freedom than American teachers did, or if they had freedom, they didn't appear to seize it. They read to their students from books and old notes, taught the same courses, gave the same assignments. Xu Ban once said to me, "The goal among Chinese professors is to get promoted higher and higher so that they will have to do less and less work, teach fewer and fewer courses, have more and more time for a rest," and this was said not as criticism but as praise, as though rest were a reasonable, admirable goal for an academic.

I found the administrative skills in the university sorely lacking. In my department, lines of communication got hopelessly crossed, and changes in the course were made too often and too quickly, without sufficient reason or planning. One week it was announced that we would spend the rest of the semester on grammar and vocabulary, and the teachers gathered and spent hours mimeographing, hand-collating, and stapling miles of exercises to this end. The following week the order was rescinded, the grammar and vocabulary exercises were tossed aside, and we were asked to collate intensive-reading and listening exercises instead.

Some days I had the creeping feeling that my cheerful, friendly teaching group were only playacting at college, as in a dream. They had a laughing, unfocused, doubting approach to their work.

The course we were teaching was state engendered and nationwide, and our examinations were administered, in effect, by the government.

I thought very little of the Chinese university, but I was impressed by its affectionate, respectful, hardworking students. I told the group of engineering students that most of all I was impressed with the remarkable patience and good-naturedness Chinese college students maintained in the face of adversity. Each day passed was a day endured for them, and they passed their days without a murmur—without a thought—of dissent.

The sun had shifted now in such a way that only I was left illuminated. The engineering students sat in the shadows, which made it difficult to see their faces. I had been talking a long time and I felt exhausted and uncertain about what I had said or how my opinions had been received. Worst of all, had I made myself and my country seem haphazard and foolish? My back was wet with sweat. I glanced at my watch, and from the back of the room I heard the gentle-eyed woman saying, "And how would American students approach adversity?"

CAO, TRANSLATOR
OF NOVELS

Ming Yu invited me to a performance by a Canadian ballet company at the Hangzhou Theater. On the evening I was preparing to leave for the ballet, a skinny man with a headful of bushy, unkempt hair walked into my room unannounced and uninvited. Leaving the door gaping open behind him, he came to the middle of the room and extended a long-fingered hand to me. "You are Rosemary," he said with authority, as though I should remember this fact and act accordingly.

I stood with my jacket halfway up my back and stared in amazement at the man's face—it was long and narrow and virtually chinless, and his teeth were so large he had difficulty getting his top lip down over them. His hair was a dusty, tangled nimbus around his head. I conceded that I was Rosemary. He grabbed my hand and shook it heartily. His hand was cold and dry, and his eyes were shot through with red. He wore a baggy blue army coat with brown mock-fur around the collar, and his apparently stiff neck forced him to turn his head from the torso. In the style of the near-blind he pressed his face up close to mine. "I am pleased!" he said happily. "How do you do? Are you busy?"

"Who are you?" I asked.

He pushed out his chest and clasped his hands behind his back. "Cao, translator of novels in the Foreign Language Department. Are you busy?"

I explained that I was on my way out to the ballet with a friend, when Ming Yu stepped into the doorway. The translator turned himself slowly around, greeted Ming in Chinese, turned back to me with some effort, and smiled broadly. "Then! I must come to see you next time!"

Ming stepped out of the doorway and let the translator pass through. When he had gone, I said to her, "What an odd man he is!"

She shrugged, brushed a lock of hair back from her face with her hand. "He is only another teacher. But rather a clever one, I think."

The Hangzhou Theater resembled a sports complex of the early seventies; it was low and wide, and its facade was a wall of double-paned floor-to-ceiling windows clouded by condensation sandwiched between the poorly sealed panes. The many shallow steps leading up to the entrance were browned with soot and strewn with candy wrappers. Inside, the lobby felt eerie and abandoned. Most of the fluorescent ceiling lights were dead, and the few that prevailed cast a metallic light on an inconsequential area behind the concession stand, the area where mops and brooms and folding chairs were kept. The green linoleum floor tiles had cracked and buckled. Tin cans and sticky papers had been swept— or kicked like leaves—into the lobby's corners. Two young women in charge of the concession stand were napping with their heads down on the counter, and this was only logical, considering that the shelves beneath them were nearly empty and the performance had already begun. Behind the women, perched atop a refrigerator, a battered pocket radio set at low volume whispered the day's news.

Ming and I ran up the side stairs and found our seats, which happened to be directly alongside Tatiana and Vladimir. I sat down next to Tatiana and spoke her name. She turned, startled, and peered hard at me through the dim light. "Rosemary!" she whispered, "You come to ballet?!" Her hair was like a furry hat, and she smelled pleasantly of fresh pepper. Vladimir sat on the other side of her in a blue Chinese cap, his mustache drooping around the corners of his mouth and glistening in the reflection of the footlights. He smiled and waved at me.

Halfway through the first piece a talkative Chinese family of four stood up in the row in front of us, clamored out to the aisle, and marched noisily out of the theater. Tatiana scowled at them as they went. "Chinese," she whispered as though this explained their behavior.

Vladimir smiled throughout the entire ballet, and each time he leaned over to whisper something to Tatiana—which he did frequently—he laid his thick-knuckled hand gently on her forearm. At some point I looked over to see Tatiana squinting down onto the stage, trying to follow the confusing story line. A pair of troubled lovers—the male lead dressed something like the joker in a deck of playing cards—danced an unhappy duet. When a second man leapt dramatically from the wings and took up dancing with the woman, Tatiana gestured at the stage and hissed, "What is *this*? An extra man for her?"

"I guess so," I said.

Tatiana looked incredulously at me, and in the daintiest way imaginable she said, *"Shit!"*

The next evening Cao, the translator, came again to my room dressed in the same blue coat. He sat low in my chair and crossed his skinny legs at the ankles. He wore black plastic loafers and no socks. His neck ailment seemed to have disappeared overnight. He rubbed his long hands together. "Yesterday when I was here, I felt strange," he said.

I asked him why; he waved his hand at the flag of the Communist Youth League hanging on the wall. "It is strange for me to see this flag on the wall."

The flag was a bright red rectangle of cotton with a gold star within a circle in one corner. It was a striking, cheerful thing I had tacked up to cover a torn patch in the room's bamboo-patterned wallpaper.

"Chinese people would not do this," Cao said.

I asked Cao if that was due to the political nature of the flag—he said it wasn't. I asked if it was perhaps illegal—he said he was sure it wasn't. I asked if it was considered offensive or disrepectful. He said, "It is not considered," and he leaned back uncomfortably in his seat and peered warily at the flag as if he feared it might fly down off the wall, wrap tight around his face, and suffocate him. He seemed to be sinking into his coat—the lobes of his ears rested now in the fur of his collar. His skin was waxy, and the rims of his eyes were pink as a guinea pig's.

"No one does it," he said. "No one would get the idea to do it. I must tell you, to see it now makes me feel very strange."

I apologized and offered to take the flag down for the duration of his visit, but Cao put his hands up before him and said in somber protest, "It is your home. You must have it as you like."

Mr. Cao was very young, but already he had a business-like, fatherly air about him. He was here to ask if I might recommend some American books on AIDS that would be acceptable for translation into Chinese. The Chinese, he said, knew very little about AIDS; many had an unwarranted fear of it and believed that nearly every foreigner was afflicted with it. To stress the depth of his compatriots' ignorance, Cao wagged a finger at me and said indignantly, "Some Chinese will even turn down a perfect opportunity to visit the West because they fear they will contract the disease!"

I was aware that foreigners were required to present proof of a negative AIDS test, or to have the test performed in a Chinese hospital, before they could be granted a Chinese work card. I had neglected to have the test done before I came to China, and the only medical form I had brought with me was a carbon copy of a prescription from the Cambridge City Hospital, a faint, wrinkled scrap of tissue paper signed in a messy blue scrawl. Driven by my exaggerated fear of Chinese hospitals, and for want of a better solution, I resorted to forgery and medical fraud: I placed a fresh sheet of carbon paper on top of the copied prescription, wrote "HIV neg." on its back, and signed a doctor's name to it. Though the carbon seemed utterly unconvincing to me, I turned it over to Xu Ban in the Foreign Affairs Office and told him it was the result of a test I had had in Boston. He was pleased with it, and three days later he appeared at my door with the work card enclosed in a red plastic case. For a month following this deception I waited in fear that the Public Security Officers would knock on my door and arrest me. They never did, and I began to think the Chinese authorities were perhaps not as vigilant as they were reported to be.

Cao was long-winded and loud—he was fairly shouting now. "Because we know nothing about AIDS, we must get our information from foreign countries. My publishing company has offered to pay me a large sum to find and translate a book on the subject. But it is impossible to find one here. I am sure that there are some such books in America, if only I could hear about them."

I happened to have in my room an American newspaper in which two novels about AIDS had been reviewed. I showed it to Cao. He drew a pair of rimless spectacles out of his coat pocket and put them on his nose. He scanned the reviews cursorily, then slapped the paper down hard on the table between us and waved his hands in objection. "These books are fiction. Why do they write fiction stories about such a thing? No, no. It is not the kind of book I want. I want something that explains the disease. Or if you don't know of those, what about some other general novels that would be appropriate for this country?"

I told Cao that offhand I didn't know of any books on AIDS that were directed at a lay audience, but that I believed he could write to the Library of Congress for more information. He reached deep inside the front of his coat, withdrew a booklet, and made note of this. And then, as though my presence had slipped his mind, he began to study my room with a keen eye, making an obvious appraisal of its furnishings and appointments, sizing up my possessions. He took in the character blocks on the shelf, the paper lantern in the shape of a fish hanging from the ceiling, the cowboy boots by the door, the portable typewriter. His disdainful gaze rested last and longest on the flag.

I saw in this interlude an opportunity to ask Cao some questions. Since September I had met several Chinese translators, all of whom were engaged in translations, from English to Chinese, of either mystery stories, detective stories, or weightless romances. I asked Cao why they spent so much energy translating this kind of work, why they didn't concentrate on more literary efforts.

Cao sighed, removed his glasses, and tucked them away with his notebook. "I do not wish to shock you, but I must say that literature is dead in China. People these days only want money and entertainment. They are losing what you would call spirituality. I must include myself among those people. I cannot lie—I, too, want money. I do not translate for fame but for money. I want better things and a better life, so I translate what I know is bad literature. I can translate good literature, but I don't want to. The publishing companies will not pay me a lot for it. The people don't want to read it."

He glanced at the few books on my shelf and said, apropos of nothing that had gone before, "My girlfriend is twenty. I am twenty-five. The first time I kissed her on the mouth, she didn't know how to react. She knows very little. She is like a child, though she is legally old enough to be married. Young people in China are still somewhat naive."

The intimacy of Cao's revelation was both surprising and familiar; I had learned already that Chinese who indulged in Western novels were, in the company of Western-ers, arrantly candid. From these novels they had constructed fantastical impressions of the Western world, and their view of the American spirit was particularly distorted. They seemed to believe an American would talk about—and do— almost anything. At the same time these readers were frus-trated; they'd let themselves in on a hive of secrets while their unreading compatriots slippered along with blinders on. Their isolation only served to encourage their confes-sions. Cao had been here ten minutes and already I knew his girlfriend didn't know how to react when he kissed her. Like the other Chinese translators, Huang and Hu, Mr. Cao—for all his self-importance—was more blunt and un-buttoned than I would ever be with him.

Cao grew contemplative now. He gazed deep into my eyes. In an accusatory tone he said, "Ming Yu is your friend."

I agreed.

"But she is not liked among her colleagues."

"Why not?"

"For one thing she is not pretty. And she is strange. And is not like other women. She is too knowledgeable and opinionated."

I reminded Cao that not a moment ago he had been complaining about the ignorance and naiveté of young Chi-nese people.

He nodded wearily. "Yes, yes, but Miss Ming is differ-ent. Sometimes we talk about her in a room, maybe a few men will be discussing these things, and everyone agrees that she would not be a good Chinese wife. On her way to the dining hall she sings out loud. Chinese women don't do such a thing as that. Chinese men like women who are pas-sive, and physically we like them to have a small mouth and beautiful features."

"Some foreigners think Miss Ming is beautiful," I said.

Cao ignored the comment. He turned in his seat and

scrutinized me. He said, "Why do you like Ming Yu?" The question was pointed and probing. He wore his inability to understand my friendship with Miss Ming defiantly across his face.

I told Cao she was independent and warm. She was friendly without being wary, and, unlike many Chinese, she shared her opinions with me.

"Well, then," he said loudly, "do you like your co-teacher, Zhen Xinqu?"

"How do you know Zhen is my co-teacher?" I said.

Cao threw up his hands and shouted almost giddily, "It is general knowledge!"

"What does that mean?"

"It means everyone knows!"

"How does everyone know?!"

Cao put his hands palms-up in front of him in a chiding-pleading kind of gesture intended to mean, "Let us be realistic." "Foreigners are very visible, and word travels fast. Anything slightly different is news. Foreigners are different, so foreigners are news."

The fact was that many things about me seemed to be general knowledge; if I went to the post office to mail a package on Monday, on Tuesday complete strangers in the university asked, "How did the mailing go?" If I had dinner in a restaurant on Yanan Road, the maids in the guest house would say upon my return, "You should have tried their duck instead of the fish." It was clear that I was being watched, not for security reasons but for sport.

I considered Cao's question about Zhen Xinqu; Zhen was eager to go to America, and because of his good behavior in the department there was no question but that he would eventually be granted the opportunity. Zhen was shrewd—he played along with the demands the department made on him even when he disagreed. He wanted to succeed, but he had a clever way of dismissing authority when he was in my company, of being honest and loose and of shrugging off the Party line. Zhen had once told me, "Mao was a dictator!"

"Zhen is a gentleman," I said to Cao. "He's hardworking, quiet, serious, and sincere. He has a good sense of humor and does what's expected of him, and I do like him."

"But these two people are very different!" Cao protested. "You cannot possibly like them both!"

I told Cao I thought this was a narrow view, that I liked Zhen and Ming for different reasons, and that in the end they were not really so different in spirit.

"Well, then," he said coyly, "do you like me?"

"You're certainly forthright," I said.

Cao looked cautiously at me, unsure whether he should be pleased by this verdict. "Forthright?"

"It means bold."

Cao frowned at his knees and flipped through the files in his mind for *bold*.

I stood up. "You can look it up when you get home," I said.

When Cao had gone, I felt anxious and unsettled. I went to the window of my room. On the fifth-floor ledge of the building under renovation beyond our wall a solitary workman in blue struggled with a heavy shovel. He worked barefoot. Some careless person had left a bag of cement out on the wide ledge, and four days of rain and wind had split it open and solidified its contents in an unmanageable heap. The workman had spent all day—and the day before—chipping at the mess with his shovel, breaking his back over work created by another man's negligence. At this construction site the men labored under enormous odds; the scaffolding was bamboo, there were no cranes, no bulldozers, no elevators or electric tools, and work piled upon work until it seemed they would never get to the bottom of it. Against the stolid background of the building the blue workman's effort seemed futile and puny. He poked repeatedly at the cement, methodically, the way a bored child pokes at an anthill with a stick. His approach seemed so listless and his purpose so absurd that I first mistook his posture for idleness—for a mere killing of time. As a rule this man's hours and days passed unchanging. Progress or not, his pay was always the same, and, modernization or not, the work was the same. Whether he poked at cement with a shovel, dug for bamboo shoots in a forest, gathered rice in a field, or banged out tin plates in a factory, it was all the same back-breaking work.

As I watched this worker, the voice of the translator crept back into mind, and before long a fierce anger overtook me; it seeped upward through my veins into my head and hands. I saw in the windowpane the faint image of my own face reflected, and the expression on it startled me.

EXAMINATION

In June my teaching group held a meeting to discuss how we would grade the final examination our students had just taken. It was a hot day, I was sick with another bad cold, and the meeting was pure chaos. We sat around the long table, with heaps of exam papers spread out before us and a pile of hard candy wrapped in colorful papers in the middle of the table, and all the teachers talked at once. As the meeting progressed, some of them began running busily in and out of the room, fetching more pens, notebooks, hot water for tea. Chen Peiling stood in his place at the head of the table pleading with the teachers, "Please keep quiet!"

It seemed the teachers were all desperate to find ways to help their students to pass the examination. They saw it as a national competition, and if other schools throughout the nation did better than Hangzhou did, we would all lose face and most likely be chastised by the head of the department for not having done our job properly.

Mrs. Lin, a heavy, older woman sitting across from me, voiced her despair: "It is always the teachers who get blamed for the success or failure of the students!" A woman beside her added a vehement, "Correct! But we know it is actually the students who should be blamed for not working hard enough!" and the rest of the group nodded and murmured their assent.

It sickened me. I wanted to defend the students, to stand up and say that if blame had to be placed, it should be placed on the administration, but that day I felt just as I had felt all year: My opinion counted for very little in this group. I could help them with English grammar, and spelling and reading and writing, but beyond that, my thoughts about teaching methods and more appropriate materials were received with polite smiles and nods, and sometimes even an utterance to the effect that my ideas were quite reasonable, and then the teachers would turn away from me again and resume their fretting. They knew how remiss the administration was, but because the habit of surrender was deep in their hearts, no one would be the first to say so.

Chen asked the teachers to exchange exam papers so that we would not be grading our own students, but no one liked Chen's idea. No one was eager to reveal to anyone else how their students had done on the test, and, too, everyone wanted to see to it that their students passed. The essay answers were graded after model answers the department had asked me to prepare. If the student's essay matched the model in thought and style, it was a success; if it differed, it failed. This method was devised in large part to make the teacher's job easier, for there were 1,400 students enrolled in this one English course and only eighteen teachers to teach them. I had made polite objections to the method, pleading that successful writing in English was founded on creativity and originality of thought. Several of the younger teachers in the group agreed with me in private, but none supported me publicly. They apologized and said, "Nothing we can do about it."

That day the teachers were putting unduly high marks on the exam papers, and the systematic way they went about creating this image of success—the absurdity of the situation—made me crazy. But I felt something parallel to what the Chinese teachers felt: The students couldn't possibly be expected to pass this examination without some kind of miracle to help them.

For my students the exam had taken place in a large classroom on the top floor of the Mathematics Building. It was a hot, overcast day, and the mosquitoes were out in angry black clouds. Hugging the seventy-six-page examinations I had hand-collated and stapled, I climbed to the fifth floor of the Mathematics Building only to discover that the door to our room had not been unlocked yet. The exam was to begin in fifteen minutes, and the students were gathering in the hallway, sweating and nervous, exhausted because they had stayed up all night studying by candlelight. My test assistant, a nervous person named Mr. Bai, who had promised to bring a cassette player for the listening section of the exam, was nowhere in sight.

I asked James, one of the Geography Department students, to bicycle across campus to the Foreign Languages Department to see if he could get a key to the room, or at least to find someone who might be able to help us.

Thrilled with the assignment, James flew so eagerly down the first flight of stairs that he stumbled on his own feet and went sprawling face-first onto the cement floor of the landing below. His eyeglasses and the fountain pens in his breast pocket went clattering across the floor. Within seconds James was on his feet again, rubbing his head and elbows, fixing the glasses on his face. Bravely he grinned up at me and at his classmates, staring in amazement from the top step. His eyes were wild.

"Ha-ha!" James said cheerfully. "I stepped wrong but am fine!" But when he bent over to collect his pens, I could see he was nearly sick with pain and humiliation and that both his bony elbows were bleeding.

"James," I said, "someone else could go if you like," and at that Elvis and Louis eagerly stepped forward to say, "We will go!"

From his spot on the landing James looked fiercely up at them and said, "No! I will go! I am fine!" His face was scarlet with determination. We listened to his hurried clacking footsteps, echoing down the five flights of stairs.

Fifteen minutes later James returned, bringing with him

a breathless old man with a key. The man pushed through the crowd of students, tried the key in the lock, jiggled it, laughed indifferently, said, "Wrong key!" and set off again down the stairs.

I stood there in the dingy hallway, surrounded by my wide-eyed students. I had no idea what to do next. I was determined not to send them home after all the work we had done preparing for this exam, all the practice tests and exercises, and essays and listening comprehension and grammar quizzes. I knew that if the students missed this exam, they might not be allowed to take it again and that they would never be more ready than they were right now.

I held the heavy stack of exam papers to my chest, picked my way among the students, leaned over the iron banister, and called out to the old man, "Hey! Comrade! Are you coming back? Are you going to help us?" My voice sounded loud and desperate as it traveled down the bleak stairwell. Two flights below, the old man stopped and turned his wrinkled face up at me in the well. He was smiling. He waved his hand and said he would try to come back with another key. He called me "little teacher."

I settled myself against the wall and looked at my watch. I noticed that my shirt and hands were black from the cheap ink smudged off the cheap newsprint, and probably my face was covered with it too. The exam should have begun ten minutes ago. As I thought about alternatives, other possible places we could take the exam, I noticed that the students were staring at me in an odd way. They looked shocked. A soft voice near me said, "Rose! You have spoken Chinese to that man!"

That was true, I had. Without thinking twice, I had spoken Chinese in front of my students, something I had never done in earnest before, and the man had understood me and responded, which usually made me want to leap up and clap my hands with glee at my own cleverness. But this time I hadn't thought twice about it. With all my attention focused on our present predicament, I had forgotten about being self-conscious.

"We did not know," said Clive, "that you could speak Chinese."

I gave Clive a shrug. "I can't, really."

Though the students knew I was learning to write Chinese characters, I hadn't told them very much about my efforts at learning to speak, because my efforts seemed so pathetic to me, and the way they laughed the few times I had said a stiff phrase or two in class had embarrassed me more than they realized. One or two of the girls who came to visit me had listened to me read some short Chinese texts from books, but beyond that I kept my progress in spoken Chinese a secret, and sometimes my successes at speaking surprised even me.

"Yes!" Clive said. "We heard you speak!" And then all at once the students began to repeat what I had said to the man. "Are you coming back?" they said. "Are you going to help us?" And to my relief and surprise, no one was laughing. I smiled into the stack of exams and shook my head.

"But it was very good!" said Clive. "Yes, excellent!" said Emmy.

I was struck dumb by the brilliant grins and bespectacled eyes looking back at me with curiosity, pride, and wonder and could think of no adequate response. In the silence that passed between us I saw how their delight in me mirrored exactly my own in them, a delight we had all been, for a long time, too shy to mention.

There was no room left for the seventy students who had gathered in the small hallway. They were sitting on the stairs three flights down, and on the landings, and standing shoulder-to-shoulder with their backs against the cool stone walls, and—remarkably—they seemed to be enjoying themselves. They liked being in crowds, they liked unusual situations, and they were used to waiting for things. Some of the girls standing near me said, "Rose, please sing American songs," and others begged, "Please tell us a story!"

These were two things my students never tired of: songs and stories. They seemed to think of me as an entertainer. And though I rarely sang for them, whenever I had the opportunity, I told them stories about America, or about my life, or about things that had happened to people I knew. But most of all the students like to hear my impressions of China, tales of trips I had taken to other Chinese cities or even things I had done in Hangzhou itself, and it was never the particular events of these stories that appealed to them, but more, my reactions to the events. They loved to hear how China surprised and pleased me, and they loved to hear my comments on the Chinese people.

That spring I had traveled three times to Shanghai and three times to Shaoxing, a small town not far from Hangzhou. The students knew Shaoxing was one of my favorite places, and that mystified them, for they thought of it as an old country town full of dusty streets and hickish people. Never mind that Lu Xun and Zhou Enlai had both been born there, or that China's best rice wine originated there; it just didn't make sense for a foreign person to have an attachment like mine to Shaoxing. And it drove them wild that what I liked about Shaoxing was precisely what they didn't like: the tiny streets and the ancient stone-and-wood houses built up along the network of canals; the square-faced old men in their elfish felt hats who rowed up the weedy canals in covered canoes; the flat green fields on the outskirts of the town; the long duck barns with their thatched roofs; and the barren red hills to the south of the town. I liked the Yu temple, with its quiet gardens and elaborate rooftops, and I liked that Shaoxing was usually uncrowded. But best of all I like Shaoxing's ancient wine shop, which looked as though it had been standing in its shady spot near the Lu Xun museum since the start of time. It was a warm place of dark wooden beams and whitewashed walls, and there were paintings and framed calligraphy on the walls, and sturdy old wooden tables and chairs. The front wall of the shop was only waist-high, and in good weather the wooden shutters were taken down, and you could feel the breeze against your face and watch the people going by on their bicycles in the shade of the trees that lined the little street. The workers there would heat wine in tin containers like inverted oil cans, then ladle the wine into ceramic bowls, and there were steamed beans to eat and squares of dofu and peanuts marinated in their shells. I found the shop peaceful and quiet. Each time I went there, I hated to leave. The calligraphy on the wall said, "Though the shop is small, its fame is large," and "Old wine will make you drunk."

While we waited for the old man from the department to return with the proper key, I told the students about my most recent trip to Shaoxing, a trip I had taken with Bruce Ford and Coburn Ward, an American professor who, with his wife, Mary, was teaching that semester at Hangzhou. The students settled against the wall and listened with their mouths open, straining not to miss a word of what I said.

Toward the end of a day of wandering, Bruce and Coby and I went to the wine shop and found it so crowded that we had to drink our wine outside in the courtyard. Before long a crowd of people gathered around us to stare, mostly at Coby and Bruce, who were both very tall. Bruce had a bushy brown beard, an uncommon sight in China, and Coby was lean, with the handsome, square-jawed look of a Texas cowboy. They were both thoughtful, soft-spoken men. Bruce was nearly fluent in Chinese, and Coby, though he had just begun studying the language, had made remarkable progress, and that, combined with his sense of humor about the perils of speaking a foreign language, made Coby a great hit with the crowd.

That day at the wine shop we met a group of young teachers from Shanghai. There were six of them sitting inside the wine room at a table near the front window, and they were listening to us over the wall. A young woman among them stood up and invited us to eat some of their peanuts. Her name was Wang Feng and she and her friends had come to Shaoxing for a little holiday. She waved the plate of peanuts gently to indicate who her friends were, and they smiled expectantly and obediently. Wang Feng had a pretty, serious face and wore gray cotton trousers and a prim white blouse with a Peter Pan collar. Her husband, sitting at her right, had a wide mouth and a lot of teeth and a very pointed chin, and though he couldn't speak English, he seemed exceedingly proud that his wife could. Wang Feng explained that she and her husband were only recently married, and she showed us the golden wedding ring she wore. She and her friends took photographs of us and asked us to sing songs with them. I talked with Wang Feng about Shanghai, which I liked almost as much as I liked Shaoxing, and she was pleased by that, since she had been born and raised in Shanghai. She smiled and stared at me and hooked her arm in mine as we talked.

As the sun began to set behind the white building, these teachers urged us to spend the night in the Chinese hotel they were staying in. Somewhat drunkenly, we agreed to do that.

The hotel, on Shaoxing's main street, was shabby, dirty, narrow, three stories high, and plastered with fake wood paneling. The manager told us that although he had a room for Coby and Bruce to share, there was no room for me that night. Politely Wang Feng suggested to the manager that I might stay in the room she, her female friends, and several other women were occupying. The manager tipped back his head and laughed, then informed Wang Feng her idea was a very bad one, for I was clearly a foreigner, and in a hotel like this foreigners and Chinese were forbidden to mix. I offered to stay in the room Coby and Bruce were staying in. The manager said that that was out of the question, for Coby and Bruce were men, and anyone could see that I was clearly a woman.

On the stairs in the Mathematics Building the students began to snicker at the mention of gender. I ignored them and carried on with the story: Wang Feng and her husband tried to persuade the manager that since there was no place else for me to go that night, he might make an exception this time and that Wang Feng and her roommates wouldn't at all mind my presence in their room. Finally the proprietor agreed.

On the way up to the room I asked Wang Feng why she and her husband did not stay in the same room together. She said, "It is not allowed in this hotel. The men go with the men and the women go with the women."

"Even married couples have to sleep separately?" I said.

Wang Feng—like the students on the stairs—laughed a long time at my obvious dismay at this rule. "Unfortunately, yes." Wang hooked her arm in mine and led me to the room, a narrow cell bursting with six sheeted cots pressed so close together that they seemed to form one huge bed. There were three other women already in the room, sitting on the cots: one was reading a magazine, one was singing and brushing her hair, and the third was washing stockings in a tin basin. When Wang and I entered, the three women stopped what they were doing and fell silent. Wang's two friends flopped down on two vacant cots and went immediately to sleep. Wang pointed to the third cot and said to me, "And you will sleep in this bed."

"Fine," I said. And then I realized that there were seven women, but only six beds in the room. "Where will you sleep, Wang Feng?" I said.

Wang Feng smiled proudly. "Also in this bed!"

I looked at the bed—hardly wide enough for one of us—and looked back at Wang Feng. I dreaded it but tried to appear appreciative as I thanked her for her generosity. I told her I hoped this sleeping arrangement would not be too uncomfortable for either one of us.

"It will not present a problem!" Wang said, waving her ringed hand between us in a gesture of comparison, "for we are both small girls!" She laughed gaily and fished a tin basin out from under the bed and went out of the room to wash up in the bathroom.

I sat on the end of the cot and looked at the other women; they were feminine and demure. They looked as though they'd been preening there since morning. Beside them I felt dusty. They stared flatly at me, and at the huge Chinese men's sneakers I wore on my feet and the two little wooden parrots I had for earrings. Blue characters across the backs of my sneakers said, *Hui Li*, "Warrior." I felt trapped and incongruous in that little room, and the wine had made me lightheaded. I pointed out the window and said cheerfully in Chinese, "So, what do you think of Shaoxing?"

At the sound of my voice the three women looked deeply offended. Their spokeswoman, the long-faced one with the comb, snapped fiercely, "We can speak English!" and they gave each other sidelong looks and returned to their various distractions—the hair, the magazine, the stockings. I turned to Wang Feng's two friends for solace, but they were fast asleep, with their mouths open and their forearms slung across their eyes.

I drank some hot water out of a thermos next to Wang Feng's bed, hoping she would return and defend me. How hostile and suspicious those three seemed! Maybe they resented being surprised by a foreigner in their room. Maybe they didn't like being seen in all their intimate disarray.

The room reminded me of a Girl Scout summer camp; it was dark, musty, hot, with fluorescent lights, a broken ceiling fan, and two narrow windows with beetles and mosquitoes smashed against their screens. The floor felt gritty, there was underwear drying on a string across the middle of the room, and I could smell the toilets festering at the other end of the hall.

It puzzled me that these vacationing women seemed to be preparing for bed, though it was still early evening and there was plenty of sunlight left.

Wang Feng came back scrubbed and smiling and sat next to me. I told her Coby and Bruce and I were going to have dinner soon and asked her if she and her husband wanted to join us.

"We have already eaten," she said. "And soon we will sleep a nap."

I had been with them for three hours and hadn't seen them eat anything but peanuts. I said, "You go to bed early."

"We like to sleep," she said.

Eventually I went out of the room to join Coby and Bruce, with the roommates looking askance at me as I went.

The students liked to hear my impressions of Shaoxing, my description of the wide main street and the people out strolling on it. The buildings were very old here, the people looked twenty years behind the people in Hangzhou, and there were few cars on the streets. That night Shaoxing had the feel of a small town in the American West. The night was warm and the moon was rising over the tops of the houses in the still-blue sky. We went up to the second floor of an old restaurant, where a large family was having a wedding party. They occupied three round tables, and the floor around their feet was covered with seeds, chicken bones, shrimp hulls, fruit peelings, and rice. The men smoked and drank a lot, and the women held babies in their laps. One of the men got up, approached our table, and without saying a word, offered us three cigarettes. Though none of us smoked, we took them, and the man went quietly away.

We ate shrimp and fish-head soup. Through the restaurant window I could see the full moon just behind Coby's head now. It was a warm yellow, and it silhouetted an iron dragon decoration on the corner of a rooftop next door.

After dinner we went to the bar in the basement of the restaurant, a strangely modern place with varnished pine tables and chairs and soft lights and mirrored walls. We drank coffee there and watched a few young people drinking Coke. And then three dark-faced men from Xinjiang came into the bar, like the bad guys in a Western movie. They were stout, heavy-cheeked, curly-haired, and had thick lips and long noses; they looked Italian. One of them had long sideburns and wore his satin blouse unbuttoned to the waist. He wore gold chains around his neck and a big leather belt cinched tight around his waist. He and his friends stood in the middle of the bar, with their hands on their hips, surveying the situation. They seemed to fill the room. The balding, heavyset one went up to the bar, bought a tin of pears, tore it open with a pocket knife, sat at a table, and ate the pears directly from the can, spearing them with his knife. One of his friends joined him while the other, the mod one with the chains and belt, strolled over to see about us. He spoke excellent *Putonghua* and he told us that he and his friends had come from Kashgar to sell nylon in Shaoxing, but they hated Shaoxing, and the food here was terrible. The man had a huge, hairy chest and peered keenly from Coby to Bruce to me and back around again with an open-mouthed smile, as though he were looking at enchanting little origami figures.

It was nine o'clock when we returned to the hotel, and the six women were already in bed, but the lights were still ablaze, obviously for my benefit, which made me feel guilty. The unfriendly spokeswoman had draped the arm of a sweater across her eyes to block out the light. I took off my shoes and pants, gulped down some water, and was just about to turn off the light when Wang Feng reached over the edge of the bed and picked up the tin basin. "Here is the basin for your feet," she whispered.

"Oh, yes," I said, "my feet," and I took the basin from her. I pulled on my pants and went out into the hallway and stood there doing nothing for what I thought was the appropriate amount of time. I hadn't had a shower in three days; my feet were the last thing I cared about, and the bathroom was so dirty and so offensive that I wouldn't even have washed my face in it.

Back I went to the room, turned off the light, and climbed into bed next to Wang Feng, feeling intrusive and strange. Wang Feng lay on the very edge of her side of the bed in what must have been an extremely uncomfortable position, and I planned to do the same until she touched my shoulder and patted the middle of the bed and whispered, "There is room for you here. You should be comfortable. And pull the blankets up high so you will be warm." Wang Feng waited till I moved closer to her, then she pulled the sheets and blankets up to my chin and literally tucked me in.

"Wang Feng," I whispered, "how old are you?"

"I am twenty-three years old."

Three years younger than I was, but she acted like my mother. I could hear her breathing beside me, could almost feel her eyes blinking in the darkness. I knew she was looking at me and I half thought she would reach across the bed and hold my hand. Eventually I fell asleep. Several times during the night I woke up to feel Wang Feng rearranging the blankets on my shoulders and murmuring softly to me in a mixture of Chinese and English, almost unconsciously. "You must keep warm," she murmured, and, "There is room for you here. Are you comfortable?" At one point, toward morning, I woke to see her leaning on her elbow and staring down at me through the dim light, and when she saw I was awake, she whispered, "Next year, when you have finished teaching in Hangzhou, you could come to Shanghai to teach. I could find you another job. We could be friends."

I could see Wang Feng's teeth shining in her smile, and though she stared at me a long time, I was completely unprepared when she reached out and brushed a lock of hair from my forehead.

The old man from the department finally showed up with the correct key and let us into the exam room. The room was hot and full of mosquitoes. The students rushed to sit down, friends sitting with friends, boys in back and girls in front. I walked up and down the aisles, handing out the exams to the students, explaining the directions to the various sections. An hour later than scheduled, we began our test.

Almost immediately loud rock-and-roll music came blasting out of the windows of the building next door, and the students nearly jumped out of their seats in surprise. They looked out the windows and then at me in a pleading way. It would be impossible for them to think with that racket going on. I shut all the windows on that side of the room, which lessened the noise but also cut off the crosswind that had kept the room from becoming an oven.

I sat down at one of the desks and looked over the exam, and what I discovered horrified me: The proofreading corrections I had made in it the week before had not been incorporated—one whole paragraph of the reading-comprehension section of the exam was missing, others had been misprinted, and there were numerous other grammatical mistakes and typographical errors that could be insurmountable obstacles for these students.

I stood up and interrupted the students to walk them through the exam, making as many corrections as I could, writing some things on the blackboard. I could hardly conceal my frustration.

The students had written through three sections of the exam by the time Mr. Bai showed up with the cassette player. Bai was a kindhearted person who always looked faint with fear and anxiety. He seemed to despise his life in Hangzhou and went about his tasks with a desperate, fatalistic grin. He told me he had spent the previous year studying English in Yugoslavia and that he had hated it and was sorry now because he would probably never have a chance to see America, his "first-choice country."

Bai came into the room red-faced and panting, gritting his teeth in a weird grin. He put the cassette player on the podium at the front of the room and came over to me. He waved widely and whispered, "Hi," which in his fear and despair he managed to make sound like a curse. Then he went back to the cassette player, knelt down, and tried to plug the machine into the wall. Eventually he looked over his shoulder at me and hissed, "Comrade! A problem!"

I got up and went over, thinking, What now? I knelt down next to Bai. "It is the wrong plug for this outfit," he said. Beads of sweat had formed under his eyes, and if I hadn't known better, I might have mistaken them for tears.

"*Outlet*, Mr. Bai," I said, taking the plug from him. Sure enough, the plug's round metal prongs wouldn't fit into the narrow slits of the outlet, a common occurrence with Chinese appliances, as though each individual factory decided to shape their plugs in whatever form struck their fancy. On his hands and knees, Bai began to giggle. A shock of his thick dark hair fell into his eyes as he shook his head. He looked at me for directions. I asked him if he would mind going back to the department and getting an adaptor, or even another machine, in the teachers' room. Bai sighed and lifted himself up off the floor so slowly and so sadly that I changed my mind and told him that if he would stay with the students, I would go back to the department and get the plug myself.

Two at a time I took the stairs and rode my bicycle furiously across the campus to the department. I ran into the teachers' room, where two ponytailed teachers named Wu and Lu were shouting agreeably across the table at each other as they collated more examination papers. They circled around and around the table, page by mistaken page. I rummaged through the cupboard for a cord and thought I would choke on my own frustration. We had spent the entire year preparing for this examination, and it was clear to me that the students were ready, but the department was not.

Teacher Lu said, "Rose, what are you looking for?"

Luckily I was speechless with anger, for I might have snapped something smart at her, something I would have regretted later on. I found a suitable cord, jumped back on my bicycle, and raced back up to the exam room. The room was roasting now, and the students seemed to be sagging over their desks. The music next door harangued on and on. Bai walked up and down the aisles among the students with his hands clasped behind his back; the back of his shirt was soaked with sweat.

I plugged the cassette machine into the wall, popped in the tape, and started the listening-comprehension section of the examination. The students were to listen to several short passages on the tape and answer subsequent questions on their exam paper. The first passage was an airline announcement:

Good afternoon, ladies and gentlemen. Captain Gibson and his crew welcome you aboard British Airways Flight 197 to New York. We are now flying at a height of thirty thousand feet. Our speed is approximately six hundred miles an hour. We will land in New York in five and a half hours. The temperature in New York is now minus three Centigrade. In a few minutes you'll be able to see the Irish coast. Our stewards and stewardesses will serve lunch in half an hour.

I cringed as I listened to it: The British narrator's accent was so regal that even I found it difficult to understand, and the tape was scratched and fuzzy, and the machine squealed and clicked, but above all the passage seemed like a taunt to me, an absurd piece of knowledge for a group of people who might never even travel as far as their own capital and who most certainly had never traveled by airplane. Such thoroughly irrelevant bits of information were common fare in this English course, and I often wondered what was the logic behind it, what was the justification, why did they want their students to learn these things? There was also a fascination with statistics, dates, and facts in these listening tapes, and the "challenge" for the students was whether or not they could remember them all. The questions that followed the passage were:

1. When was the announcement made?
2. At what time of the day was the announcement made?
3. Where is the plane now?
4. When will the plane reach its destination?

The boys at the back of the room screwed up their faces, straining to hear the tape, and some of them stood up and even came partway down the aisle to hear it better. And then the machine began to chew up the tape, and we had to stop it.

I could not look at Bai, or at anyone else. I wanted to hurl the crappy little Chinese machine through one of the windows and watch it go crashing down onto the bicycles parked below.

The students waited to see what I would do.

Sentence by sentence I listened to the rest of the tape, stopping the machine after each sentence and repeating it clearly for the students. Mr. Bai settled himself into one of the little desks and listened, mouth agape.

Cars are an important part of life in the United States. Without a car most people feel that they are poor, and even if a person is poor, he doesn't feel really poor when he has a car. Henry Ford was the man who first started making cars in large numbers. He probably didn't know how much the car was going to affect American culture. The car made the U.S. a nation on wheels, and it helped make the United States what it is today. There are three main reasons the car became so popular in the United States. First of all, the country is a huge one and Americans like to move around in it. The car provides the most comfortable and cheapest form of transportation. With a car people can go anyplace without spending a lot of money. The second reason cars are popular is the fact that the United States never really developed an efficient and inexpensive form of public transportation. Long-distance trains have never been as common in the United States as they are in other parts of the world. Nowadays there's a good system of air service provided by planes. But it is too expensive to be used frequently. The third reason is the most important one, though; the American spirit of independence is what really made cars popular. Americans don't like to wait for a bus or a train or even a plane. They don't like to have to follow an exact schedule. A car gives them the freedom to schedule their own time. And this is the freedom that Americans want most to have. The gas shortage has caused a big problem for Americans. But the answer will not be a bigger system of public transportation. The real solution will have to be a new kind of car, one that does not use so much gas.

The first question was, "When do most Americans feel they are poor?"

Mr. Bai listened intently to the story, and when the exam was over, he approached me and said sweetly, "You have a beautiful voice, more beautiful than the voice on the tape."

The students filed out of the room, looking miserable. They were dying of heatstroke and anxiety. I knew they knew a lot more about English than this bad test could ever prove and that if they got stranded on a street in New York, or if they got jobs as travel agents, they would be able to express themselves quite capably, and that was what mattered.

As we sat in the teachers' room that June day, I decided I didn't care that the grades were inflated. Though I would have wished for far more for these students, this seemed, in some small way, like justice.

THE EAST
IS RED

Mao said China had two powerful enemies: American imperialists and Soviet revisionists. The border clashes with the soviets plunged the whole nation into a state of alarm. This was during the Cultural Revolution, the late sixties. Mao said, "Prepare for possible war, for possible natural disasters; work for the people." We were to dig tunnels deep, store food, and never be monopolized. The whole nation started digging. The tunnels snaked underground, intertwining, meeting, overlapping. Every afternoon in school we practiced running for shelter from air raids. I remember in one rehearsal a muddy wall collapsed because of the people rushing for the tunnel. Nobody was hurt in that accident, but in others people died.

On a late July day, the hottest day of the year, I rode my bicycle to Ming Yu's new apartment in a building on the far side of the campus. The campus was flat and deserted, the sky was like a sheet of hot metal, the air seared my lungs and burned the sweat off my face. My eyes felt like dry stones in their sockets. My brother James, who had come to China to visit, followed gamely behind on a rented bicycle too small for his large frame. He squinted fiercely in the sun. His face and hands, like mine, were burned red. James had arrived in China in June, and in a month of traveling here had lost a great deal of weight.

I pedalled on.

The hallway of Ming Yu's newly constructed building was awash in trash: empty drink cans, orange peels, balled-up wrappers, piles of dust. Big black bootprints went—absurdly—up a wall.

When I knocked on Ming Yu's door she responded slowly. The door opened a crack, revealing only half of Ming's face, which looked puffy and yellowish, the color of a newly hewn pine plank. Her hair hung uncombed around her face, her speech was slow and thick.

"You returned," she said, opening the door a little wider. She was dressed in an old sleeveless cotton blouse and baggy shorts, the summer clothes of a small child. Her bare arms and legs were thin, her eyes looked enormous. She was barefooted. Before I could hold a hand out to her or say a word of greeting she disappeared into the bathroom.

"Ming Yu," I said after her, "are you all right?" She didn't answer.

I waved James into the room, and we sat down. The room was hot and stuffy and the homemade curtains drawn across the windows lent the room a false twilight. The walls were cream colored, like toffee. On Ming's desk six ten-pound notes—probably from George Greatorex—lay spread out in a fan shape. James picked up a heavy Chinese book that lay on the bed and held it up for me to see. "What's this?" he whispered. His eyes were sharp blue in his hot face.

"It looks like *Self-Criticism*," I said.

When Ming came out of the bathroom she was dressed in a different blouse and a skirt. Her face was washed and her hair was combed and she seemed a bit livelier. When she saw James on the bed she stepped backward in surprise; she obviously wasn't expecting him.

I said, "Ming Yu, this is my brother."

James stood up and shook Ming's hand. She stared at

him, her tiny hand lost in his. James was a foot-and-a-half taller than she, and probably twice her weight—he could have picked her up over his head a flung her across the room like a sack of leaves.

With his height and his light hair, James was an arresting sight to the Chinese, and everywhere we had traveled that summer he drew a crowd, which he then proceeded to delight with magic tricks, and with his beguiling friendliness. Young Chinese women sang songs for him on the train and begged him to write to them when he returned to America. Little children held his hand and called him "Uncle," and put their fingers behind his ears, searching for coins that weren't there. A soldier had unscrewed the badge from his cap and handed it over as a gift the instant James expressed an interest in the characters on it. Old men said to me, "Tell you brother he is very interesting."

Ming Yu sat next to me on the bed and explained that she had two abscessed teeth and had been lying in bed for a week in pain, waiting for the swelling to go down so the teeth could be pulled. She had had no pain killer. She looked exhausted but smiled brightly at us, glad of our company.

James looked around the room and said suddenly, "Miss Ming, you have no fan here." I knew he was thinking, How could a person live in a place like this without a fan? Why would anyone tolerate it?

Ming nodded her head, snapped her fingers in her lap. "Correct."

"Are you going to get one?" James asked.

"I think so."

"When are you going to get one?"

"Next year, perhaps."

James leaned forward in his chair, as if to hear Ming's tiny voice better. "Next *year*?"

"I think so."

He shook his head in disbelief. Ming smiled that accepting smile that seemed to say, I know what you're thinking and why you're thinking it, but this is the way it is. She asked us about our trip.

We had done most of our traveling with Mary and Coby Ward, had been to Inner Mongolia, to Datong, Beijing, Qingdao, and Shanghai. We had met a man whose nose and upper lip had been chewed off by a wolf when he was a baby and who spoke with his hand held constantly before his face in an effort to spare us the gruesome sight and himself our reactions. We had seen a truck flatten a fruit stand and several people standing at it; a six-year-old girl, thirty pounds overweight, breakdancing expertly in the aisle of a train; shirtless, netless beekeepers going about their work protected only by the smoke of their cigarettes; and Mao in his glass case. We had seen the Great Wall. On our way back to Shanghai from Qingdao we had shared a berth in a train with two prostitutes. When I spoke to one of them in English she said with a babyish pout, "I can't understand English."

"Where are you going?" I asked her in Chinese.

"To Shanghai."

I pointed to the woman beside her. "Is she your sister?"

"No, she's my friend."

The speaker had a wide, plain face and thick upper arms and was the friendlier of the two. The other was pretty, sharp-eyed, distant, and coy. Their dresses were diaphanous togalike wraps, like silk bedsheets. They sat with their knees apart and the skirts of their dresses hanging down between their legs, sweating and fanning themselves. They looked worn out. The silent one kept hiking her red dress up higher and higher on her thighs until we could all see the lace edges of her underwear.

I asked the young woman if she and her friend were workers. She looked at the friend, then back at me. "We're ... ahh ... typists," she said hesitantly, and she lifted her hands in front of her and wiggled her fingers at me, demonstrating her typing technique. She had amazingly long fingernails, which would have rendered her hands entirely useless at even the most modern of typewriters. With interest she pointed at James. "Is he your husband?"

"He's my older brother."

"He's good looking. What does he do?"

"He's a pianist," I lied, wiggling my fingers back at the woman.

All night long the two women scurried in and out of the berth, whispering and giggling and slamming the door shut.

We told Ming Yu stories of our trip. "I think you have been to more places in China than I have," she said.

In a few days we would leave China; James by plane and I by boat to Hong Kong.

I invited Ming Yu to join us at the Hangzhou Hotel for a drink later that afternoon.

"I will meet you there," Ming said.

The bar in the Hangzhou Hotel was carpeted, dark, and cool. Mary, Coby, James, and I sat in soft armchairs and listened to the piano player, the only Chinese person here, a middle-aged woman with a kind face and a silk dress down to her shins. At nearby tables sat a Taiwanese couple, a few quiet Japanese, some American businessmen, and a German family. Mary and Coby, usually humorous and spirited, sipped their drinks silently; like us they were tired and sunburned. I waited for Ming Yu, hoping she would enjoy a break from her room, that she would get cool and be able to relax. I waited a long time, then with a pang of regret I realized Ming Yu might not have been able to get past the doorman: ordinary Chinese were not usually allowed into this luxury hotel. I hurried out to the front door and found Ming Yu chatting with the doorman on the steps. She was dressed in blue sleeveless blouse and skirt and had a soft white sweater knotted around her waist. Her hair fell around her face and over her shoulders. She was smiling and seemed neither annoyed nor anxious. I took her by the arm and brought her inside, my foreign features validating her.

In the bar, Ming Yu sipped orange soda and looked around at the dark comfortable room, at the people in their good clothes, drinking and speaking several languages. Eventually James urged Ming to sing a song at the piano.

Ming held her glass shyly before her lips. "What shall I sing?" she said.

"How about 'The East is Red,'" said James. Ming laughed, but got up and went over to the piano player and asked in English if she knew how to play "The East is Red."

The piano player laughed and tilted her curly head at Ming. "Are you *sure* you want that one?" she asked.

Ming nodded. The pianist shifted on her bench and struck a chord. Ming sang in Chinese:

"The East is red, the sun rises,
  Then in China appears Mao Zedong.
  He brings happiness to the people.
  He is the savior of the people."

Beside the enormous black piano Ming looked tiny, but she was the most compelling presence in this room full of people, and the only person who truly belonged here. Ming sang the song with great feeling, and no one was laughing at what had become, over the years, a laughable song. She sang beautifully. On the last note everyone in the bar applauded loudly and appreciatively, and even the skeptical piano player turned to Ming to offer her praise.

Ming sat down again in her seat at our table and clapped a hand over her embarrassed smile.

The night before I left China Ming Yu came to Shanghai on the train to say good-bye to me. She had planned to stay in a Chinese hotel, but I insisted that she stay with me in my room at the Peace Hotel; the room was enormous and there was an extra bed there for her. Ming agreed. We spent a day wandering around Shanghai together. I bought a Shanghai brand watch, a clock-sized industrial-looking machine with digits that glowed green in the dark. The watch was too large for my wrist, but I strapped it on anyway, much to Ming's amusement. I bought Ming a silk scarf and gave her what little money I had left over. We walked a lot that day in the oppressive heat, and we spoke very little.

In the evening, back at the hotel, Ming rummaged in her cotton bag and pulled out a large paper fan tied around with green ribbon. "It is for you," she said, handing it to me.

I untied the fan and opened it; it had two rosewood stays, its paper was rice-white, and across one side of it three delicate shrimp were painted in black ink; on the other side of the fan a few lines from a Chinese poem had been written.

"I asked an artist friend to paint it for you," Ming said. She sat in an armchair by the window and recited the poem for me:

"How sad I am, looking back. All my friends are now gone and how many I still have left. My white hair is white for nothing, and I laugh at everything in the world. If you ask what can make me happy: I see the blue mountains so charming and so graceful, and I guess the blue mountains see me in the same way. The feeling and appearance are alike. With a cup of wine I am sitting in the window facing south, my hand stroking my hair. I'm thinking of Yuan Ming, the poet, writing his poems; this may be the feeling he had at that time. The people who know fame and are after it in such a possessed way live an extravagant life but they never know the real taste of wine, and I shout back, and the cloud begins to fly and the wind begins to blow.

"I don't regret not having seen the ancient people, but I regret that the ancient people cannot see me, a wild person. And there are only a few, just a few, who really know me."

Ming Yu stared around the hotel room, silent for a moment; she seemed to be taking in every detail, the telephone, the air conditioner, the mouldings, the mirror, the desk. This was an old hotel and had always been a place for foreigners and wealthy Chinese. "I often walked past this hotel and wondered what was inside. Now I know," she said with satisfaction. "The windows are pretty and the ceiling is so high, and the air is very cool here."

Through the hotel window we could see the lights of boats on the river, and hear the bleating horns of ships. People sat in their underwear on bamboo chairs on the sidewalk below us.

Ming said, "Tomorrow you will leave."

"Yes."

"Will you come back?"

"Before I do I'll see you in America, I'm sure."

Ming smiled and leaned back in her chair. "I will miss you," she said.

"I will miss you more," I said.

That night as we went to sleep I watched Ming Yu pull the blankets up to her chin. She stared thoughtfully at the ceiling, as though already in a dream. She smiled to herself and sighed, "I never thought that on the hottest day of the year I would be wearing blankets to bed."

I shut my eyes. I saw Ming Yu as a child, digging tunnels deep down in cool darkness, surrounded by the soft damp earth. She worked with a little shovel, her hair in a ribbon-tied ponytail, her hands and face muddy, a red armband on her upper arm identifying her as a Little Red Guard, digging deep.

POSTSCRIPT

11/88

Dear Rose:

You are studying Chinese characters so I will tell you my opinion about them. I think Chinese have many virtues such as filial piety. They also have many weaknesses. Compared with Americans, Chinese are content with things as they are and are dilatory in doing things. Many officials are mediocre and unambitious persons. They care about nothing but make money for themselves. We call them "Official resellers."

Now, more and more, lazy people are becoming beggars and taking begging as their jobs. They have an "advanced" way of begging because they always tell lie. Various beggars join together at night and become a gang of beggars. Some beggars are very rich and they usually spend money on gambling and whoring. So social atmosphere is becoming worse.

Perhaps you have not been to Chinese countryside. I will tell you about the people in my hometown. Some are very rich, while most people are still very poor. Whomever they are, they have nothing to do but gamble during their spare time, as they have received so poor education. Even some little kids are able to gamble affected by their fathers. I don't know what kind of person these kids will become in the future. They are likely to be thrown in prison.

American pioneers were active in developing the western country under so arduous condition, but most contemporary Chinese are unwilling to work in the western part of our country because of the execrable physical condition there. Chinese are proud of the Great Wall all the time, but it also shows our ancestors' incapability. Why did they only construct it to defend enemies rather than launch an attack? Some people are afraid that Chinese won't be pure Chinese if we learn too much from foreign coutries. Many fine students want to study abroad but the government is afraid that they will not come back! Is there anybody who doesn't wish his motherland rich and strong?

I am very happy, though sometimes I complain. I never feel vacuous. I have been teaching myself Japanese for a year and can read Japanese articles . . .

Your student,
Mark

7/3/89

Dear Rosemary,

Thank you very much for your concern. I and my family are well. The newspapers sent by you are useful. Thank you.

On June 3, I went along Changan Avenue with my friends all day. I was too tired. I went to bed at night. So I couldn't give an eyewitness account of the incident. But I know there is a real matter. An acquaintance of mine was killed at the night of June 3. A bullet passed through his head. He went out only to have a look. He was 39 years old. He was a manager of a private company. He signed a contract with a publishing company to publish a dictionary on commerce. He also had two children of less than 13 years. How talented he was! He should have maken an all out effort. But . . . Rose, I feel very depressed.

I believe what you have heard and seen are much more than I have. Now the passage of information are blocked. What we've heard are from VOA, BBC, etc. Since the movement has been defined as turmoil, police whistle sounds frequently (the objects are young men). So residents only say to each other the words, "Don't talking about state affairs."

Everything seems to be back to normal, but it's difficult to say whether it's true or not. It's very difficult to forecast [what] the situation [will be] when the troops withdraw. My acquaintance's brother ever want to go to Tian'an Men square to reason it out.

The movement made me understand many things. The most important thing is that politics is dirty. This is the best gift to me from the movement. I also realized that life is too short. Rose, it is not easy for a person to go through to the end of his road safely and soundly.

I believe history. I insist on believing that, no matter how long the history will give a just appraisal of it.

During this year of my graduation I experienced too many things. Many factors make me intend to go out of Beijing. But my parents don't agree with me. The earliest time of my leaving may be at the end of this year. How's your everything going? I wish you everything smoothly.

Yours sincerely.
Tess

July 12, 1989

Dear Rosemary,

Thank you very much for your latest letter and I am very sorry that I have delayed it for such a long time. I am anxious to write to you as much as I can, but I am not able to write . . . ! Can you imagine?

You know, I used to be very happy, but I am no longer happy now. I am in tears more than once. but I never cry before.

Now I am very well, but I usually feel I stand at the

crossroad. I stay at home and help my parents do farming. I often go to swim. My summer vacation lasts to Sept 1.

I am sorry that I cannot write this letter very long. I believe that history will give a fair judgment in near future.

With best wishes!
Yours,
Mark

November 22, 1989

Rosie:

... I guess you don't know much of what is happening here in Hangzhou. All the students are doing introspection and making confessions. We were asked to study the documents. All the work—teaching and learning—stopped for several days on end. Then we were issued questionnaires to fill in. On it, several items were listed. We were asked have you ever:

1) been in any demonstrations.

2) put down signatures on big posters, or small posters announcing the wish to go on strike or to boycott classes.

3) written anti-revolutionary slogans, and radical posters.

4) organized any society or organization for the same purpose.

There are many things to be reported. You have to write the time, place, frequency and companies. Everybody was required [to do this]. I didn't write. When I asked them why should I fill in the form the leader said, "It's required by the top. If you ask us why, we have to ask the top why."

They don't know this very act is violating man's rights. It assumes that everybody is guilty without any proof. But to this flagrant breach of law nobody dares to speak up. When I said that I'll hold out people all responded in the same way: "Do you want to ruin yourself? If you want to stay here all your life and you don't care about the treatment you'll get, then do as you please. Otherwise, avoid the bomb." I didn't fill in the form. I avoided it in a roundabout way. The leader said I was the only that hadn't done the required confession. To me, I don't have the obligation to tell them my thoughts. If I trust the leader, I tell him, or if he is my priest, I do that, but nobody can claim to that. Not even my own father. Now everybody knows the best way to survive is to achieve conformity with the central government. . . .

A true man is a man who will fight if he is deprived of his inherent right to act according to his free will. Only animals are content to be led by the nose. As they say, many people choose to be animals. Now you can hear only one voice—that is the voice of the Central Government. I am thinking of the first line of a poem: "The red microphone in the red hall is governing the whole world . . ."

Now it is very quiet and the voice of the Central Government is very clear. It is quiet everywhere you go: the political arena, the battle field, the writers, the news media, the music hall, inside the atrium . . . I like the quietness. I have missed it for a long time. It is a pleasure that I have never dreamed of having. My mind has never achieved such a clean, vast exultation. I'm afraid of being overwhelmed if I let myself indulge in the nullifying peace and tranquility . . .

Love,
Ming

11/25/89

Dear Rosemary,

Thank you very much for our kind letters and postcard. I am very sorry that I have made you worry about my classmates and me so much! I wrote a letter to you soon after I read the letter you wrote in early August. I wonder why you didn't receive it.

Now I am doing at school. All your Chinese students are all right, I think. Including Madeleine and Louis. I can not tell you more about Madeleine, because I don't know of her very much, but she looks like very happy. . . . Louis usually play Majiang for amusement or gamble in his spare time.

Our brains were poured into something but they flowed away soon. Most students don't work hard now. One reason is that a Chinese student doesn't have the right to choose subjects he studies—no matter he likes it or not. of course, there are many other reasons—perhaps more important.

I am not going to take TOEFL test. One reason is money. I am still working hard at English. Perhaps chances will come to me in the future. I worry about that I won't have a good job after I graduate. I hope you won't write too many letters to your Chinese friends . . . One is the money—it's too expensive for an average Chinese to post an overseas letter. The other is that this can avoid unnecessary and unexpected troubles. I can feel your love forever, and love is not measured by the number of letters . . .

I send my best wishes to you and your family, to all those who love the people as well.

Your friend,
Mark

ABOUT THE AUTHOR

Rosemary Mahoney was born in 1961 in Boston, Massachusetts. She won the Charles E. Horman Prize for fiction writing as an undergraduate at Harvard, and received her MA from Johns Hopkins University. She is also the recipient of a Henfield/Transatlantic Review Award for Creative Writing. This is her first book.